ASP.NET 2.0
DEMYSTIFIED

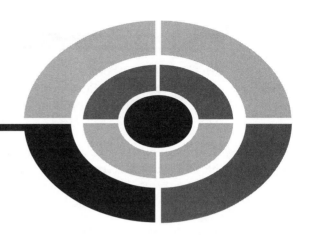

ASP.NET 2.0 DEMYSTIFIED

JIM KEOGH

McGraw-Hill/Osborne

New York   Chicago   San Francisco   Lisbon   London
Madrid   Mexico City   Milan   New Delhi   San Juan
Seoul   Singapore   Sydney   Toronto

The McGraw·Hill Companies

McGraw-Hill/Osborne
2100 Powell Street, 10th Floor
Emeryville, California 94608
U.S.A.

To arrange bulk purchase discounts for sales promotions, premiums, or fund-raisers, please contact **McGraw-Hill**/Osborne at the above address.

ASP.NET 2.0 Demystified

1234567890 FGR FGR 0198765

ISBN 0-07-226141-2

Acquisitions Editor
Wendy Rinaldi

Project Editor
Carolyn Welch

Acquisitions Coordinator
Alexander McDonald

Technical Editor
Ron Petrusha

Copy Editor
Bob Campbell

Proofreader
Susie Elkind

Indexer
Claire Splan

Composition
ITC

Illustration
ITC

Cover Series Design
Margaret Webster-Shapiro

Cover Illustration
Lance Lekander

This book was composed with Adobe InDesign.

This book is dedicated to Anne, Sandy, Joanne, Amber-Leigh Christine, and Graff, without whose help and support this book couldn't have been written.

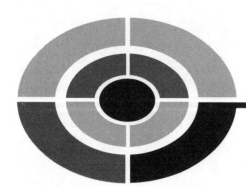

ABOUT THE AUTHOR

Jim Keogh is on the faculty of Columbia University and Saint Peter's College in Jersey City, New Jersey. He developed the e-commerce track at Columbia University. Keogh has spent decades developing applications for major Wall Street corporations and is the author of more than 65 books including *J2EE: The Complete Reference, Java Demystified, JavaScript Demystified, Data Structures Demystified, XML Demystified*, and others in the Demystified series.

CONTENTS AT A GLANCE

CONTENTS

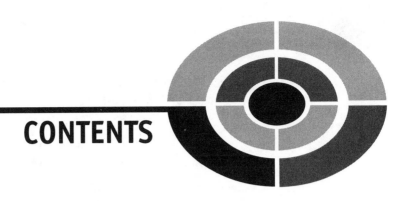

CONTENTS

CONTENTS

INTRODUCTION

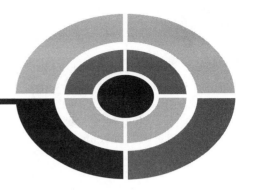

Most of us have gone online to check our bank account, pay bills, or place an order from an e-commerce web site, and we were probably amazed at how these companies were able to display our personal information on their web pages.

Within seconds of entering our user ID and password we can view our records on the screen. This seems like a miracle considering the amount of time you spend creating your web page. At first you might think they have an army of web builders quickly looking up your information in their databases and then creating a customized web page for you. That's not practical, so there might be a secret method they use—and there is.

The secret is ASP.NET.

Web developers us ASP.NET to perform tasks normally performed by employees to serve the needs of their customers, such as:

- Verifying that the person is a customer
- Understanding the needs of the customer
- Retrieving the customer's information from the company's database
- Building a web page
- Transmitting the customized web page containing customer information to the customer

ASP.NET is server-side software used to create interactive, dynamic web sites that can interface with databases that are also used by other corporate systems such as accounting, order entry, and shipping systems.

If you want to learn how to build high traffic web sites, then you've purchased the right book because ASP.NET has been adopted by some of the most popular, high demand sites on the Internet.

The Home Shopping Network uses ASP.NET to process orders from thousands of customers every day. Microsoft uses ASP.NET for their web site to meet the needs of their customers 24 hours a day, seven days a week.

You might be a little apprehensive learning ASP.NET, especially if you are a web developer and not a computer programmer. ASP.NET can be mystifying; however, it becomes demystified as you read *ASP.NET 2.0 Demystified* because your knowledge of HTML is used as the foundation for learning to write ASP.NET dynamic web pages.

As you'll see when you write your first ASP.NET application, each element of ASP.NET is introduced by combining a working web page with just the ASP.NET element you need. You already know 90 percent of the code that creates the web page because it is HTML. The remaining 10 percent of the code is ASP.NET, which is clearly explained in every chapter.

Like many developers, you probably learn by doing. You'll like reading *ASP.NET 2.0 Demystified* because it uses a hands-on approach to teaching ASP.NET. You can copy examples illustrated in this book from our web site and experiment with each ASP.NET concept presented in this book. Load the web page and see the effect of ASP.NET. Copy the ASP.NET and reload the web page and see how the web page reacts without the ASP.NET. You can then incorporate the ASP.NET into your own web page and move on to the next topic.

By the end of this book you'll be able to make your own classy web site that will leave even the sophisticated web surfer in awe and web developers scratching their heads, asking, "How did he do that?"

A Look Inside

ASP.NET can be challenging to learn unless you follow the step-by-step approach that is used in this book. Topics are presented in the order in which many developers like to learn them, starting with basic components and then gradually moving on to those features found on classy web sites.

Each chapter follows a time-tested formula that first explains the topic in an easy-to-read style and then shows how it is used in a working web page that you can copy and load yourself. You can then compare your web page with the image of the web page shown in the chapter to be assured that you've coded the web page correctly. In addition, each chapter also includes a practice quiz and answer section. There is little room for you to go wrong.

Chapter 1: An Inside Look at ASP.NET

Ever wondered how high traffic web sites work? Scratch the surface and you'll be surprised what you won't find—web pages. Few static web pages are stored on these web sites because nearly all their web pages are generated by a program tailored to meet the needs of each visitor to the web site. You can make your web site come alive with a professional flare by using ASP.NET. In Chapter 1, you'll learn everything you need to get started to put ASP.NET to work for you on your web site.

Chapter 2: The ASP.NET Web Page

The content of a dynamic web page is a blend of HTML markup code and source code, and can include data retrieved from a database or from a nonweb-based application, depending on the nature of your application.

In this chapter, you'll learn how to build an ASP.NET web page using the Visual Web Developer. The Visual Web Developer is an all-in-one editor and development environment where you build ASP.NET applications by dragging and dropping elements and source code from a toolbox onto your ASP.NET page. Best of all, the Visual Web Developer writes the code for you.

Chapter 3: Building an ASP.NET Web Page Application

Building web pages dynamically is more involved than creating static web pages because you must design, develop, and test the client-side and server-side of the application. The client-side is what the visitor sees. The server-side is the ASP.NET program that interacts with a database and generates the web page.

In this chapter, you'll learn techniques developers use to create the server-side program that generates an ASP.NET web page. You'll find this more challenging than building static web pages, but the step-by-step instructions presented in the chapter get you up and running in no time.

Chapter 4: Variables and Expressions in ASP.NET

The ASP.NET engine is the brain behind every ASP.NET application because it processes and responds to requests from visitors to your web site. Your job is to write instructions that tell the ASP.NET engine how to process and respond to those requests.

You'll write these instructions using Visual Basic .NET. In this chapter, we'll explore the foundation of nearly every instruction that you'll write. These are values, variables, and expressions. If you know how to add 1 + 1, then you will breeze through this chapter.

Chapter 5: Conditional Statements

Commercial web sites powered by ASP.NET make intelligent decisions on the fly while processing a visitor's request, such as validating his or her login and knowing what personal information should be displayed on the web page.

You can write instructions telling ASP.NET how to make decisions by using conditional statements. You'll learn how to write conditional statements in this chapter that tell ASP.NET when to make a decision, how to make a decision, and what to do after a decision is made.

Chapter 6: Arrays

Visitors to your web site want information and they want it fast. Developers meet this demand by placing large amounts of information in memory in an array so the information can be retrieved at nearly the speed of light.

In this chapter, you'll learn about arrays and how to use them in your ASP.NET application to store and manipulate large amounts of information.

Chapter 7: Subroutines and Functions

An ASP.NET application is inherently complex because it requires a lot of instructions. This makes an ASP.NET application difficult to write, difficult to read, and difficult to change. Developers reduce the complexity of an ASP.NET application by grouping the application into logical pieces that are later assembled into the complete application.

Groups are called a subroutine and function and in this chapter you'll learn how to use subroutines and functions to simplify the complexity of your ASP.NET application.

Chapter 8: Drop-Down Lists, Radio Buttons, Check Boxes

Visitors to your web site expect to see web forms that contain drop-down list boxes, radio buttons, check boxes, and other graphic user interface (GUI) controls found

on commercial web sites. These controls enable visitors to pick and choose selections using a mouse, and minimize the amount of information they need to enter from the keyboard.

You're already familiar with these GUI controls since they are widely used on e-commerce web sites. In this chapter, you'll learn how to create these GUI controls on your ASP web page. You'll also learn how to retrieve values selected by visitors to your web site.

Chapter 9: Databases

Many commercial web sites are data driven and use the web to enable customers to complete transactions online. The heart of a data-driven web site is the database that contains account information, product information, and other data that is necessary for a transaction.

This is the first of four chapters that teach you how to create a data-driven web site. In this chapter, you'll learn database concepts and how to design a database for your application.

Chapter 10: Interacting with Databases

Your ASP.NET application must use a series of routines behind the scenes that, among other things, links your web site to a database. This connection enables you to store information in the database and retrieve information from the database, which can be incorporated directly into your web page.

In this chapter, you'll learn how to create an ADO.NET connection that becomes your pipeline into popular commercial database management software (DBMS), such as Microsoft SQL Server, Oracle database server, and Microsoft Access. You'll also learn how to write simple SQL statements in a query that direct the DBMS to perform tasks that are commonly used in many commercial web sites.

Chapter 11: SQL

Real world ASP.NET web applications require sophisticated queries to retrieve information from multiple tables, perform complex calculations, and efficiently organize information so it can be displayed on a web page.

In the previous chapter you learned how to connect your application to database management software and how to request and store data in a database by writing simple queries. This chapter focuses on writing sophisticated queries that perform commonly used tasks in commercial applications.

Chapter 12: Binding Data to Controls

An efficient way to streamline your data-driven ASP.NET application is to link data directly to web controls so data automatically appears every time a web page is displayed. For many applications, the data is information stored in a database. In this chapter, you'll learn how to bind data contained in a database to a web control and then use that data and web control in your application.

Appendixes

This book also includes a final exam (Appendix A) and final exam answers (Appendix B). The questions in the final exam are practical and are drawn from all chapters in the book. Take the exam when you have finished all the chapters and have completed all the quizzes.

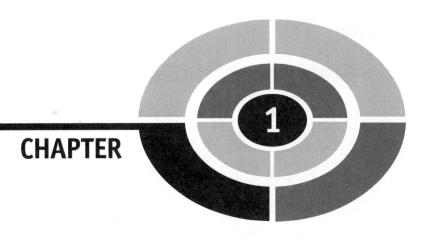

CHAPTER

An Inside Look at ASP.NET

Scratch the surface of an e-commerce web site and you'll be surprised at what you won't find—web pages. Few web pages are stored in files on an e-commerce web server, because a program generates nearly all web pages that visitors see. Programs also respond to requests visitors make, such as to display their account status and to process an order. And programs are used to personalize web pages.

Web pages you build are static web pages, since their content stays the same once you save the pages to your web server. Web pages generated by a program are dynamic web pages because the program can tailor the content of the web pages to meet the needs of each visitor to the web site.

You can make your web site come alive with a professional flare by using ASP .NET to create dynamic web pages that individually respond to each request made by visitors to your site. You'll learn everything you need to know to put ASP.NET to work for you throughout this book, beginning with an introduction to ASP.NET in this chapter.

The Static over Static Web Pages

Before embarking on a journey into the world of ASP.NET, let's quickly review how static web pages are used on a web site so that you can later appreciate the power of dynamic web pages. A *static* web page is a web page whose content doesn't change after the developer saves the web page to the web server. The web page simply remains the same until the developer replaces it with an updated static web page (Figure 1-1).

With one exception, static web pages are not tailored to each visitor, since every visitor to the web site sees exactly the same web page. In order to personalize the content of the web page, the developer must know something about the visitor and then update and replace the existing web page on the web server. Obviously, this is impossible to do for every visitor.

The exception is to personalize a web page by using a client-side script such as JavaScript that is incorporated into the web page. JavaScript is a limited object-oriented programming language that developers use to enhance the capabilities of HTML.

A developer uses JavaScript to create portions of the web page dynamically after the browser loads the web page. For example, the visitor's name might have been saved to a cookie during a previous visit to the web site. On the next visit, the JavaScript reads the cookie and then uses the visitor's name to write a personal greeting on the web page.

Developers also use JavaScript to dynamically modify an HTML form while the visitor is interacting with the form. For example, the visitor might be prompted to enter a telephone number onto the form. The JavaScript then properly formats the telephone number.

It is important to remember that scripts written in JavaScript or a similar scripting language run on the visitor's computer. ASP.NET runs on the web server, which gives developers far-reaching capabilities to tie together corporate databases and

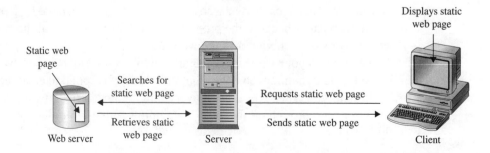

Figure 1-1   A static web page is stored on a web server and sent to a browser.

non-web applications into a web page. Pick up a copy of my *JavaScript Demystified* (McGraw-Hill/Osborne, 2005) if you want to learn more about how to enhance your web page with JavaScript.

Serving Up Static Web Pages: Are You Being Served?

A web server is like a sales clerk who stands behind the counter waiting to respond to customers' requests.

The customer in this case is called a client, which is typically the browser used by the visitor to retrieve the web page. However, a client can be any program that accesses the Internet, such as Microsoft Office products and customized programs that you might write yourself using Visual Basic, C++, or other popular programming languages.

The client requests either to receive a file or to run a program. The file is usually a web page, but it could be a file containing a graphic image, a Flash movie, an audio file, or a Java applet used by a browser plug-in.

The program on the server side can perform any number of operations, which may include processing information supplied by the visitor and generating dynamic web pages. You'll learn more about this throughout this chapter.

The client's request takes the form of a URL such as www.mywebsite.com/ FileName and is followed by a series of strange-looking characters. The first part of the request (www.mywebsite.com) identifies the domain on the web server. The second part is the name of the file located within the domain. The strange-looking characters form the query string, which is information that the server-side program needs to process the client's request.

When a request is received, the web server locates the file and sends the file to the client; then it waits to receive another request from any client. The client then processes the file; if the file is a web page, the browser displays its content on the screen (Figure 1-2).

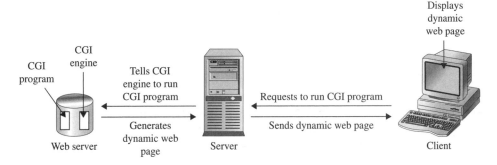

Figure 1-2   A dynamic web page is generated by a program and sent to a browser.

CGI stands for *common gateway interface*, and it refers to software running on the server that is called when a client submits a form. The CGI program uses information contained in the form to process the client's request.

The Pros and Cons of Static Pages

Static web pages have been the mainstay of web sites for decades because they are relatively simple to build and easy to host, and because for many web sites they effectively present information to visitors.

Static web pages are simple to build because they can be created by dragging and dropping HTML elements using a web development tool such as Dreamweaver or FrontPage.

Static web pages are easy to host because you don't require additional software on the web server such as the ASP.NET engine, which you'll learn about later in this chapter. All you require is a web server to host a static web page.

Static web pages effectively present information to visitors to a web site because many web sites display information that doesn't change frequently and doesn't require the personalization and interactions found on e-commerce web sites.

However, static web pages do have drawbacks, one of which is the lack of a capability to personally communicate with visitors—a requirement of many enterprises. Businesses that use the web as a source of revenue or to improve customer support require web pages to give visitors a warm, cozy, personalized experience that can only be achieved by dynamically generating web pages.

For example, static web pages are incapable of displaying customer account information because account information could change frequently during the day, requiring the developer to manually update the page, and there would simply be too many static web pages—one per account. Also, static web pages are incapable of enacting e-commerce business strategies such as dynamic pricing, where a business adjusts the selling price of an item according to the customer's profile stored in a database.

Businesses turn to dynamic web pages to provide customers with the up close and personal relationship expected when doing business online.

Dynamic Web Pages: Viagra for Web Sites

A dynamic web page is a web page that doesn't exist until a program generates it in response to a request from a client. Sounds a bit like web magic. One second there isn't a web page, and then poof—there it is.

Here's the trick: A dynamic web page contains the same HTML markup code as a static web page, except the code is written by a program at the time that the web server receives the client's request. The HTML markup code isn't written to a file. Instead, it is sent directly to the client.

Here's how this works. Typically, index.html is the first web page a client requests from a web site. This is a static web page in many cases, because the client's request usually doesn't identify the visitor. You've seen this happen whenever you go online to view your benefit statement. The first web page that appears prompts you to log in.

The second request usually contains information that identifies the visitor, such as an employee ID and password, and asks the web server to run a program rather than return a web page. You might be wondering how the client knows what program to run. The URL for the program is contained in a hyperlink on the first web page requested by the client.

When this URL is requested, the web server passes the request to software that is specifically designed to run the program, which is commonly called an *engine*. For example, if the URL is for a myprogram.aspx, the web server passes the request to the ASP.NET engine to run this program.

The information provided by the client is used by the program to customize the next web page that is sent to the client. How the program customizes the web page depends on the nature of the application.

For example, a program that validates your login executes when you submit your employee ID and password to gain access to the benefits web site. If your login information is invalid, the program generates a dynamic web page prompting you to re-enter it. If it is valid, then the program retrieves your benefits information from the company's database and generates a dynamic web page that blends your benefit information with general information that explains the status of your account (Figure 1-3).

A dynamic web page looks the same as a static web page to a client. In fact, you couldn't tell the difference if you viewed the source code of both of them. Another way of looking at this is that you already know how to write most of the program that generates a dynamic web page, since you know how to write a web page using HTML.

Parles-tu Visual Basic .NET?

Do you speak Visual Basic .NET? Visual Basic .NET is one programming language that developers use to write ASP.NET programs to generate dynamic web pages. (Another language is C#.) Any .NET-compliant programming language can be used to write an ASP.NET program.

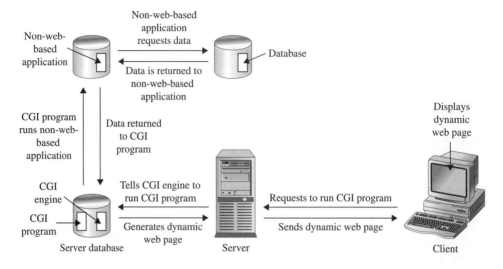

Figure 1-3 Dynamic web pages usually blend general information with personalized information obtained from a database.

The Pros and Cons of Dynamic Pages

The capability to create web pages dynamically opens new horizons for developers, for now they can create web-based applications that can tap into corporate databases and that can interact with existing non-web-based applications.

You've probably experienced such interactions when making an online purchase, but you may not have realized what was happening behind the scenes. You entered your credit card information into a web page and clicked the Submit button, which kicked off a program on the web server that probably passed along your credit card information to a non-web-based application for validation. This application determines if your credit card is valid by comparing your information with information stored in a database. Once your card is validated, a web page confirming your purchase is dynamically created and sent to your browser.

You simply can't do this with a static web page.

Here are some other benefits of using dynamic web pages:

- **They save money and trouble updating applications**   Before web-based applications were developed, the IT department had to install software on every computer in the company each time an application was upgraded. Today many of the applications are stored on a web server and are accessed using a browser.

- **They give you access from any place with an Internet connection**   A web-based application is never out of reach from anyone who is authorized to access it.

- **They increase customer satisfaction**   Customers go online rather than wait in line registering for class, placing an order, paying a bill, or checking their account status.

You can't do this with a static web page.

And there are drawbacks to using dynamic web pages, too:

- **Security**   A web-based application that generates dynamic web pages might expose corporate applications and databases to hackers.

- **Decreased customer satisfaction**   There is a tendency to keep customers at arm's length and force the customer to do business with the firm online, while concealing ways in which a customer can talk to a company representative.

- **Complex programming**   Creating dynamic web pages and linking them to corporate databases and non-web-based applications requires programming, something that isn't necessary when using static web pages.

- **Additional software**   An engine—not a web server—executes programs. Therefore, the engine must be installed and maintained. The web server processes static web pages without requiring help from an engine.

Are You Ready for Some ASP.NET?

ASP.NET is the latest incarnation of Microsoft's Active Server Pages and is the engine that executes ASP.NET web pages. An ASP.NET web page is the program that you create to generate a dynamic web page, which you'll learn how to do in the next chapter. For now we'll take a few moments to introduce the concept of an ASP.NET web page.

Two sets of instructions must be executed in order for a visitor to view a dynamic web page. The first set is executed on the web server. Developers call this the server side. The second set is executed on the visitor's computer. Developers call this the client side. Both sets of instructions are written in an ASP.NET web page.

The ASP.NET web page is organized into two sections that correspond to the two sets of instructions. These are the HTML markup code section and the controls section.

The HTML *markup code* section contains HTML markup code that forms the dynamic web page sent to the visitor's computer by the ASP.NET engine. These instructions are executed on the client side by the browser.

The *controls* section contains instructions that tell the ASP.NET engine how to generate the dynamic web page. These instructions are executed on the server side by the ASP.NET engine. The controls section is divided into two subsections called HTML controls and web controls. You'll learn the difference between these two subsections in the next chapter.

The ASP.NET engine that executes the ASP.NET web page needs to run within the .NET Framework. This simply means that the ASP.NET engine needs help from a group of programs and related files that are collectively called the .NET Framework. There are two key elements of the .NET Framework: .NET programming languages and Framework classes.

A .NET programming language is a language developers use to write instructions telling the ASP.NET engine what to do. VB.NET and C# are each a .NET programming language. Framework classes are like building blocks used to write ASP.NET web pages. You'll learn more about Framework classes in the next chapter.

Building an ASP.NET Web Page

An ASP.NET web page can be built using an editor such as Microsoft's Notepad that comes with Windows. All that's needed is for you to write the HTML markup code section and the control sections using VB.NET or C#, and then save the page to a file that has the .aspx file extension. You'll learn how to do this in the next chapter.

The next step is to execute your ASP.NET web page. This is the tricky part because to do this, you need a web server that has access to the ASP.NET engine, and chances are you don't have these on your computer. Don't be too concerned, because you have three options available, depending on which operating system you have running on your computer.

ASP.NET Web Matrix Web Server

ASP.NET Web Matrix is your best option if you are running Windows NT, Windows XP Professional, Windows XP Home, or Windows Server 2003 (unlikely unless your computer is also running a web server) on your computer because it is a free, all-in-one development tool and web server.

It'll take you about five minutes to download this tool, and ASP.NET Web Matrix installs in no time. You'll also need to download and install the .NET Framework if

you don't already have it installed on your computer. (.NET Framework is already installed if you are running Microsoft Windows Server 2003, Windows 2000, or Windows XP.) The .NET Framework is also free. You can download it from www .asp.net or http://msdn.microsoft.com/net.

The greatest benefit of using the ASP.NET Web Matrix is that you can build your ASP.NET web page using WYSIWYG (what you see is what you get) by dragging and dropping components from a toolbox onto the page. And you can test your ASP.NET web page with a click of a button, since the ASP.NET Web Matrix has the Web Matrix Web Server built in.

ASP.NET Web Matrix has its drawbacks. First, it doesn't run on Windows 98 or Windows ME, and besides, the ASP.NET Web Matrix Web Server is limited to requests coming from the computer running it. This means that you cannot access the ASP.NET Web Matrix Web Server from outside your computer even if your computer is connected to the Internet, because the ASP.NET Web Matrix web server is not designed as a product web server.

Web Hosting

If you're running Windows 98 or Windows ME or simply don't want to download the ASP.NET Web Matrix to your computer, then you'll need to make arrangements with a web hosting company to run your ASP.NET web page.

A web hosting company provides space on its web server for your web site, usually for a nominal monthly charge. The company will also help you register your own domain name (e.g., www.mydomain.com) and link your domain to your web site.

TIP: *Go to www.netsol.com to find out what domains are still available.*

There are thousands of web hosting companies. Visit www.hostindex.com or www.tophosts.com for a listing of web hosting companies and their offerings. When selecting a web hosting company, make sure that the company supports ASP.NET. If it doesn't, then their web servers cannot handle your ASP.NET web pages.

You can get your feet wet with ASP.NET without spending money for web hosting by using the educational package offered by www.brinkster.com. The educational package provides you with a free web hosting account that you can use to run your ASP.NET web page. You simply copy and paste your ASP.NET web page into a text area available on the www.brinkster.com web site to upload your ASP.NET web page to their web server. Visit www.brinkster.com for complete instructions on how to do this.

Internet Information Server (IIS)

You can install Microsoft's Internet Information Server (IIS) if you are running a Windows 2000, Windows XP Professional, or Windows 2003 web server. However, Internet Information Server is a bit of overkill, since it is the web server used by many web-hosting companies.

Developers rarely run such a powerful web server on their desktop, since they can use the ASP.NET Web Matrix web server to test and debug their ASP.NET web pages.

Publishing Your ASP.NET Web Page

The last step in creating an ASP.NET web page is to publish it on your web site. The process of publishing your ASP.NET web page is basically the same process used to publish a static web page: you copy the ASP.NET web page file to the proper location on the web server using the File Transfer Protocol utility that is built into most browsers.

The exact location to place your ASP.NET web page file is up to you. Many developers store all their ASP.NET web pages in the same subdirectory on the web server to keep their web site files organized.

You won't be able to FTP your files if you are using the www.brinkster.com educational package, since FTP is provided only to paid accounts. Instead, you'll need to copy and paste your ASP.NET Web Page into their web page.

Here are a few things to review before publishing your ASP.NET Web Pages:

- Make sure your web hosting company supports ASP.NET. Some support ASP, but not ASP.NET.

- Make sure that the hyperlink that references your ASP.NET web page has the path to the subdirectory that contains the ASP.NET web page file and includes the filename; otherwise, an error is displayed by the browser.

- Make sure you thoroughly test your ASP.NET web page and stamp out all bugs.

- Make sure that resources used by your ASP.NET web page such as databases and non-web-based applications, if any, are available to your ASP.NET web page.

- After publishing your ASP.NET web page, pretend to be a visitor to your web site and make sure that your ASP.NET web page is accessible and working properly online.

Looking Ahead

ASP.NET is used to generate dynamic web pages in response to requests made by visitors to your web site. Dynamic web pages are web pages that don't exist on a web server. Instead, a program generates them.

The content of a dynamic web page can be tailored for each visitor according to information provided by the visitor. For example, it could contain the visitor's account status or order information that is retrieved from databases and non-web-based applications.

The program that generates the dynamic web page is called an ASP.NET web page. An ASP.NET web page contains two sets of instructions. These are HTML markup code and controls. The HTML markup code forms the dynamic web page that is sent to the client. Controls are instructions that tell the ASP.NET engine how to generate the dynamic web page. The ASP.NET engine is the application on the server side that executes the ASP.NET web page.

In the next chapter, you'll learn how to create ASP.NET web pages using the ASP.NET Web Matrix.

Quiz

1. ASP.NET web pages are written using
   a. VB.NET
   b. C#
   c. C++
   d. VBScript

2. The ASP.NET engine requires
   a. .NET OS
   b. .NET Framework
   c. .NET Source Code
   d. None of the above

3. ASP.NET can be used to create
   a. E-commerce web sites
   b. Intranet web sites
   c. Corporate web sites
   d. All of the above

4. ASP.NET web pages run on

   a. The server side

   b. The client side

   c. Both the server side and the client side

   d. None of the above

5. The ASP.NET engine runs on

   a. The server side

   b. The client side

   c. Both the server side and the client side

   d. None of the above

6. The .NET Framework contains

   a. Customer information

   b. Classes

   c. Account information

   d. All of the above

7. You can write an ASP.NET web page using any editor.

   a. True

   b. False

8. All dynamic web pages must be generated by ASP.NET web pages.

   a. True

   b. False

9. There is a visible difference between HTML markup code in a static web page and a dynamic one.

   a. True

   b. False

10. A dynamic web page cannot contain images or audio.

    a. True

    b. False

Answers

1. a. VB.NET and b. C#
2. b. .NET Framework
3. d. All of the above
4. a. The server side
5. a. The server side
6. b. Classes
7. a. True
8. b. False
9. b. False
10. b. False

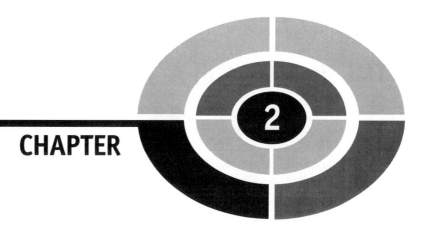

CHAPTER 2

The ASP.NET Web Page

An ASP.NET web page is an extension of HTML markup code that includes instructions called source code that tell the ASP.NET engine how to generate a dynamic web page. The content of a dynamic web page is a blend of HTML markup code and source code; it can include data retrieved from a database or from a non-web-based application, depending on the nature of your application.

In this chapter you'll learn how to build an ASP.NET web page using the ASP.NET Web Matrix Project, which is an all-in-one editor and development environment that enables you to drag and drop HTML elements and source code from a Toolbox onto your ASP.NET web page. Best of all, the Visual Web Developer writes the code for you.

HTML and XHTML: A Short Review

Before plowing ahead learning how to create an ASP.NET web page, let's take a very brief side trip to review HTML and XHTML. Skip this section if you already know how to build static web pages using HTML and XHTML; otherwise, refresh your memory by reading the rest of this section.

HTML markup code consists of tags that tell the client, which is usually the browser, how to display information contained in the web page and instruct it on how to link to other pages and files.

An HTML tag has a start tag (<TagName>) and an end tag (</TagName>). Information that is affected by the tag is placed between these tags. For example, suppose you want text to appear in italics. Here's what you write. The <i> is the start tag and the </i> is the end tag. The text "Some text" is the text that the browser displays in italics.

```
<i>Some text.</i>
```

There are many tags that can be used to describe how information contained in a web page should be displayed on the screen.

TIP: *Some HTML tags have only a start tag and not an end tag, such as <br>, which signifies a new line and the <hr> tag that tells the browser to draw a horizontal line.*

HTML tags are typically grouped together so that multiple tags can apply to the same information. This is referred to as nesting the HTML tags. Let's say that you want the previous example to display in bold italics. Here are the HTML tags that you need to write: The italics tag (<i>) is nested within the bold () tag. This tells the browser to display the text "Some text" in bold italic.

```
<b><i>Some text.</i></b>
```

You can change the order of nested tags as long as the tags are properly nested. Properly nested HTML tags require that each end tag appear in the reverse sequence from the start tags. The preceding example is properly nested; however, the next example is improperly nested because the bold end tag () comes before the italic end tag (</i>).

```
<b><i>Some text.</b></i>
```

TIP: *HTML tags are not case sensitive.*

XHTML is a variation of HTML that is used to create the HTML markup portion of an ASP.NET web page and requires stricter formatting than that found in HTML. XHTML is a blend of HTML and Extensible Markup Language (XML), which among other things has strict tag formatting.

XHTML is case sensitive and requires all tags to be in lowercase. Furthermore, all XHTML tags must have an end tag, including HTML tags such as <br> and <hr> that don't require an end tag in HTML.

TIP: *Combine the start and end tags into one tag by using the form <TagName />, such as <hr />.*

Kick-Starting Visual Web Developer

You can create an ASP.NET web page by using a simple text editor such as Notepad that comes with Windows. However, you'll find yourself having to write each line of HTML markup code and source, which is time-consuming and tedious.

Many professional developers choose to use a development environment that includes a WYSIWYG editor that you can use to drag and drop elements onto the ASP.NET web page. You don't have to write all the code, because the WYSIWYG editor writes some of it for you.

The Visual Web Developer is a commonly used WYSIWYG editor for building ASP.Net web pages. The Visual Web Developer is a component of Microsoft Visual Studio 2005, which is available at www.microsoft.com.

Once Microsoft Visual Studio 2005 is installed, start by following these steps:

1. Click the Windows's Start button.
2. Select Programs.
3. Select the Microsoft Visual Studio 2005 folder.
4. Select the Microsoft Visual Studio 2005 application.

After Visual Studio 2005 is displayed, select File | New Web Site and then select the ASP.NET Web Site icon to create a new ASP.NET web page. A screen opens displaying two tabs along the bottom-left corner: Design and Source.

The Design tab (Figure 2-1) is used to design the content of your ASP.NET web page by dragging HTML elements from the Toolbox and dropping them onto the page. Anything you drop on the Design tab appears on the ASP.NET web page.

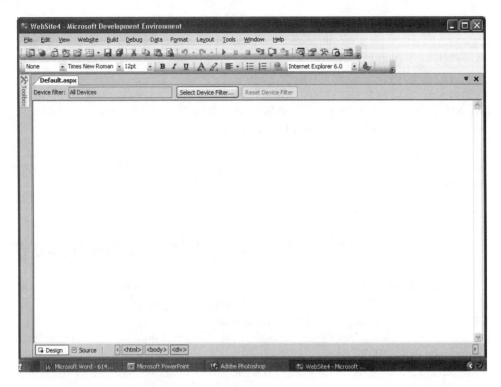

Figure 2-1 The Design tab is where you design content for your ASP.NET web page.

You display the Toolbox by selecting the Toolbox tab located in the upper-left side of the window (Figure 2-2). Place the mouse cursor on the Toolbox tab and wait a second for the Toolbox to open.

The Source tab displays the HTML markup code for the ASP.NET web page. The Visual Web Developer generates this code for you, although you can enter HTML markup code there too.

Notice that the Design tab is empty. This is because you haven't designed your ASP.NET web page yet. However, the Source tab contains HTML markup code. At first this may seems unusual, but it isn't, because the Visual Web Developer automatically creates the basic HTML server control that is required for all ASP.NET web pages.

An HTML server control looks like HTML markup code, except that an HTML control contains the runat="server" attribute (Figure 2-3). The runat="server" attribute tells the ASP.NET engine to run the HTML server control on the server

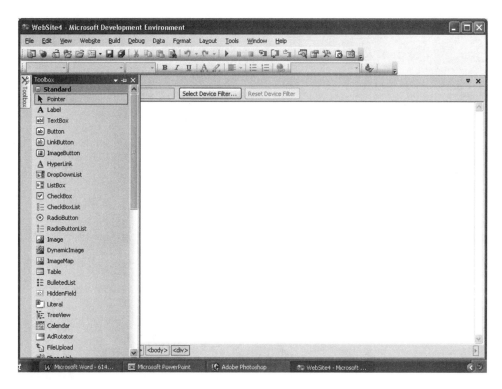

Figure 2-2   The Toolbox contains controls that you drag and drop into your web page.

side rather than on the client side (see Chapter 1). You'll learn how the HTML control is run on the server side in the section "HTML Server Controls" later in this chapter.

For now it is important to understand that in the absence of the runat="server" attribute, the ASP.NET engine treats the HTML markup as an HTML control, but not an HTML server control. This means that the HTML markup code is sent directly to the client (i.e., browser) by the ASP.NET engine if you leave out the runat="server" attribute.

Tools of the Trade

Along the left side of the Visual Web Developer is the Toolbox that contains elements and controls that you can drag and drop onto your ASP.NET web page in the Design tab.

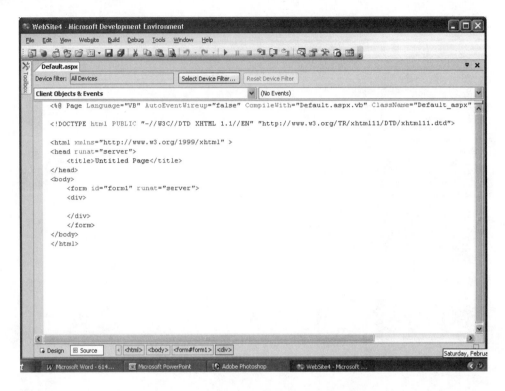

Figure 2-3 The Code tab displays an HTML control that is generated for you.

The Moment of Truth: Creating Your First ASP.NET Web Page

Let's create the traditional first ASP.NET web page—Hello world! Here's what you need to do:

1. Select the Design tab.

2. Select the Toolbox panel.

3. Drag and drop the Label from the Standard section of the Toolbox onto the Design tab. Remember that the open space in the Design tab is the ASP.NET web page that the client will see. Drag and drop by pointing to the Label in the Toolbox. Hold down the left mouse button while moving the mouse cursor from the Toolbox to the ASP.NET web page in the Design tab.

4. Release the mouse button and you'll notice that the Toolbox automatically closes.

5. Point to the label on the Design tab. Select the right mouse button to display a pop-up menu and then select the Property option to display the Property panel.

6. Select the label on the Design tab and then locate the Text property in the Appearance section of the Property panel. Enter **Hello world!**

7. Move the mouse cursor to anywhere on the Design tab and then click the left mouse button. "Hello world!" appears on the ASP.NET web page (Figure 2-4). You may have to drag the sizing box that appears around the label to resize the label so that the text appears on one line.

That's all you need to do.

Select the Code tab and you'll see code that Visual Web Developer wrote for you. You must admit that dragging and dropping is more convenient that writing the code yourself.

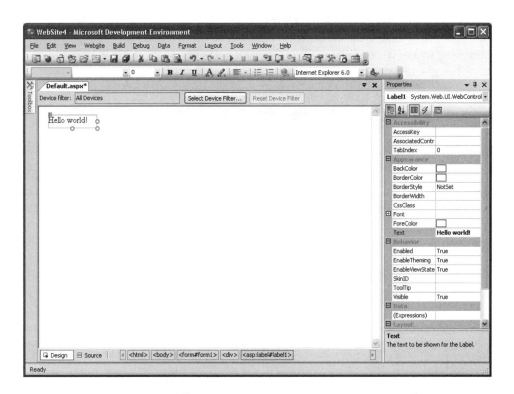

Figure 2-4   Dragging and dropping the label is easier than writing the code yourself.

Testing Your ASP.NET Web Page

You can test your ASP.NET web page by pressing CTRL-F5. Visual Web Developer cranks away and opens the web page in your browser (Figure 2-5).

Very little can go wrong with the Hello world! web page. However, a real-world ASP.NET application is more complex than the Hello world! web page and must be thoroughly tested before you release it on your web site.

In order to thoroughly test your ASP.NET application, you'll need to run it using the debugger that comes with Visual Web Developer. The debugger is a tool that is used to execute your web page so that you can see what happens when each instruction executes.

You'll find the debugger by selecting the Debug menu option. Don't do this now, because we'll show you how to use the debugger later in this book.

Writing HTML Code Yourself: Watch Out!

There are still some diehards among us who like to get their hands dirty and write HTML markup code themselves. Dragging and dropping is simple for lazy developers. If you're one of those hands-on developers, though, then there are a few facts you need to know before you starting writing HTML markup code using Visual Web Developer.

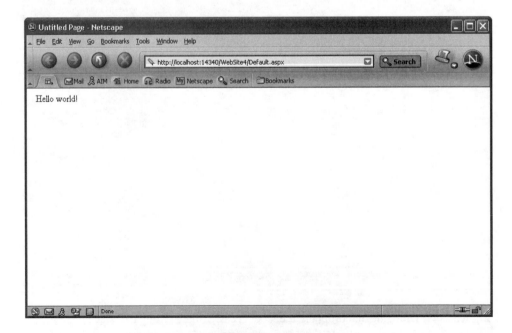

Figure 2-5   Test your ASP.NET web page by selecting CTRL-F5.

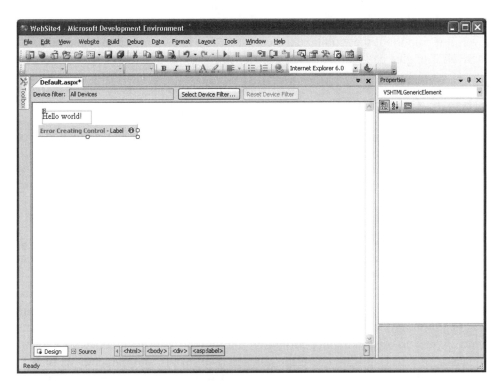

Figure 2-6   An error is displayed if you write buggy code.

The Source tab of the Visual Web Developer is the place to insert your own HTML markup code into the ASP.NET web page. Code that you enter here is properly displayed when you switch to the Design tab. However, you must make sure that you properly write your code; otherwise, you'll see an error displayed in the Design tab (Figure 2-6).

Digging into the Source Code

The source code section of the ASP.NET web page contains instructions written in a .NET-compliant programming language such as Visual Basic .NET or C#. Source code tells the ASP.NET engine how to generate the dynamic web page in response to a client's request. Source code is inserted into the ASP.NET web page using the Source tab.

You'll learn how to write source code in the remaining chapters; for now, however, it is important that you take a closer look at what source code is and how the ASP.NET engine calls it.

Object-Oriented Programming: A Class Act

Source code is written using object-oriented programming. Object-oriented programming is a style of programming that resembles the way we naturally look at things. We see the world as objects such as a computer keyboard. We don't see the world as a group of parts such as keys, springs, diodes, and other components of the keyboard.

An object is defined as having data and actions. For example, a keyboard has a specific length and width. These are two of many data that defines the keyboard. Also, a key on the keyboard can be pressed and released. These are two actions that also define the keyboard.

In *object-oriented* programming, a *class* defines an *object*. Data that is associated with the object is called a *property,* and actions are called *methods*. It is important to keep in mind that a class is a definition and not a real object. Some developers who are new to object-oriented programming find this a difficult concept to grasp.

Think of a class as a stencil of the letter *W*. The stencil isn't the letter W. Instead it defines what the letter *W* looks like. A real *W* is created when you place the stencil on a piece of paper and trace the stencil. The real *W* is seen once you remove the stencil from the paper. You can use the stencil over and over again to create many copies of the letter *W,* and all those copies are identical because they come from the same definition.

In object-oriented programming, copies of a class are called *instances,* or simply objects. Each instance is identical to other instances of the same class. That is, each instance has properties and methods that are defined in the class. For example, when we create an instance of the keyboard, the instance will have a width and length and keys that can be pressed and released.

Visual Basic .NET (and C#) use the .NET Framework library of classes that you'll be using to build the source code for your ASP.NET web page.

Classes will have properties whose values you can modify and other properties that cannot be modified. For example, you can't change the width and length of a keyboard, but you might be able to select the color of the keyboard.

A class has built-in methods and methods that you write. For example, pressing and releasing a key on the keyboard are built-in methods of a keyboard. Picking up and moving the keyboard is a method that you define (i.e., you can use one hand or two).

Let's take a look at a method that you'll use when writing source code for your ASP.NET web page. This is the Response.Write() method, which is used to send a response to the client who initiated the request.

Response is the object, and Write() is the built-in method. Notice that a dot is used to link them together. In a sense this is saying to the ASP.NET engine, use the Write() method that is defined in the Response object. Developers refer to this as calling the method. You'll learn a lot more about calling methods throughout this book.

The Write() method sends a series of characters from the ASP.NET engine to the client, which is usually a browser. These characters are typically HTML markup code that creates the dynamic web page. Characters are placed within quotations between the parentheses as shown in the following example, which causes "Hello world." to be displayed in bold on the client's computer.

```
Response.Write("<b>Hello world.</b>")
```

Events: I'll Wait for Your Call

The source code portion of an ASP.NET web page is subdivided into one or more groups, each of which is associated with an event. An *event* is an action such as your pressing ENTER on the keyboard. The source code that is associated with the event is called an *event handler.*

When an event occurs, the ASP.NET engine executes any source code in the event handler that is associated with the event. Developers say that an event has fired when an event occurs, causing its event handler to execute.

For example, a 911 operator might receive a call for an ambulance. This is an event. The 911 operator follows a specific set of instructions when a call for an ambulance is received. These instructions (source code) are the event handler that dispatches an ambulance.

TIP: *Programming languages that execute source code in response to an event are called event-driven programming languages. Programming languages that execute source code in sequence are called procedural programming languages.*

There are many events that can happen, which you'll learn about throughout this book. For now let's take a look at an event that you'll respond to most often. It is called the Page_Load event. As the name implies, the Page_Load event occurs whenever the client loads the ASP.NET web page. Associated with this event is the Page_Load event handler. The Page_Load event handler contains source code that executes each time the ASP.Net web page is loaded by a client.

You'll need to define the Page_Load event handler. Here's how this is done:

1. Select the Source tab.
2. Change AutoEventWireup to True.
3. Click the right mouse button.
4. Select View Code from the pop-up menu.
5. Enter the following source code:

```
Sub Page_Load(sender as Object, e as EventArgs)
    Response.Write("<b>Hello world.</b>")
End Sub
```

That's all you need to do!

Let's walk through this example. First of all remember that we're using Visual Basic .NET as the programming language for the source code, so your source code will look different if you decide to use C# to write it.

Sub and End Sub define the sequence of source code instructions that forms the event handler. Sub is short for subroutine. Each event handler must have a unique name. Page_Load is the name of this event handler.

ASP.NET passes the event handler two pieces of information in order for it to process the event. First, the event handler needs to know who made the request, and then it needs to know any additional data about the event.

These are given to the event handler by the ASP.NET engine and are stored in arguments that are identified within the parentheses of the event handler. You don't need to know about arguments right now, because you'll learn about them later in this book. However, if you can't wait, then read the next section, "Arguments: A Preview"; otherwise, skip that section.

Between the Sub and End Sub lines is where you place the source code that you want the ASP.NET engine to execute whenever the Page_Load event occurs. Source code is executed sequentially. You'll learn how to write source code throughout this book.

Our example has one line of source code that sends Hello world. to the client when the client loads the ASP.NET web page. You probably recognize this as HTML markup code.

Arguments: A Preview

The term argument might sound strange to you; however, think of an argument as information. For example, a person's name, the address of the emergency, and the nature of the emergency constitute information (arguments) that the 911 operator needs to respond to a call for an ambulance.

The developer needs a way to identify arguments (information) so that it can be referenced in the event handler. This is done by assigning a name to the argument and by identifying the kind of augment within the parentheses of the event handler.

Think of this as the form that the 911 operator fills in when an emergency call is received. The form has Caller, Address, and Nature of Emergency as labels. The 911 operator writes down the name of the caller, the address of the emergency, and the nature of the emergency alongside the corresponding label.

While the emergency call is being processed, the 911 operator and other emergency personnel refer to the labels (Caller, Address, Nature of Emergency) whenever this specific information is required. For example, the paramedic might radio the 911 operator, "We're at the address speaking to the caller." The 911 operator and the paramedics refer to the form for the specific address and the caller's name.

The argument name is like the label on the form. The ASP.NET engine "writes" the specific information to each label. Developers call this assigning a value to the argument. You'll learn more about this in the next chapter.

The Page_Load event handler has two arguments. The first argument is called sender and is a kind of Object. You'll recall that an Object is an instance of a class. This identifies the source of the event. The second argument is called e and is a kind of EventArgs, which is information about the event. You'll learn more about this later in the book.

Defining the Source Code Portion

Before event handlers can respond to an event, you need to define the source code portion of your ASP.NET web page. You do this by defining a Page directive and a script. A directive tells the ASP.NET engine how to execute the source code. You'll learn about directives later in this book. For now it is important for you to understand the Page directive in order to test the source code.

A directive begins with <%@ and ends with %>. Between these are the directive name and any directive attributes. A Page directive tells the ASP.NET engine how to execute the source code portion of the ASP.NET web page. It uses the Language attribute to tell the ASP.NET engine which programming language is used to write the source code. Here's the Page directive that is written for you by Visual Web Developer. The AutoEventWireup attribute is set to True, but you'll need to set this to False.

```
<%@ Page Language="VB" AutoEventWireup="False"
CompileWith="Default.aspx.vb"
ClassName="Default_aspx" %>
```

Beneath the Page directive is a script. A *script* consists of one or more lines of code that can be executed at the server or at the client. For example, any code written in JavaScript is a script that is executed by the client. Event handlers are part of a script that is executed by the server.

You define a script by using the <script> … </script> HTML markup code. The <script> start tag must include the runat="server" attribute, which tells the ASP.NET engine that the script is to be executed by the server.

Here's the complete source code portion of our example. Make sure that the Source tab contains this source code and then test it (see the section "Testing Your ASP.NET Web Page" earlier in the chapter).

```
<script runat="server">
    Sub Page_Load(sender as Object, e as EventArgs)
        Response.Write("<b>Hello world.</b>")
    End Sub
</script>
```

HTML Server Controls

As you learned in Chapter 1, you can drag and drop elements from the Toolbox onto the Design tab and the Visual Web Developer automatically writes the corresponding HTML markup code for you and displays it in the HTML tab. Every time the ASP.NET engine encounters HTML markup code on your ASP.NET web page, the ASP.NET engine passes it along to the client without modifying the code.

HTML server controls take the form of HTML markup code but contain the runat="server" attribute, which tells the ASP.NET engine that this is an instruction for the ASP.NET engine and not HTML markup code that is passed along to the client. You insert HTML controls on your ASP.NET web page by hand.

Earlier in this chapter you learned about classes, methods, and properties. The .NET Framework that you installed to run the Visual Web Developer contains a library of classes that are used to create source code for an ASP.NET web page. Think of this as a library of source code that other programmers wrote and you can use in your ASP.NET web page.

An HTML control tells the ASP.NET engine to use the corresponding .NET Framework class in place of the HTML control. The class contains related methods and properties used by the ASP.NET engine to generate the corresponding HTML markup code.

Web Controls

Web controls are similar in concept to HTML controls in that they are instructions to the ASP.NET engine to use the corresponding class in the .NET Framework to generate HTML markup code. HTML server controls are closely tied to the output HTML control; ASP.NET server controls are not.

Web controls are declared using the following format:

```
<asp:WebControlName runat="server" Property1="Value1"></asp:WebControlName>
```

The declaration begins with <asp: followed by the name of the web control. Next is the runat="server" property, which tells the ASP.NET engine to run the code. Depending on the nature of the web control, there may be other properties. If so, then they are also listed along with their values. The name of the property and its value are dependent on the web control. The web control ends with the end tag.

You insert web controls on your ASP.NET web page by dragging and dropping them from the Web Controls portion of the Toolbar onto the Design tab. When the ASP.NET engine encounters a web control, it uses the corresponding .NET Framework class to generate HTML markup code that is sent to the client.

HTML Server Controls vs. Web Controls

HTML server controls seem to do the same thing as web controls. Why both? HTML controls are used to make it easy to import and export dynamic web pages between ASP.NET and ASP, since no changes are necessary. On the other hand, changes must be made when web controls are used, since they are not compatible with ASP.

Besides the compatibility issue, web controls have more properties than HTML controls, giving you greater control than with the comparable HTML control. Web controls can be dragged and dropped from the Toolbox, whereas HTML controls must be entered by hand.

Looking Ahead

The Visual Web Developer is a development environment that is used to build and test ASP.NET web pages. It has two sections that are identified by tabs: Design and Source. The Design tab is where you drag and drop elements and controls to form the ASP.NET web page. The Source tab is where you enter source for your ASP.NET web page that instructs the ASP.NET engine how to generate the dynamic web page.

The Toolbox contains all the elements that you need to build an ASP.NET web page. You insert them into the Design tab by dragging and dropping them from the Toolbox.

Once you've built your ASP.NET web page, you must test it by pressing CTRL-F5 to pop up the web page in the browser.

Now that you have a good understanding of how to create an ASP.NET web page using the Visual Web Developer, it is time to create a more robust ASP.NET web page than Hello world!—which you'll do in the next chapter.

Quiz

1. An HTML server control is

   a. Another term for HTML markup code

   b. Instructions for the ASP.NET engine to use an HTML class in .NET Framework

   c. Instructions for the ASP.NET engine to use a web control class in .NET Framework

   d. Another term for web control

2. A class is an instance of an object.

   a. True

   b. False

3. The Response.Write() method

   a. Sends HTML controls to the client

   b. Sends web controls to the client

   c. Sends characters to the client

   d. None of the above

4. An event handler is

   a. Something that occurs while the ASP.NET executes

   b. A block of code that executes in reaction to a specified event

   c. Another term for an event

   d. Code that sends an event to an ASP.NET web page

5. Page_Load

   a. Is the way a client requests a page from the web server

   b. Starts the web server

   c. Starts the ASP.NET engine

   d. Is the name of the event handler for the Page_Load event

6. An ASP.NET web page is divided into an HTML portion and a source code portion.

   a. True

   b. False

7. Event handlers must be defined within the script tag.

   a. True

   b. False

8. A method is

   a. An action associated with a class

   b. Data associated with a class

   c. An instance of a class

   d. None of the above

9. The runat="server" attribute means

   a. Start the web server

   b. Start the ASP.NET engine

   c. Execute the code on the server side

   d. None of the above

10. The sequence <%@ Page Language="VB" %> is a directive.

   a. True

   b. False

Answers

1. b. Instructions for the ASP.NET engine to use an HTML class in .NET Framework

2. b. False

3. c. Sends characters to the client

4. b. A block of code that executes in reaction to a specified event

5. d. Is the name of the event handler for the Page_Load event

6. a. True

7. a. True

8. a. An action associated with a class

9. c. Execute the code on the server side

10. a. True

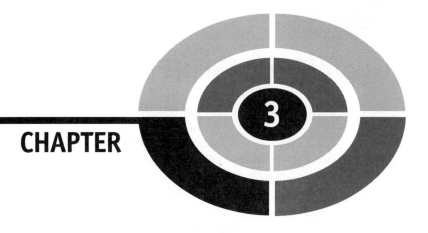

Building an ASP.NET Web Page Application

Developing an ASP.NET web page application is more involved than creating a web site using static web pages because you must design, develop, and test both the client side and the server side. The client side is what the visitor sees. The server side is how the ASP.NET web page generates what the visitor sees.

As you learned in previous chapters, an ASP.NET web page application can link together web pages with databases and non-web-based application, which is something that cannot be done using static web pages. It is for this reason that an ASP.NET web page application can be more challenging to build than a web site that has only static web pages.

In this chapter, you'll learn techniques developers use to create an ASP.NET web page application.

Designing an ASP.NET Web Page Application

All applications, including an ASP.Net web page application, are developed using the same general road map, called the application life cycle. The *application life cycle* divides the development process of an application into phases, each of which must be completed before the next phase can begin. A phase specifies things that must be done in order to create the application successfully.

The life cycle that we'll use have five phases: design, development, testing, implementation, and maintenance. You might come across other versions of the life cycle that have different phases, but they generally all help you accomplish the same objective: to create an application.

You might be wondering why they call this a life cycle. The reason is that the road map to creating an application is similar to the development of living things. Think about plants. A new plant develops from a seed, matures, and dies. During this cycle it gives off other seeds that begin the life cycle again.

An application also dies when it outlives its usefulness. Usually by this time, the application has been modified many, many times in order to conform to changing business requirements. At some point, developers decide it is more economical to build a replacement application than to simply continue to modify the existing application. When this happens, the existing application dies. The developers start at the beginning of the life cycle to create the replacement application.

Design Phase

The first phase of the life cycle is the *design* phase. This is where you determine the objective of the application. That is, what is the application going to do? You then define all the features that will be necessary to reach the objective.

Let's say that you're a building a house. In the design phase, you determine your housing needs and relay this to the architect. The architect draws up a detail plan for the house based on your needs.

Your goal for the design phase is to develop a detail plan for building your application. This plan must describe how both the user side and the server side look and work.

It is best to begin your design using a top-down approach. First, determine what your application is going to do, such as accept an online order.

Client Side

Next, focus on the information needed to achieve this objective. That is, what information is necessary to place an order online? Make a list and describe each piece of information by name, kind of information (e.g., money, quantity, name, calculation), and source.

For example, you'll need to display product information on the screen before the customer places the order. Typically, product information includes a product name, a product description, a product number, a price, and possibly a product picture. This information is generated by the ASP.NET engine using product data stored in a database.

Once you make a list of this information, then design the user interface. A user interface is the client side of an application that the visitor uses to interact with your application. The list of information is your guide to determine what HTML elements are needed to design the user interface. For example, labels can be used to display a product name, a product description, a product number, and a price. An image element is used to display a product picture.

Your user interface design must define how the user interacts with your web page. Suppose you expect the visitor to place an order using your web page; you must then decide how they are going to place the order. That is, what information must they enter, where do they enter this information, what button do they click to submit the order, and so on. This is all part of the design phase.

TIP: During the design phase, focus on what you need and not how you are going to build it. Building occurs in the development phase.

Your job is to describe the user interface and how it works the best way you can without building it. This plan is then given to a developer to build, although in some situations you'll be both the designer and the developer.

Server Side

During the design phase, you must specify what you want to happen on the server side of your application. Remember from previous chapters that the server side is where the ASP.NET engine processes requests and generates a dynamic web page that is sent to the visitor. Therefore, you must explicitly itemize steps needed to process the request and generate a dynamic web page.

These steps depend on the nature of your application. Some applications will require the ASP.NET engine to retrieve data from a database and insert that data, such as product information, into a dynamic web page. Other applications might require the ASP.NET engine to access a non-web application, for instance, to verify login information provided by the visitor.

Whatever the process, it is your responsibility to list all the steps in the process so that a developer can write the code to have the ASP.NET engine perform those steps. The best way to specify a process is by using pseudocode. Pseudocode is an informal language that is a mixture of plain English and a programming language.

Let's say that you want the process to verify login information provided by the visitor. The ASP.NET engine calls a non-web application to do the verification, and that application sends back an approval or rejection notice.

Here's the pseudocode that describes this process:

```
Read ID and password submitted by visitor
Send ID and password to verification program
if verification program approves then
    Dynamically create an approval web page and sent it to the visitor
else
    Dynamically create a rejection web page and sent it to the visitor
end if
```

Everything except the if...else...end if is in plain English. The if...else...end if is part of a programming language that specifies a condition for making a decision. If the condition is true, then one set of instructions is executed. Another set of instructions is executed if the condition is false.

A developer translates pseudocode into a programming language that the ASP.NET understands. As a designer, you only need to describe every process as best as you can using pseudocode.

Development Phase

The *development* phase is the segment of the life cycle where your application is built. It is here that a developer brings your plans to life by creating the user interface and the server-side processing. Think of this as the general contractor taking the plans for your house from the architect and then building your house.

You might be the developer of your application, but typically in larger commercial applications, there are teams of designers and developers working on the project. Therefore, it is important that the plans clearly convey the specification for the application; otherwise, times may come during development when the builder will be left wondering what you want to happen.

Imagine if the architect planned for a window but didn't specify its location. The carpenter is left wondering and might put the window where he/she thinks it belongs, but not necessarily where the architect wanted it.

Throughout the remaining chapters of this book you'll learn the techniques for building an application.

Testing

Testing is the third and probably the most important phase of the life cycle because this is where you identify flaws in your planning and development. Testing is where you determine if the application performs as planned.

There are various types of testing. Four important tests are unit testing, integration, quality assurance, and user acceptance.

Unit testing is where a piece of the application called a *unit* is tested. For example, a unit might be verification of login information. Typically, a unit test is performed by the developer who built the unit.

Integration testing is where all the pieces (i.e., units) are tested together to determine if they work. On large commercial applications, there is usually a group of technicians who perform integration testing. These technicians are not usually developers of the application.

Quality assurance testing is where a group of testers verify that the application performs according to specification. Their objective (among others) is to try to break the application before the application is used for business. Each time they find a problem, called a bug, they report it to the developer for fixing and further testing.

User acceptance testing is where members of the business unit who are going to use the application to run the business verify that the application meets their objectives. Think of this as walking through your new house for the first time. You open every door and window and go into every room—and, of course, flush the toilet.

Once the users accept the application—and the application passes all the other tests—the application is ready to be used by the business.

Implementation

Implementation is where the business uses the new application and turns off older applications that are being replaced. This is a critical moment because in some situations, the business cannot fall back on the older application once the new application is in place.

In large commercial applications, teams of technicians from various areas of the firm develop a formal implementation plan that specifies everything that must be in place before they turn off the old application and turn on the new application. Furthermore, the implementation plan also specifies how to test once the new application is installed—and steps to take if the new application fails the test.

Typically, implementation occurs over a long weekend. This gives the team time to install and test the new application—and time to back out the new application and reinstall the older application in case the installation of the new application fails.

TIP: *You won't have to develop an elaborate implementation plan for most of your applications unless they are large commercial applications.*

Maintenance

Maintenance is the last and longest phase of the life cycle. This is where your application is used to run the business. Needs of a business change, and therefore your application will need to reflect those changes by adding new features to the application. These changes are made during maintenance of the application.

The maintenance phase begins as soon as the business unit begins using the application. It continues until it is decided that it is more economical to create a replacement application than it is to change the current application. This results in the life cycle starting over again.

Designing Your First ASP.NET Web Application

Let's design a simple ASP.NET web application. The application will create a new account number for a visitor and display it on the screen. Although an application that creates a new account number usually gets the new account number from a database, our application will generate the number by combining the visitor's first and last names with the number 54321. We'll do it this way because you haven't learned how to interact with a database yet.

The first step in the design process is to clearly state the objective of the application. The objective of our application is to use a visitor's first and last names to create a new account number.

The next step is to list the information that we need. Here's the list:

- Visitor's first name
- Visitor's last name
- New account number

Client Side

Next we need to focus on the user interface. The user interface should have a place for the visitor to enter his or her first name and last name and a button that can be clicked to submit this information to the server side for processing.

Once the server side generates the new account number, we'll need to display the visitor's first and last names and the new account number. We don't need the button displayed. Furthermore, we must make sure that the visitor cannot edit the first and last names and the new account number once they are displayed.

Server Side

Our design must specify how the server side is going to process the request for a new account number. The objective of the server side is to read the visitor's first and last names, combine them with the number 54321, and then display the new account number on the screen.

However, we need to be very specific in how we describe this process; otherwise, the developer won't know what we want the ASP.NET engine to do. We specify the process using the following pseudocode.

```
Read the visitor's first name
Read the visitor's last name
Create the new account number by combining the visitor's
first name and last name with 54321.
Make the visitor's first name read only
Make the visitor's last name read only
Make the Create new account number button invisible
Display the new account number as read only
```

Notice how specific we have to be when describing how the ASP.NET engine processes the request for a new account number. We need to state that the visitor's first and last names and the new account number are displayed as read only. Read only means that the visitor can see the information but cannot change it.

Developing Your First ASP.NET Web Application

Now it is time to transform your design into a working ASP.NET web application. We'll begin by creating the user interface and then write the program on the client side to create and display the new account number.

Start by opening a new ASP.NET web site in the Visual Web Developer (see "Kick-Starting Visual Web Developer" in Chapter 2).

Our design calls for two screens. One screen prompts the visitor to enter first and last names and then click a button to get a new account number. The other screen displays the first and last names and the new account number.

We can achieve the same results by using one screen that includes all the elements. We'll then use the Visible property to make an element visible or invisible, depending on the activity that is occurring at the time. Setting the Visible property to True makes an element visible on the screen. Setting the Visible property to False hides the element.

For example, initially, the label and text box for the new account number are invisible. Once the visitor enters his or her name and clicks the button, the new account number label and text box will be visible and the button will be invisible.

Here are the steps to create the user interface for our application:

1. Drag and drop a Label.
2. Change the Text property under Appearance in the Properties panel to **First Name:** and press ENTER.
3. Drag and drop an HTML Textbox and place it alongside the label.
4. Change the ID property in the Properties frame to FName (Figure 3-1) and press ENTER.

TIP: *The ID property is used on the server side to identify a specific control.*

5. Select the first name label and use the sizing handles to stretch the label box so that there is a space between it and the text box, if needed.
6. Press ENTER to move to the next line.
7. Drag and drop a Label.
8. Change the Text property in the Properties frame to **Last Name:** and press ENTER.
9. Drag and drop a Textbox and place it alongside the label.
10. Change the ID property in the Properties frame to **LName** and press ENTER.

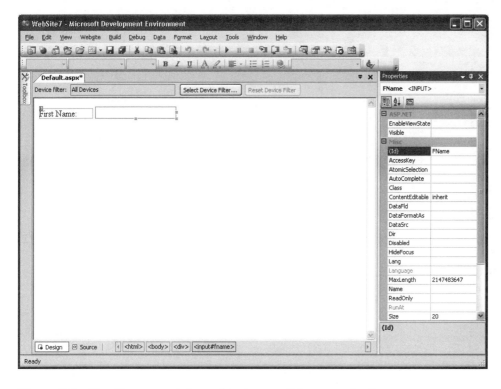

Figure 3-1   The ID property is located at the top of the properties list.

11. Select the last name label and use the sizing handles to stretch the label box so that there is a space between it and the text box, if necessary.

12. Press ENTER to move to the next line.

13. Drag and drop an HTML Button.

14. Change the Value property to **Create New Account Number**.

15. Change the ID property to **CreateAccount** and press ENTER.

16. Press ENTER to move to the next line.

17. Drag and drop a Label.

18. Change the Text property to **New Account Number**.

19. Change the ID property to **NewAccountNumberLabel**.

20. Change the Visible property to False and press ENTER.

21. Drag and drop a Textbox and place it alongside the label.

22. Change the ID property in the Properties frame to **NewAccountNumberTxBx**.

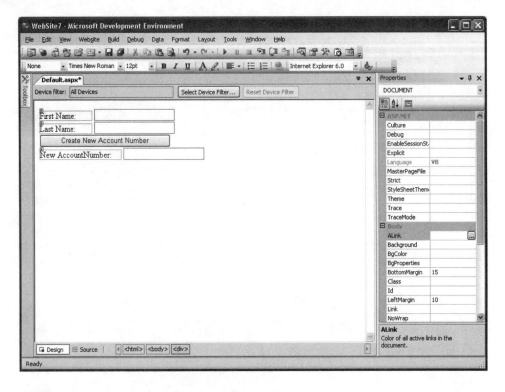

Figure 3-2 Here is the user interface for your application.

23. Change the Visible property to False and set the ReadOnly property to ReadOnly, and then press ENTER.

24. Select the new account label and use the sizing handles to stretch the label box so that there is a space between it and the text box.

Figure 3-2 shows the completed user interface for your application. Select the Source tab and you'll see the code that the Visual Web Developer generated for you as shown here:

```
<%@ Page Language="VB" AutoEventWireup="false" CompileWith="Default.aspx.vb"
ClassName="Default_aspx" %>
<!DOCTYPE html PUBLIC "-//W3C//DTD XHTML 1.1//EN"
"http://www.w3.org/TR/xhtml11/DTD/xhtml11.dtd">
<html xmlns="http://www.w3.org/1999/xhtml" >
<head runat="server">
    <title>Untitled Page</title>
</head>|
<body>
```

```
    <form id="form1" runat="server">
    <div>
        <asp:Label ID="Label1" Runat="server" Text="First Name:" Width="102px"
Height="19px"></asp:Label>
        <input id="FName" type="text" />
        <br />
        <asp:Label ID="Label2" Runat="server" Text="Last Name: " Width="102px"
Height="19px"></asp:Label>
        <input id="LName" type="text" />
        <br />
        <input id="CreateAccount " type="button" value="Create New Account Number" />
        <br />
        <asp:Label ID="NewAccountNumberLabel" Runat="server" Text="New AccountNumber: "
Width="158px"
            Height="19px" Visible="False"></asp:Label>
        <input id="NewAccountNumberTxBx" type="text" visible="false" />
    </div>
    </form>
</body>
</html>
```

Server-Side Development

Now we'll turn to the server side and write the code that is necessary to generate the new account number. Select the Create New Account Number button and press the right mouse button to display the pop-up menu. Select Run At Server Control.

Double-click the Create New Account Number button to create an event handler that responds when the visitor to your web site clicks the Create New Account Number button.

This automatically displays a screen that contains the Partial Class Default_aspx, in which the Sub...End Sub for the button's Click event handler is already inserted. All you need to do is insert the code that you want to execute when the event occurs.

First let's make the new account number label and text box visible by changing its Visible property to True. You do this by using the assignment operator as shown here:

```
NewAccountNumberLabel.Visible = True
NewAccountNumberTxBx.Visible = True
```

We use the ID of the element to identify the element that we want to change. We use the name of the property to specify what we want to change. The ID and the name of the property must be separated by a dot.

The value of the property is changed by using the equal sign followed by the new value. In both of these statements we're telling the ASP.NET engine to change the Visible property to True, making these elements visible.

TIP: *Each property has its own values. Review the property in the Property pane to determine available values for a particular property.*

Next let's create the new account number. Remember that according to the design the new account number is a combination of the first name, the last name, and the number 54321. Therefore, we must write code that reads the first and last names that are entered by the visitor and then combine them with 54321.

The visitor enters the first name in the text box that has the ID FName. The value entered into the text box becomes the value of the Text property for the text box. In order to access the value of a text box from within the code, we need to reference the text box's Text property as shown here:

```
FName.Value
```

Remember that FName is the ID you gave to the text box when you created the user interface. Value is the name of its Value property. We link them together using a dot. Therefore, anytime we want to refer to the contents of the first name text box, we simply use FName.Value. The same is true for the last name text box, except we use the ID for that text box, which is LName.

The plus sign is used to combine values. If we're using a literal value such as the number 54321, then we must enclose the literal value within quotations, such as "54321". If we're using the contents of a text box, then we use the ID followed by the Value property as shown in the previous paragraph.

Here's how we create the new account number:

```
FName.Value+LName.Value+"54321"
```

Our next job is to store the new account number into the new account number text box. This is done by using the equal sign to copy the new account number into the Text property as shown here:

```
NewAccountNumberTxBx.Value = FName.Value+LName.Value+"54321"
```

The NewAccountNumberTxBx is the ID for the text box that will contain the new account number, and Text is the Text property for that text box. At this point in the code, the new account is created and stored in the new account number text box.

We have one final step before the out event handler is completed. We need to hide the Create New Account button. To do this, we simply change its Visible property to False as shown here:

```
CreateNewAccount.Visible = False
```

Figure 3-3 shows you how your Code tab should look after entering code for the event handler. Notice that we indented the code. This makes it easy for you to read.

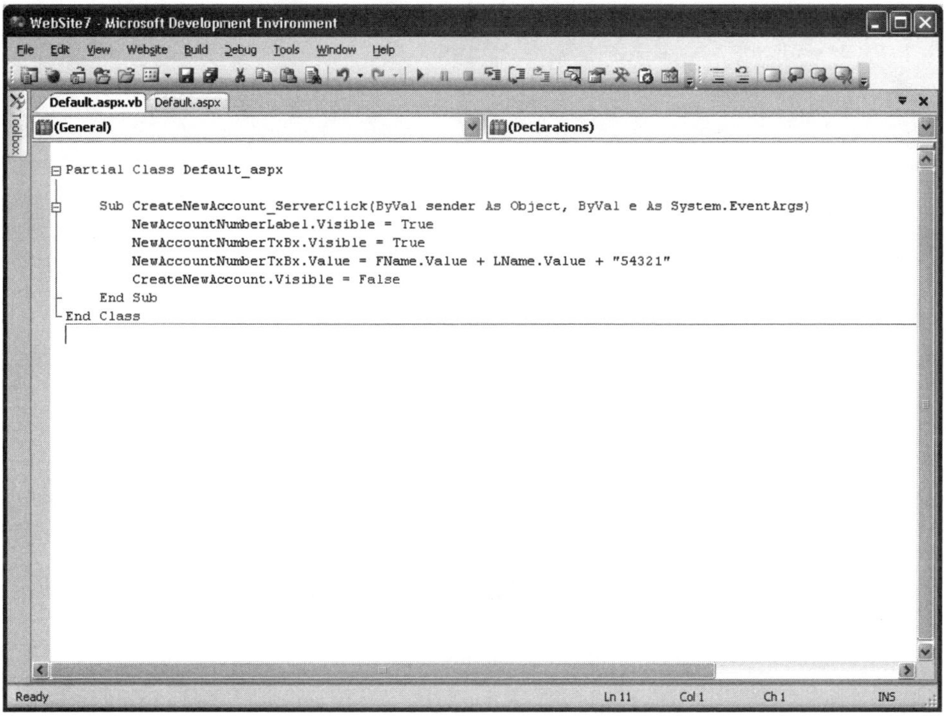

Figure 3-3   Here is the code for your application.

Running an ASP.NET Web Page Application

The moment of truth has arrived. It is time to run your ASP.NET web page application. All you need to do is to run the application by pressing CTRL-F5 in the Visual Web Developer. In a large commercial application, you would follow more elaborate testing procedures, as described in the earlier section of this chapter "Testing."

Here's how to test your application:

1. Press CTRL-F5.

2. Enter **Bob** into the first name text box and **Smith** into the last name text box (Figure 3-4) or use any name.

3. Click Create New Account Number.

4. The ASP.NET engine follows instructions that you wrote in the event handler to generate the new account and displays it on the screen (Figure 3-5).

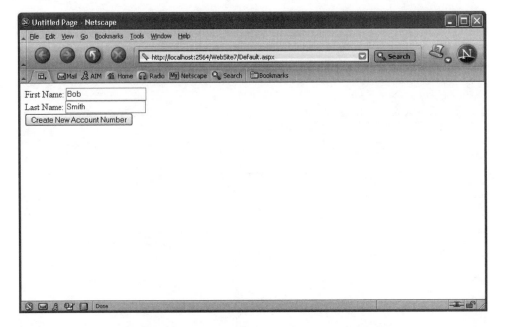

Figure 3-4 First enter a name and then click Create New Account Number.

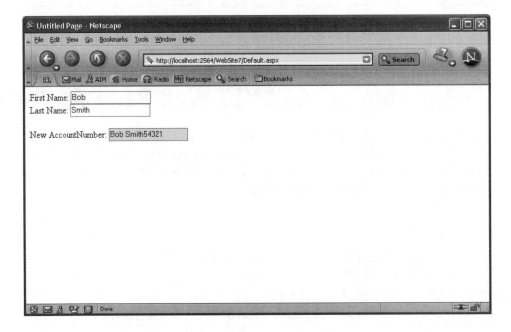

Figure 3-5 The server side generates the new account number.

Implementing an ASP.NET Web Page Application

As mentioned previously in this chapter, implementing an ASP.NET web page application is the process of making the application available to the business unit. This can be an involved process. ASP.NET files must be stored in the proper directories within the proper server. Any databases used by the application must be available. Non-web-based applications, if any, must be accessible to the ASP.NET application. And all these components must work together perfectly.

You must also develop and follow an implementation plan for turning the old application off and the new application on without disrupting business operations. This entails a great deal of planning, which is beyond the scope of this book.

However, implementing your simple application requires you to place the ASP.NET application file in the appropriate directory on your web server. You'll also need to create a static web page called index.html that has a hyperlink to your ASP.NET application. This too must be placed on the web server.

The visitor then will request the index.html web page and click the hyperlink to run your application.

Looking Ahead

In this chapter you learned how to use the life cycle to create an ASP.NET web page application. The life cycle defines five phases: design, development, testing, implementation, and maintenance. Each application that you build will pass through each of these phases.

The design phase is when you identify the objective of the application and specifically how it achieves that objective. The development phase translates the design into a working application. The testing phase tracks down bugs and design flaws and fixes them. The implementation phase turns off the old application and turns on the new application. The maintenance phase is where minor modifications are made to the application to conform to changes in the business.

You also learned in this chapter how to identify the elements in your code by using the ID property and how to change the value of a property. In addition, you learned how to read the value the user entered into a text box and use that value within the code of your application.

Now that you know how to build a simple ASP.NET web page application, we'll move on to learn new programming techniques that are used to create commercial

ASP.NET web page applications. In the next chapter, you'll learn about variables and expressions. Variables are used to store information into memory, and expressions are used to manipulate that information within your application.

Quiz

1. The ID property is
    a. Used as the text for an element
    b. Used as the value for an element
    c. Used to uniquely ID an element
    d. None of the above
2. The design phase is where you write code for your application.
    a. True
    b. False
3. You prevent a visitor from changing the value of a text box element by
    a. Setting the Visible property
    b. Setting the Invisible property
    c. Setting the ReadOnly property to True
    d. None of the above
4. Values can be combined by using
    a. The equal sign
    b. The assignment operator
    c. The equivalence operator
    d. The plus sign
5. You store information into a text box from within your code by using
    a. The equal sign
    b. The copy property
    c. The equivalence operator
    d. The plus sign
6. The testing phase is where bugs are discovered and fixed.
    a. True
    b. False

7. You create an event handler for a button control by double-clicking a button on the Design tab.

   a. True

   b. False

8. You can change the property of an element by

   a. Using the Property pane

   b. Using the Visible property of the element

   c. Using the ReadOnly property of the element

   d. None of the above

9. CreateAccount.Visible = False means

   a. Making an element visible

   b. Making an element invisible

   c. Making an element accessible

   d. None of the above

10. Literal values must be enclosed with quotations in your code.

   a. True

   b. False

Answers

1. c. Used to uniquely ID an element

2. b. False

3. c. Setting the ReadOnly property to True

4. d. The plus sign

5. a. The equal sign

6. a. True

7. a. True

8. a. Using the Property pane

9. b. Making an element invisible

10. a. True

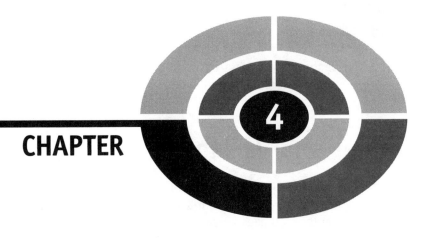

Variables and Expressions in ASP.NET

The brain behind every ASP.NET application is the code executed by the ASP.NET engine that processes and responds to requests from visitors to a web site. As you've seen in previous chapters, code consists of instructions that tell the ASP.NET engine how to process and respond to requests. Your job is to write that code.

Code for ASP.NET web pages is written using one of two programming languages: Visual Basic .NET or C#. A programming language is similar to English in that it has words that are grouped to form sentences. Throughout this book you'll learn how to write the words and sentences of Visual Basic .NET to tell ASP.NET what to do when a request is received from a visitor to your web site.

In this chapter, we'll explore the foundation of nearly every line of code that you'll write. These are the values, variables, and expressions that are used beginning

in the next chapter to tell your browser how to make decisions. If you know how to add 1 + 1, then you will breeze through this chapter.

Values and Variables

ASP.NET web pages contain a lot of information along with a few pictures sprinkled about to catch your attention. You place information that you want to display on the web page between a variety of HTML tags, such as between the open and close level-1 heading tags, <h1> and </h1>. Information placed on the screen is referred to as a *value*. Some developers call this a literal because it is exactly the information you want displayed. Values can also be placed in the code of your ASP.NET web page.

Values

As mentioned, any information that you place in the code of an ASP.NET web page is called a value. For example, "Hello world!" is a value. The number 10 is also a value. So is True, which is the value you assigned to the Visible property in the last chapter to make an HTML element visible on the web page.

As you can imagine, all kinds of values can be used in the code portion of your ASP.NET application, depending on the nature of your application. For example, a person's first name is a value and so is their street address. Their user IDs and passwords are also values.

Values are grouped into four categories: numbers, strings, Boolean values, and dates.

Number

A number is, well, a number that can be directly used in a calculation. Numbers are written in code without enclosing them in double quotations. For example, 10 is a number, which seems obvious until you run into something like this "10", which is a string and not a number value. More about strings in a moment.

Numbers are further categorized as integers and decimal values. An *integer* is a whole number that can be positive or negative. That is, the number doesn't have a fractional component. A *decimal* is a mixed number that can have a whole number and a decimal value. It too can be positive or negative. Developers refer to decimal values as floating-point values.

String

A *string* is a series of characters that are enclosed within quotations. "Hello, world!" is a string, and so is "121 Gordon Street". Notice that a string can contain numbers, but those numbers won't normally be used in a calculation.

However, numbers that are contained within a string can be used in a calculation if the string is converted to a number. For example, "10" is a string and not a number value. Removing the quotations transforms the string into a number. You'll learn how to convert strings to number values and number values to strings in the section "Casting: Converting Data Types" later in this chapter.

Boolean

A Boolean value is either true or false and cannot be any other value; it is written using the word True or False without placing it in quotations. This can be a little confusing at first because the words True and False look as if they are strings and should be enclosed in quotations. If you enter "True" in your code, you'll be entering a string. If you enter True, you'll be entering a Boolean value.

Boolean values are used a lot for setting the property values of HTML elements. You've seen this in the previous chapter, where you assigned True to the Visible property to make an HTML element appear on the web page.

Date

A date value is a date or a portion of a date. For example, 1/1/07 is a full date. January is a portion of that date, as are the day and year. Time is also considered part of a date. A date is written using a standard date format and is enclosed within pound signs (#1/1/07#).

Variables

Values are fine to use, if you know what the value is when you write your code. However, most times the value isn't known until your ASP.NET engine is ready to process a request. Let's say that ASP.NET needs to calculate the sales tax on the purchase price of an item. You probably know the percentage value of the sales tax when you write the ASP.NET web page, so you can write the value of the percentage into your code. However, you don't know the purchase price of the item until the customer selects the item while your ASP.NET web page runs. This poses a dilemma. How can you write the sales tax calculation into your code without knowing the purchase price of the item?

The solution is to use a variable in place of the purchase price. Think of a variable as an empty cardboard box sitting on a table. You place a label on the box on which you write a name. You place a value inside the box. Each time you want to refer to the value, you simply refer to the name of the box.

Let's return to our sales tax example to see how this works. First we'll need a box to store the purchase price. Let's write PurchasePrice on the label of the box. We could write any name on the label, but it is less confusing if the name used represents the value stored inside the box.

Next, we'll write the math expression to calculate the sales tax.

```
PurchasePrice * .06
```

TIP: *The asterisk (*) is the symbol for multiplication.*

Notice that we use the name on the label of the box when we're referring to the purchase price in this calculation. We could have used the actual purchase price, but we don't know the purchase price until the customer enters the purchase price into the ASP.NET web page. Until then, all we can do is refer to the box where the purchase price will be stored.

When the ASP.NET engine sees PurchasePrice in the code, it knows that PurchasePrice is a label for a box that contains the value of the purchase price. The ASP.NET engine then goes to the box, copies the value, replaces PurchasePrice with the value, and performs the calculation.

The box is actually a piece of computer memory. The label on the box is a variable name and is used to refer to a location in computer memory.

Data Types: What Kind of Data Is in the Box?

A *variable* is a temporary storage place—a box—in computer memory where values are placed while the ASP.NET engine is processing a request. You need to specify the type of information that can be placed into the box. You do this by specifying a data type for the variable.

A *data type* describes the kind and range of values that can be placed into the box. There are 15 date types in Visual Basic .NET. We are covering the ten data types that you'll use the most. The ten data types that you'll need to know are:

Integer

As you learned previously in this chapter, an integer is a whole number. An Integer data type specifies a temporary memory location that can hold a whole number.

However, the number must range from −2,147,483,648 to 2,147,483,647. Any number outside of this range won't fit into this location.

Long

The Long data type specifies a temporary memory location that can hold a whole number within the range −9,223,372,036,854 to 9,223,372,036,854,775,807. This hold values smaller and greater than the Integer data type can hold.

Short

The Short data type is used to store whole numbers in the range −32,768 to 32,767.

Single

The Single data type is used to store mixed numbers, which are called floating point. A mixed number contains both a whole number and a decimal value. It can hold negative values ranging from −3.4028235E+38 through −1.401298E−45 and positive values ranging from 1.401298E−45 through 3.4028235E+38.

TIP: *The E specifies the number of decimal places for the number. For example, 7.52E−8 is 0.0000000752.*

Double

The Double data type is used to store more precise mixed numbers. Negative numbers can range from −1.79769313486231570E+308 through −4.94065645841246544E+308, and positive numbers can range from 4.94065645841246544E−324 through 1.79769313486231570E−308.

TIP: *Precision is the accuracy of a number to a specific decimal value.*

Decimal

The Decimal data type provides more precision and is much less subject to rounding errors than the Single and Double data type. The Decimal data can store a whole number; the largest it can store is 79,228,162,514,264,337,593,543,950,335, and the smallest is −79,228,162,514,264,337,593,543,950,335. The Decimal data type can also store up to 28 decimal places. The largest of these is 7.9228162514264337593543950335.

Boolean

The Boolean data type is used to store a Boolean value, which is described previously in this chapter. These values are either True or False.

String

The String data type is used to store a string, which is a series of characters that are enclosed within quotations.

Date

The Date data type is used to store dates.

Object

The Object data type is used to store any kind of data; however, you should use another data type in preference to using an Object data type, if possible. When you use an Object data type, Visual Basic .NET has to convert the data stored in the Object to the proper data type before processing the data. This takes up more computing time than if you used the proper data type and also runs the risk of errors while your application is running.

Declaring a Variable

Remember that the box in the preceding section is really called a variable. Before you can use a variable, you must tell the ASP.NET engine to create a variable by *declaring* a variable in the code of your ASP.NET web page.

In order to tell the ASP.NET engine to do anything, you must write a *statement* within the code of your ASP.NET web page. Think of a statement as a sentence that tells the ASP.NET engine to do something. The statement must contain words that the ASP.NET engine understands. Those words are contained in the Visual Basic .NET programming language.

The statement that tells the ASP.NET engine to create a variable has three parts.

Dim

Dim is a word that tells the ASP.NET engine that you want to create a variable.

Variable Name

The variable *name* is the name you give to this variable. Think of this as the label on the box that we spoke about earlier in this chapter. A variable name must begin with either an alphabetic character or an underscore.

If it begins with an alphabetic character, then you don't need any other character in the name, although typically the variable name will have additional characters.

If it begins with an underscore, at least one other character must follow the underscore.

A variable name can have from 1 character to 16,383 characters. Variable names are not case sensitive, so salary and SALARY are the same.

It is best to choose a variable name that reflects the data stored in the variable. Let's say that you are going to use the variable to store a person's first name. You could name the variable A, but the letter *A* doesn't imply the contents of the variable. FirstName or FName might be a better choice for the name of the variable because it gives you a clue as to the data stored in the variable.

The variable name must be unique within the scope of the variable (see the later section "Scope").

As Data Type

The data type describes the kind and at times the size of the data that can be stored in the variable (see the earlier section "Data Types: What Kind of Data Is in the Box?"). The data type can be

- Integer
- Long
- Short
- Single
- Double
- Decimal
- Boolean
- String
- Date
- Object or a specific type of object

Now that you know the rules for declaring a variable, let's declare a variable for a person's first name. The following is a statement that tells the ASP.NET engine to create a variable called FirstName as a String:

```
Dim FirstName As String
```

You use this same format to create any variable, except you use the appropriate variable name and data type.

Here are a couple of techniques that you can use to declare more than one variable in the same statement. If you are declaring variables of different data types, then you can use one Dim keyword followed by each declaration. A comma must separate declarations as shown here:

```
Dim FirstName As String, HireDate As Date, Salary As Decimal
```

If the variables are the same data type, then you only need to specify the data type once as shown here:

```
Dim FirstName, LastName As String
```

Initializing a Variable

Declaring a variable simply tells the ASP.NET engine to create a variable. It doesn't place a value in the variable. This isn't a problem, because the ASP.NET engine assumes that another statement later in your code will tell it to place a value in the variable.

The ASP.NET engine automatically places a zero in all numeric variables and a false in a Boolean variable; strings are left empty (as what are called null strings), and objects are left empty because the ASP.NET engine doesn't know what kind of data will be assigned to an object.

Developers typically place a value in a variable when the variable is declared. This is called *initializing* the variable because this is the initial value assigned to the variable. You initialize a variable by using the equal sign to assign a value to the variable as shown here:

```
Dim FirstName As String = "Bob"
```

In a statement that declares multiple variables, you can initialize some variables and leave others uninitialized except for any default value that the ASP.NET engine assigns to them. The next statement initializes the HireDate only:

```
Dim FirstName As String
Dim HireDate As Date = #1/1/2007#
DimSalary As Decimal
```

Scope

As you learned in the preceding chapter, statements are typically grouped into event handlers and functions (you'll learn about functions later in this book). No event handler or function knows what's going on inside any other one.

Suppose you have two HTML button elements on your ASP.NET web page. We'll call them Add and Remove. You will have a click-event handler for each of them. Each event handler is a group of statements.

Statements in the event handler for the Add button cannot access statements in the event handler for the Remove button. Statements in the event handler for the Remove button are said to have different *scope* than for the event handler for the Add button.

If you declare a variable called FirstName in the Add button event handler, you can declare another variable called FirstName in the Remove button event handler and the variables won't conflict with each other. This is because the variable is *out of scope* from the other event handler.

The scope of a variable is determined by where the variable is declared in your code.

Assigning a Value to a Variable

It is very common for the value of a variable to change while the ASP.NET engine processes a request. The current value of the variable is overwritten by the new value. Think of this as replacing the value in the box (variable) with another value.

You assign a value to a variable by using the name of the variable, the equal sign, and then the new value. For example, suppose we want to change the value of the FirstName variable from "Bob" to "Mary". Here's what we need to do:

```
Dim FirstName As String = "Bob"
FirstName = "Mary"
```

The first statement declares the variable and initializes it with "Bob". The second statement tells the ASP.NET engine to replace the value of FirstName with "Mary".

Operators and Expressions

Many statements that you'll write include an expression that tells the ASP.NET engine to perform a mathematical operation. Math may not be one of your strong points, but that shouldn't stop you from learning how to write a mathematical

expression, simply because you already know how to do it. You've probably written the following. You may think of this as a simple addition problem, but it is technically a mathematical expression that performs two operations. First 1 and 1 are added together, and then the sum is placed on the left side of the equal sign:

```
2 = 1 + 1
```

Here's another mathematical expression that you've already seen:

```
FirstName = "Mary"
```

In this example, the ASP.NET engine is told to assign "Mary" to the FirstName variable.

Let's take a closer look and see how to write an expression.

Parts of an Expression

A mathematical expression consists of two parts. These are the operand(s) and the operator. An *operand* is the value. An *operator* is the symbol that tells the ASP.NET engine how to evaluate the mathematical expression using the operand.

Think of operands as the numbers and the addition symbol as the operator. The ASP.NET engine evaluates this mathematical expression by adding the value on the right side of the operator to the value on the left side of the operator.

```
1 + 1
```

Multiple Operations

The assignment operator is an operator that tells the ASP.NET engine to perform another operation. The left side of the assignment operator must be a single value. The right side can be a single value or an expression. Let's insert the assignment operator into the previous mathematical expression and see how the second operation is evaluated.

```
= 1 + 1
```

The ASP.NET engine is told to perform two operations. The first operation is to add the value on the left side of the plus sign to the value on the right side of the plus sign. If you could see the mathematical expression after the first operation is completed, it would look like this:

```
= 2
```

The second operation is performed once the first operation is completed. This operation uses the assignment operator (equal sign) to assign the result of the expression on the right side to the operand on the left. Here's how this mathematical expression looks after the assignment operation is completed:

```
2 = 2
```

Performing more than one operation in the same mathematical expression can lead to confusion—not for the ASP.NET engine, but for you and me, because we may be unsure of the order in which the operations are performed.

Two operations were performed in the previous example: addition and the assignment operation. ASP.NET performed addition before performing the assignment operation. However, you won't know which operation is performed first until you read the section "Order of Operations" later in this chapter.

Types of Operators

Visual Basic .NET has four types of operators. These are arithmetical operators, logical operators, assignment operators, and comparison operators.

Arithmetical Operators

Let's begin with arithmetical operators (see Table 4-1). No doubt these are familiar to you because they are they same operators that you use to perform everyday arithmetic. However, at least one of these operators is probably something you haven't seen before.

This is the modulus operator (Mod). The modulus operator tells the ASP.NET engine to divide the value on its left by the value on its right. The modulus operator returns the remainder. This is shown in the following examples:

- 23 Mod 10 is equal to 3.
- 7 Mod 10 is equal to 7.

Operator	Description
+	Addition
–	Subtraction
*	Multiplication
/	Division
Mod	Modulus
^	Exponent
\	Integer division

Table 4-1   Arithmetical Operators

Logical Operators

Logical operators combine two logical expressions into one expression. A *logical* expression is an expression that evaluates to either true or false. The concept of a logical expression might be new to you because we normally don't write logical expressions during the course of the day.

Logical expressions are used in conjunction with other statements to tell the ASP.NET engine to make decisions. You'll see how this is done in the next chapter, but for now suppose your ASP.NET engine needs to validate a user ID. Here's the logical expression that you'll need to use:

```
if userID = "Bob" then
    'Some statements
end if
```

The expression is userID = "Bob". We placed the expression in an if...then statement so that you don't confuse this logical expression with the expression that assigns the value "Bob" to the variable userID. Besides, this example illustrates how a logical expression is typically used in an application.

As you'll learn in the next chapter, the if...then statement tells the ASP.NET engine to evaluate the logical expression and to execute a group of statements if the logical expression is true. That is, if the value of the variable userID is "Bob", then the logical expression is true; otherwise, the logical expression is false and the group of statements are skipped.

Let's look at each of the different logical operators ASP.NET offers.

And Logical Operator

It is common that you'll combine two logical expressions together to form a third logical expression. This probably sounds confusing, but let's take a look at an example to illustrate this technique.

Suppose the visitor to your site entered "Bob" as the user ID and "Bob555" as the password. We need to ask the ASP.NET engine to determine if both are valid. Looking at the preceding example, you probably realize that we'll use a logical expression to evaluate each of them.

The first logical expression is

```
userID = "Bob"
```

and the second logical expression is

```
password = "Bob555"
```

However, both logical expressions must be true in order for the user ID and password to be valid. Therefore, we need to join these to form a third logical expression by using the And logical operator. The And logical operator tells the ASP.NET engine that both expressions must be true for the third logical expression to be true.

Let's place these logical expressions in an if...end statement so that you can see how this works.

```
if userID = "Bob" And password = "Bob555" then
   'Valid login
end if
```

If the value of the userID variable is "Bob", then the userID = "Bob" logical expression is true. If the value of the password variable is "Bob555", then the password = "Bob555" logical expression is true. If both logical expressions are true, then the login is valid and statements within the if...then statement are executed by the ASP.NET engine. However, the third logical expression is false if either the first logical expression or the second logical expression is false. Both must be true for the third logical expression to be true.

Or Logical Operator

The Or logical operator provides another way for you to join together two logical expressions. The Or logical operator also forms a third logical expression. However, the third logical expression is true if either the first logical expression or the second logical expression is true.

This too might sound confusing, so let's create another example to illustrate how this works. Suppose there are two valid user IDs. These are "Bob" and "Mary". For now we won't require a password. We'll use the following logical expressions to determine if the value of the userID variable is either "Bob" or "Mary":

```
if userID = "Bob" Or userID = "Mary" then
   'Valid login
end if
```

Here are the three logical expressions that are shown in this example:

```
UserID = "Bob"

if userID = "Bob" Or userID = "Mary" then
   'Valid login
end if
```

If the value of the userID variable is Bob, then the first logical expression is true, and so the third logical expression is true also. It doesn't matter if the second logical expression is true or not, because we used the Or logical operator to join together the first and second logical expressions.

If the value of the userID variable is Mary, then the second logical expression is true, and so the third logical expression is true also. It doesn't matter if the first logical expression is true or not.

XOr Logical Operator

There can be rare occasions when you want a group of statements to execute only if the first logical expression or the second logical expression is true—but not if both logical expressions are true. To do this, we need to join together the first and second logical expressions using the XOr logical operator.

The XOr logical operator tells the ASP.NET engine to evaluate both logical expressions. As long as only one of them is true, then the third logical expression is true; otherwise, the third logical expression is false.

Let's see this in action. The first logical expression in the following example determines if the value of the doorOne variable is "Open". The second logical expression determines if the value of the doorTwo variable is "Open". The third logical expression is true if only one of the doors is open. The third logical expression is false if both doors are closed or if both doors are open.

```
if doorOne = "Open" XOr doorTwo = "Open" then
   'Only one door is open
end if
```

Not Logical Operator

The Not logical operator reverses the logic of a logical expression. For example, we can tell the ASP.NET engine to determine that the value of the user ID is not "Bob" by using the Not logical operator. This is like saying, "I passed that test—not!" meaning that you didn't pass the test.

Here is how we write this expression:

```
if Not userID = "Bob" then
   'The value of the userID is other than "Bob"
end if
```

The ASP.NET engine initially evaluates the userID = "Bob" expression to determine if this expression is true. If it is true, then the Not logical operator tells the ASP.NET engine to reverse this logic, making the expression false. Likewise, if the user ID is not "Bob", the Not operator reverses this logic, making the logical expression true.

AndAlso

The AndAlso logical operator combines two logical expressions. If the first logical expression isn't true, then the ASP.NET engine doesn't evaluate the second logical expression. The second logical expression is evaluated only if the first logical expression is true.

TIP: *This replaces the And operator.*

The following example illustrates how to use the AndAlso logical operator. If the value of var1 is equal to or greater than var2, then the first logical expression is false, and therefore the third expression is also false. The ASP.NET engine doesn't evaluate the second expression.

```
if  var1 < var2 AndAlso var3 > var4 then
   'Execute these statements
end if
```

OrElse

The OrElse logical operator works much like the AndAlso logical operator. However, if the first logical expression is true, then the ASP.NET engine doesn't evaluate the second logical expression.

TIP: *This replaces the Or operator.*

The following example shows you how to use the OrElse logical operator. If the value of variable var1 is less than the value of variable var2, then the first logical operator is true and the third logical expression is true. Therefore, ASP.NET skips the second logical expression:

```
if  var1 < var2 OrElse var3 > var4 then
   'Execute these statements
end if
```

Assignment Operator

The assignment operator (Table 4-2) assigns the value from the right side of the operator to the variable on the left side of the operator, as you saw done earlier in this chapter when you assigned a value to a variable as shown here:

```
Dim FirstName As String
FirstName = "Bob"
```

Typically, the assignment operator is used with an arithmetic operator to perform two operations in one. In the next example, we'll take a look at the += assignment operator to see how two operations are combined into one operator.

You are familiar with the first two lines of this example. Each declares a variable and initializing it with a value. The last line is new to you. The += assignment operator tells the ASP.NET engine to add the value of variable b to variable a and then replace (assign) the value of variable a with the sum of variable a and b.

```
Dim a As Integer = 10
Dim b As Integer = 2
a += b
```

Operator	Description
=	Assign
+=	Add value and then assign
−=	Subtract value and then assign
*=	Multiply value and then assign
/=	Divide value and then assign
\=	Integer division and then assign
^=	Exponentiation assignment

Table 4-2 Assignment Operators

No doubt this is confusing, so let's take apart the last line to see the two actions the ASP.NET engine is taking. First it is told to add the values stored in variable a and variable b. The sum is 12. This is the same as the following:

```
a + b
```

Next the ASP.NET engine is told to replace the value of variable a, which is 10, with the sum, which is 12. This is the same as the following:

```
a= a + b
```

The value of variable a is 12 after the ASP.NET engine finishes.

The other combinations of operators shown in Table 4-2 cause the ASP.NET engine to perform actions similar to that of the += operator, except each performs a different combination of operations. For example, the −= operator subtracts variable b from variable a and then assigns the difference to variable a.

Comparison Operators

A comparison operator (Table 4-3) compares two values. The result of the comparison is either true or false. Typically comparison operators are used to set the

Operator	Description
=	Equivalence
>	Greater than
<	Less than
>=	Greater than or equal to
<=	Less than or equal to
<>	Not equal

Table 4-3 Comparison Operators

criteria for ASP.NET to make a decision using the if...then statement. You were briefly introduced to the if...then statement previously in this chapter. You'll be formally introduced to it in the next chapter.

The first comparison operator on the list is the equivalence operator (=), which you already learned how to use when you learned how to use logical operators.

The equivalence operator tells the ASP.NET engine to compare the value on its right side to the value on its left side. If these values are the same, then the expression is true; otherwise, the expression is false.

In the next example the ASP.NET engine is told to compare "Bob" with the value of the variable userID. If they are the same, then statements within the if... then statement are executed; otherwise, those statements are skipped.

```
if userID = "Bob" then
    'Execute these statements
end if
```

Next on the list is the greater-than operator (>). The greater-than operator tells the ASP.NET engine to determine if the value on the left side of the operator is greater than the value on the right side of the operator.

Here's how this works:

```
Dim a As Integer = 10
Dim b As Integer = 2
if a > b then
    'Execute these statements
end if
```

The ASP.NET engine is told to determine if the value of a is greater than the value of b. If so, then the expression is true; otherwise, the expression is false. This expression is true because 10 is greater than 2.

Next we'll look at the less-than operator (<). The less-than operator tells the ASP.NET engine to determine if the value on the left side of the operator is less than the value on the right side of the operator. If this is the case, then the expression is true; otherwise, the expression is false.

The last line in the next example determines if the value of variable a is less than the value of variable b. This expression is false because 10 is not less than 2:

```
Dim a As Integer = 10
Dim b As Integer = 2
if a < b then
    'Execute these statements
end if
```

The next two comparison operators on the list combine two operations into one. These are the equal-to or less-than operator (<=) and the greater-than or equal-to operator (>=).

The equal-to or less-than operator tells the ASP.NET engine to determine if the value on the left side of the operator is less than or equal to the value on the right side of the operator. If so, then the expression is true. If not, then the expression is false.

The greater-than or equal-to operator performs a similar operation except that the value on the left side of the operator must be either greater than or equal to the value on the right side of the operator; otherwise, the expression is false.

The last two lines of the following example show how to use these operators. The first of these expressions is false because the value of a is greater than the value of b. The second expression is true for the same reason:

```
Dim a As Integer = 10
Dim b As Integer = 2
if a <= b then
    'Execute these statements
end if
if a >= b then
    'Execute these statements
end if
```

Order of Operations

Test your skills in arithmetic. Is the answer to the following expression 56 or 110?

```
10 * 5 + 6
```

It depends.

If addition is performed before multiplication, then the answer is 110.

If multiplication is performed before addition, then the answer is 56.

You can avoid any confusion by learning the order of operation. The order of operation is a set of rules that specifies the order in which an expression is evaluated by the ASP.NET engine. These are the same rules that you learned back in your high school math class. Here is the order of operation:

1. Calculations in parentheses are performed first. When there is more than one set of parentheses, the expression in the inner set of parentheses is performed first.

2. Exponentiation operations are performed next.

3. Multiplication and division are next. If both operations are at an equal level of precedence, then perform calculations left to right.

4. Modulus operations are performed next.

5. Addition and subtraction are next. If both operations are at an equal level of precedence, then perform calculations left to right.

If you forget the order of operations, simply use parentheses to tell the ASP.NET engine the order to evaluate an expression. Portions of an expression that are enclosed within parentheses are evaluated before those portions that are outside of the parentheses.

Suppose you write the following expression but you are unsure which operation is performed first. By placing parentheses around the addition expression, you force ASP.NET to add those values before performing multiplication. The value of this expression is 110:

```
10 * (5 + 6)
```

Concatenation

Another operator that you'll probably use frequently is the concatenation operator, which is symbolized as & or +. Concatenation means that one string is joined with another string to form a third string.

TIP: *Remember that a string is a series of characters that are enclosed within quotations.*

The following example shows how to do this. Here we declare and initialize a variable called FullName. We initialize it by concatenating two strings using the concatenation operator. The value of FullName after concatenation is completed is "Bob Smith":

TIP: *Notice there is a space between the last b and the last quotation mark. The space separates the first name from the last name when the words are joined together.*

```
Dim FullName As String = "Bob " & "Smith"
```

Constants

You can use literal values such as the number 10 and the name "Bob" directly in your code as you've seen throughout this chapter. However, there might be occasions when you want to use the same literal value over and over again within your code.

Let's say that your state sales tax is 6 percent and you need to use the state sales tax several times throughout your code. One alternative is to simply use the literal value .06 whenever you need to refer to the sales tax in a calculation.

A better way is to define a *constant* as .06 and use the constant instead of the literal value .06.

Developers prefer to use a constant to using a literal value for a couple of reasons. First, a constant has a name that usually implies that purpose of the literal value that is represented by the constant. For example, we could call the constant SalesTax. This is more informative as you read your code than if you simply read the literal value .06.

Another reason is that you can easily update your code should the value of the sales tax change. Suppose you use the literal sales tax value in ten places within your code. If the sales tax changes, you'll need to replace all ten values with the updated value. This is time-consuming and leaves open the chance that you might overlook a few of those places. If you use a constant, however, you only need to change this in one place—where you define the constant—and that change affects your entire code.

Here's how to declare a constant:

```
Const SalesTax As Single = 0.06
```

You'll notice that this statement is very similar to the statement used to declare a variable, except that we use Const instead of Dim. Typically, you'll define a constant at the beginning of your code.

Casting: Converting Data Types

As we mentioned previously in this chapter, there is a difference between 10 and "10". The first is a number, and the second is a string. You can use a number in an arithmetical operations, but you can't use a string in arithmetic without first converting the string to a numeric data type. In other words, remove the quotations from "10".

The task of converting from one data type to another is called *casting* and is performed by calling an appropriate conversion function (see Table 4-4). Each function converts a literal value, the contents of a variable, or the results of an expression into a particular data type. The function then returns the converted value.

Let's see how this works. We'll convert "10" to the number 10, which is an Integer data type. To do this, we'll use the CInt() function. As you'll learn in later chapters, there are three parts to a function:

- Function name
- Arguments
- Return value

Convert To	Conversion Function
Integer	CInt()
Long	CLng()
Short	CShort()
Single	CSng()
Double	CDbl()
Decimal	CDec()
Boolean	CBool()
String	CStr()
Date	CDate()
Object	CObj()

Table 4-4   Conversion Functions

The function *name* is what the function is called; CInt() is a function name.

Arguments are values the function needs to perform its task. These values are placed within parentheses that appear to the right of the function name. Some functions require one argument. Other functions require multiple arguments, and still others don't require any arguments. It all depends on the specific function. More on this when we talk about functions later in this book. For now, just remember that conversion functions usually require one argument, which is the value that is being converted.

The *return* value is the value that the function returns to your program after it performs its task. The value returned by a conversion function is the converted value. You typically assign the return value to a variable, although occasionally the return value is used directly in an expression.

Let's get back to converting the string "10" to the number 10. Here's how this is done:

```
Dim TenAsANumber As Integer
TenAsANumber = CInt("10")
```

The value of the TenAsANumber variable is 10 and not "10". You can use TenAsANumber in a calculation.

Here's another way you can use the CInt() function. In this example "10" is assigned to a variable and then the variable is passed to CInt(). This has the same effect as if we passed the function a literal value:

```
Dim TenAsAString As String = "10"
Dim TenAsANumber As Integer
TenAsANumber = CInt(TenAsAString)
```

Looking Ahead

In this chapter you learned how to store information into memory using variables and then use operators to tell the ASP.NET engine how to manipulate variables and literal values. Think of a variable as a box in computer memory where you store data. The box has a label called a variable name and can hold a specific type of data, which is called a data type.

You create a variable by declaring the variable, which you do by specifying the variable name and the data type of the variable. A value can be placed into a variable by using the assignment operator either when the variable is declared or after the variable is declared.

You also learned about various operators that are available in Visual Basic .NET. An operator is a symbol that tells the ASP.NET engine to perform a specific operation. An operator usually requires two operands, although some operators require one operand. An operand is a value or variable that is used by an operator.

Operators and operands are joined together to form an expression. An expression is used in a statement to give an instruction to the ASP.NET engine.

One of the many instructions that you'll give an ASP.NET engine to perform is to make a decision. You were introduced in this chapter to how this is done through use of the if...then statement. You'll learn more in the next chapter about the if...then statement and how to have the ASP.NET engine make decisions.

Quiz

1. "Bob" is a(n)

   a. Integer

   b. Short

   c. Long

   d. None of the above

2. A comparison operator is used to define the condition for ASP.NET to make a decision.

   a. True

   b. False

3. Initialization is assigning

   a. The first value to a variable

   b. A value to a variable

   c. A string to a variable

   d. An integer to a variable

4. The < operator is used to determine if the value on the left side of the operator is

   a. Equal to the value on the right side of the operator

   b. Not equal to the value on the right side of the operator

   c. Less than the value on the right side of the operator

   d. Greater than the value on the right side of the operator

5. A variable is

   a. A temporary storage place in memory

   b. A constant value

   c. A value that cannot be changed

   d. None of the above

6. String values must be enclosed within quotations.

   a. True

   b. False

7. An expression using the XOr operator is true if both the logical expressions joined together by the XOr operator are true.

   a. True

   b. False

8. The AndAlso logical operator tells the ASP.NET engine

   a. Not to evaluate the second logical expression if the first logical expression is true

   b. To evaluate the second logical expression if the first logical expression is true

   c. Not to evaluate the second logical expression if the first logical expression is false

   d. None of the above

9. The Not operator tells the ASP.NET to

   a. Skip evaluating the expression

   b. Skip evaluating the expression only if the expression is false

   c. Reverse the logic of the expression after evaluating the expression

   d. None of the above

10. You can convert from one data type to another using casting.

    a. True

    b. False

Answers

1. d. None of the above. It is a String.

2. a. True

3. a. The first value to a variable

4. c. Less than the value on the right side of the operator

5. a. A temporary storage place in memory

6. a. True

7. b. False. The XOr operator returns true only if the two logical expressions have different values.

8. c. Not to evaluate the second logical expression if the first logical expression is false.

9. c. Reverse the logic of the expression after evaluating the expression

10. a. True

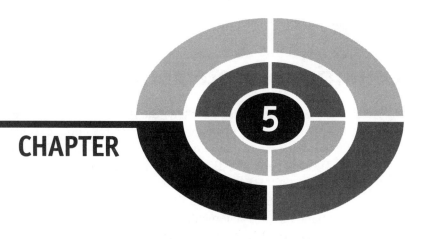

CHAPTER

5

Conditional Statements

The ASP.NET engine performs intelligently if you give it the intelligence to make decisions on the fly while processing requests from visitors to your web site. Commercial web sites do this all the time to personalize a visitor's experience by tailoring the content to match the visitor's behavior.

The secret to giving the ASP.NET engine intelligence to make a decision is to combine a conditional expression that you learned to write in the last chapter with a conditional statement, which you'll learn to write in this chapter.

This mix enables you to tell the ASP.NET engine

- When to make a decision
- How to make a decision
- What to do after a decision is made

Conditional Statements

A *conditional statement* tells the ASP.NET engine to evaluate a condition. Using the result of the evaluation, the ASP.NET either executes code or skips over code. For example, a conditional statement tells the ASP.NET engine to compare a user ID with valid user IDs. If there is a match, then one set of code is executed; otherwise, a different set of code executes.

There are three types of conditional statements. These are the If...Then statement, the case statement and the loop.

The If...Then statement tells the APS.NET engine to execute one or more statements if a conditional expression is true, for instance, if a user ID matches one of the valid user IDs. You'll see how the If...Then statement works in the section "The If...Then Statement" of this chapter.

The case statement compares a selection to one or more known values. Each known value is referred to as a *case*. Each case has one or more statements that are executed if the selection matches the case. This is used frequently in menus where a person enters a selection and then the selection is compared to menu options. If there is a match, then the menu option is processed. You'll see how this is done in the section "The Case Statement" of this chapter.

The loop statement tells the ASP.NET engine to repeatedly execute statements as long as a condition is true. If the condition is false, then statements are not executed. Think of a quiz game where a contestant can continue to play as long as he correctly answers each question. The conditional statements might ask, is the answer correct? If so, then play on. If not, then stop. You'll learn more about how to use a loop statement in the section "Loops" of this chapter.

The If...Then Statement

The If...Then statement enables you to have the ASP.NET engine execute some statements only if conditions are right while the ASP.NET engine is processing the visitor's request.

There are four versions of the If...Then statement. Let's begin by looking at the simplest version. The other versions work basically the same way but offer additional features. The If...Then statement has four parts. These are the If...Then keywords, the conditional expression, the code block that contains statements that are executed if the expression is true, and the End If keywords.

Here's how the If...Then statement is structured:

```
If conditional expression then
   'This is the code block. Place statements here
End If
```

When the ASP.NET engine comes across this code, it evaluates the *conditional expression*. The *conditional expression* evaluates to either a true or a false. If true, then statements within the code block are executed by the ASP.NET engine. The code block is the space between the If...Then keywords and the End If keywords. However, these statements are skipped over by the ASP.NET engine if the *conditional expression* evaluates to false.

The If...Then Statement in Action

Let's take a look at how to use the If...Then to validate a user ID. In this example, we'll prompt the visitor to enter a user ID and click the Submit button. The ASP.NET engine then determines if the user ID is valid or not. If the user ID is valid, then the ASP.NET engine displays text stating "Valid User ID". If the user ID is invalid, then the ASP.NET engine doesn't display anything new.

Notice that this example is very similar to the example shown in Chapter 3 in that the web page is designed with all the objects on it and then we hide those objects we don't want shown by setting the Visible property to false.

This example contains a label and text box object for the user ID, a Submit button, and a label and text box object for the login status (Figure 5-1). The label and text box for the login status are invisible when the visitor is prompted to enter a user ID.

Let's begin by opening a new Web Site project. Here's what you need to do:

1. Select File | New Web Site.
2. Select Visual Basic as the Project Types.
3. Double-click ASP.NET Web Site.
4. Select the Source tab and enter the code shown at the bottom of this list.
5. Press CTRL-F5 to run the application.
6. Enter the user ID **Bob** and click Submit (Figure 5-2).

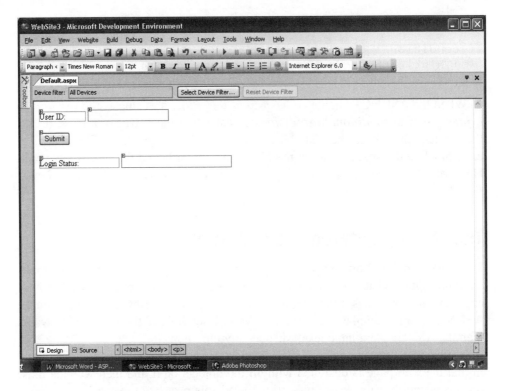

Figure 5-1 Here is how this example looks in the designer.

7. If the text of the UserID text box is Bob, then the ASP.NET engine does the following:

a. It sets the Enabled property of the userID text box to false, which prevents the visitor from changing the contents of this text box.

b. It sets the Visible property of the LoginStatus label to true, making the LoginStatus label visible on the web page.

c. It sets the Visible property of the LStatus text box to true, making the LStatus text box visible on the web page.

d. It places the text "Valid User ID" into the LStatus text box.

e. It sets the Enabled property of the LStatus text box to false, preventing the visitor from changing its contents.

8. The status of the validation process is then displayed on the web page (Figure 5-3).

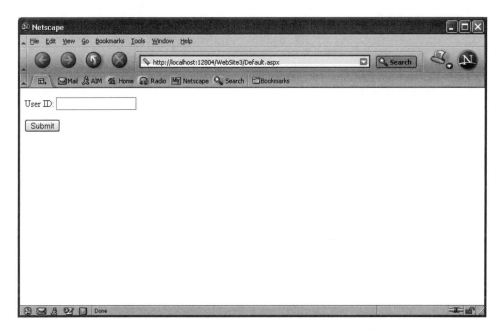

Figure 5-2   The visitor is prompted to enter a user ID into the application.

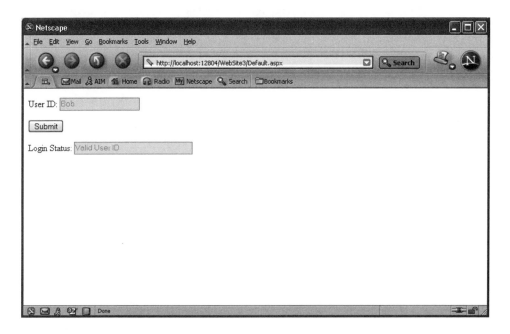

Figure 5-3   Here is what the visitor sees if a valid user ID is entered.

```
<script runat="server">
Sub Submit_Click(ByVal sender As Object, ByVal e As System.EventArgs)
    If UserID.Text = "Bob" Then
        UserID.Enabled = False
        LoginStatus.Visible = True
        LStatus.Visible = True
        LStatus.Text = "Valid User ID"
        LStatus.Enabled = False
    End If
End Sub
</script>
<html>
<head>
</head>
<body>
    <form id="Form1" runat="server">
        <p>
            <asp:Label id="Label1" runat="server" Width="92px">User ID:
            </asp:Label>
            <asp:TextBox id="UserID" runat="server"></asp:TextBox>
        </p>
        <p>
            <asp:Button id="Submit" onclick="Submit_Click" runat="server"
Text="Submit"></asp:Button>
        </p>
        <p>
            <asp:Label id="LoginStatus" runat="server" Width="156px"
Visible="False">Login
Status: </asp:Label>
            <asp:TextBox id="LStatus" runat="server" Width="210px"
Visible="False"></asp:TextBox>
        </p>
    </form>
</body>
</html>
```

The If...Then...Else Statement

The next version of the If...Then statement is the If...Then...Else statement. The If...Then...Else statement simply tells the ASP.NET engine, "If the condition is true, then execute these statements, or else execute these other statements."

There are six parts to the If...Then...Else statement. The first three parts are the same as the first three parts of the If...Then statement. The fourth part is the Else keyword. The fifth part is a second code block that contains statements that are executed if the conditional expression is false, and the sixth part is the End If keywords.

Here's how to construct the If...Then...Else statement:

```
If expression Then
    'Place statements here that are executed if the condition is true
Else
    'Place statements here that are executed if the condition is false
End If
```

If the condition is true, then only statements placed in the first code block are executed. The ASP.NET engine skips statements in the second code block.

If the condition is false, then only statements placed in the second code block are executed. The ASP.NET engine skips statements in the first code block.

What follows is a revised version of the previous example. The only difference is that the ASP.NET engine is provided a statement to execute if the user ID doesn't match a valid user ID.

The revision takes places in the code that is executed when the visitor clicks the Submit button as shown here. This is what the ASP.NET engine is told to do:

1. Set the Enabled property of the UserID text box to false to prevent the visitor from changing its contents.

2. Set the Visible property of the LoginStatus label to true.

3. Set the Visible property of the LStatus text box to true.

4. Determine if the value of the UserID text box is Bob.

5. If it is, then set the Text property of the LStatus text box to "Valid User ID."

6. If it isn't, then set the Text property of the LStatus text box to "Invalid User ID" (Figure 5-4).

7. Set the Enabled property of the LStatus text box to false so that the visitor cannot change the validation status.

```
Sub Submit_Click(ByVal sender As Object, ByVal e As System.EventArgs)
    UserID.Enabled = False
    LoginStatus.Visible = True
    LStatus.Visible = True
    If UserID.Text = "Bob" Then
        LStatus.Text = "Valid User ID"
    Else
        LStatus.Text = "Invalid User ID"
    End If
    LStatus.Enabled = False
End Sub
```

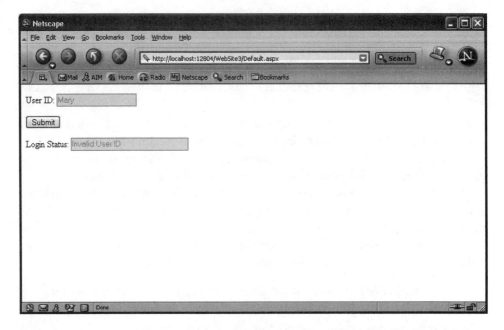

Figure 5-4   The visitor is told whenever an invalid user ID is entered into the application.

The If...Then...Elseif Statement

Another version of the If...Then statement is the If...Then...Elseif statement. This is similar to the If...Then...Else statement, except that the ASP.NET engine executing it evaluates another condition if the first condition is false.

The If...Then...Elseif statement tells the browser, "If the condition is true, then execute statements in the first code block, or else evaluate another condition. If the other condition is true, then execute statements in the second code block. If the second condition is false, then skip statements in the second code block."

Here's how to write the If...Then...Elseif statement:

```
If expression Then
   'Place statements here that are executed if the first condition is true
Elseif expression
   'Place statements here that are executed if the second condition is true
End If
```

Let's modify the previous example to illustrate how to use the If...Then...Elseif statement in your application. In this example, we'll tell the ASP.NET engine that Bob and Mary are valid user IDs. Here is the code:

1. Set the Enabled property of the UserID text box to false to prevent the visitor from changing its contents.

2. Set the Visible property of the LoginStatus label to true.

3. Set the Visible property of the LStatus text box to true.

4. Determine if the value of the UserID text box is Bob.

5. If it is, then set the Text property of the LStatus text box to "Valid User ID."

6. If it isn't, then determine if the value of the UserID text box is Mary.

7. If it is, then set the Text property of the LStatus text box to "Valid User ID."

8. Set the Enabled property of the LStatus text box to false so that the visitor cannot change the validation status.

```
Sub Submit_Click(ByVal sender As Object, ByVal e As System.EventArgs)
    UserID.Enabled = False
    LoginStatus.Visible = True
    LStatus.Visible = True
    If UserID.Text = "Bob" Then
        LStatus.Text = "Valid User ID"
    Elseif UserID.Text = "Mary"
        LStatus.Text = "Valid User ID"
    End If
    LStatus.Enabled = False
End Sub
```

If...Then...Elseif...Else Statement

The last version of the If...Then statement is the If...Then...Elseif...Else statement. This statement is a combination of the second and third versions of this code, except there is another Else part to the statement.

The If...Then...Elseif...Else statement tells the ASP.NET engine, "If the condition is true, then execute statements in the first code block, or else evaluate another condition. If the other condition is true, then execute statements in the second code block, or else execute statements in the third code block if the second condition is false."

Here's the structure of the If...Then...Elseif...Else statement:

```
If expression Then
    'Place statements here that are executed
    'if the first condition is true Else if (expression)
    'Place statements here that are executed if the second condition is true
Else
    'Place statements here that are executed if the second condition is false
End If
```

Notice that the If...Then...Elseif...Else statement contains three code blocks. Statements in the first code block execute if the first conditional is true. Statements in the second code block execute if the second conditional is true. Statements in the third code block execute if the second conditional expressions are false.

Let's revise our previous example to use the If...Then...Elseif...Else statement. This is nearly identical to the previous example except that the ASP.NET engine is told to display "Invalid User ID" in the LStatus text box if the user ID is neither Bob nor Mary.

Here's what we do:

1. Set the Enabled property of the UserID text box to false to prevent the visitor from changing its contents.

2. Set the Visible property of the LoginStatus label to true.

3. Set the Visible property of the LStatus text box to true.

4. Determine if the value of the UserID text box is Bob.

5. If it is, then set the Text property of the LStatus text box to "Valid User ID."

6. Determine if the value of the UserID text box is Mary.

7. If it is, then set the Text property of the LStatus text box to "Valid User ID."

8. If it isn't, then set the Text property of the LStatus text box to "Invalid User ID."

9. Set the Enabled property of the LStatus text box to false so that the visitor cannot change the validation status.

```
Sub Submit_Click(ByVal sender As Object, ByVal e As System.EventArgs)
    UserID.Enabled = False
    LoginStatus.Visible = True
    LStatus.Visible = True
    If UserID.Text = "Bob" Then
        LStatus.Text = "Valid User ID"
    Elseif UserID.Text = "Mary"
        LStatus.Text = "Valid User ID"
    else
        LStatus.Text = "Invalid User ID"
    End If
    LStatus.Enabled = False
End Sub
```

The Nested If...Then Statement

We purposely used simple examples in this chapter so that you don't become confused as you learn how to write the If...Then statement. Real-world ASP.NET applications make decisions more complex than those shown in this book. Let's look at a more challenging example of the If...Then statement, one that is similar to those you'll find in real-world applications.

Let's say that you built an ASP.NET web page that displays and processes an order form that requires a customer to enter country and postal codes among other information regarding the order. You probably want to have data validated on the client side and then have the ASP.NET engine validate the data too.

Here are the decisions that the ASP.NET engine must make:

1. Did the customer enter a country code?

2. Did the customer enter a postal code?

3. If the customer entered both a country code and a postal code, then is the country code a valid country code?

4. If the country code is a valid country code, then is the postal code a valid postal code for that country?

By now you realize that a series of If...Then statements are used to make these decisions. However, positioning them can be tricky because a second decision is made only if a first condition is true; otherwise, the second decision is skipped.

The solution is to use a nested If...Then statement. Nested simply means that one If...Then statement is within the code block of another If...Then statement. This is illustrated in the next example.

Assume that if the CountryCode variable and the PostalCode variable have a value of less than 1, then the customer didn't enter them on the order form. Also assume that another process validated the country code and postal code and assign a value to the Valid variable indicating if these codes are valid.

The code follows this paragraph. Notice that this is more complicated to read that other examples of the If...Then statements that you've seen in this chapter. This is because we are asking the ASP.NET engine to make up to a four-step decision. First the ASP.NET engine evaluates the value of the CountryCode variable to determine if the visitor entered the country code. Next it determines if the visitor entered the postal code. The third step is to determine if the country code is valid. And the last decision is to determine if the postal code is valid.

```
If CountryCode > 1 Then
   If PostalCode > 1 Then
      If CountryCodeValid == Valid Then
         If PostalCodeValid == Valid Then
            //Valid country code and valid postal code
         Else
            //Invalid postal code
         End If
      Else
         //Invalid country code
      End If
   Else
      //Postal code is blank
   End If
Else
   //Country code is blank
End If
```

The Case Statement

The If statement can become unwieldy when there are a series of decisions that have to be made on the basis of a single value. Think of this: Suppose you offered ten menu options on your web site. You'll need a very long If...Then...Elseif statement to determine which option the visitor selects. Each menu option needs its own If...Then or Elseif followed by a conditional expression to determine if the visitor's selection matches the menu option. This becomes unnecessarily complicated. You can avoid writing a series of If statements by using a case statement.

A case statement tells the ASP.NET engine to compare a selected value with a series of case values. If the selected value matches a case value, then statements placed beneath the case value are executed.

There are five parts to a case statement:

- The Select Case keywords
- The Select value, the value to be compared to case values, which can be an expression
- The Case keyword
- The Case value—the value compared to the select value
- The End Select keywords

Here's how a case statement is structured. Only two case values are shown here, but you can have as many case values as your application requires:

```
Select Case value
   Case first Case value
       'Statements that are executed if the select
       'value matches the first case value.
   Case second Case value
       'Statements that are executed if the select
       'value matches the second case value.
End Select
```

Here's how the Select Case statement works:

1. The ASP.NET engine compares the select value to the first Case value.

2. If there is a match, then statements beneath the first Case value are executed and the rest of the Case values are skipped.

3. If there isn't a match, then the ASP.NET engine skips statements beneath the first Case value and compares the select value to the next Case value and repeats this process.

4. If none of the Case values match the select value, then none of the statements beneath any of the Case values are executed.

Try this next ASP.NET web page and see how the Select Case statement works. This example is very similar to the If...Then...Elseif example that you saw earlier in this chapter; however, the If...Then...Elseif statement is replaced with a Select Case statement.

Here we are telling the ASP.NET engine to compare the value of the UserID text box with Bob and Mary. If there is a match, then set the LStatus text box accordingly:

```
Sub Submit_Click(ByVal sender As Object, ByVal e As System.EventArgs)
   UserID.Enabled = False
   LoginStatus.Visible = True
   LStatus.Visible = True
   LStatus.Text = "Valid User ID"
   LStatus.Enabled = False
   Select Case LStatus.Text
      Case "Bob"
         LStatus.Text = "Valid User ID"
      Case "Mary"
         LStatus.Text = "Valid User ID"
   End Select
   LStatus.Enabled = False
End Sub
```

A Variation of the Case Statement

Sometimes you'll want one or more statements to execute if the Select value doesn't match any of the Case values. Think of this as the default action. You can specify a default action by using a Case Else in the case statement.

The Case Else is positioned at the end of the Case values and basically tells the ASP.NET engine that "If the select value doesn't match any of the Case values, then execute statements placed beneath the Case Else clause."

Here's how to use Case Else:

```
Select Case value
   Case first Case value
      'Place statements that are executed if the
      'select value matches the first Case value.
   Case second Case value
      'Place statements that are executed if the
      'select value matches the second Case value.
   Case Else
      'Place statements that are executed if the select
      'value matches none of the Case values.
End Case
```

Let's revise the previous example to include a Case Else that sets the value of the LStatus text box to "Invalid User ID" if the value of the UserID text box doesn't match any Case values. Here's the revised code:

```
Sub Submit_Click(ByVal sender As Object, ByVal e As System.EventArgs)
   UserID.Enabled = False
   LoginStatus.Visible = True
   LStatus.Visible = True
   LStatus.Text = "Valid User ID"
   LStatus.Enabled = False
   Select Case LStatus.Text
      Case "Bob"
         LStatus.Text = "Valid User ID"
      Case "Mary"
         LStatus.Text = "Valid User ID"
      Case Else
         LStatus.Text = "Invalid User ID"
   End Select
   LStatus.Enabled = False
End Sub
```

Loops

A *loop* is used to execute one or more statements repeatedly without your having to write those statements more than once in your code. A loop is something you wish you had back when you were in school and the teacher told you to write "I will keep quiet in class" 25 times on a piece of paper. A loop lets you write it once and have the ASP.NET engine write it 25 times.

There are three types of loops. These are the For loop, the Do While loop, and the Do Until loop.

The For Loop

The *For loop* tells the ASP.NET engine to execute statements within a specific number of times. This is like saying, "Write 'I will keep quiet in class' 25 times." The ASP.NET exits the For loop and continues with the next statement below the loop once the maximum value is reached.

There are five parts to a For loop:

- The For keyword
- The For variable, which stores the current count
- The count range—a starting value and an ending value
- The code block that contains statements that are executed each time the For loop is executed
- The Next keyword

Here's how to structure a For loop:

```
For i = 1 to 10
    'Place statements here
Next i
```

The For variable is like any variable that you use in your program (see Chapter 4), except it serves as the loop counter.

The count range specifies the starting and ending values for the count. In this example, the count range is from 1 to 10. When the For loop begins, the start value, which is 1, is assigned to the For variable. The next time the For loop loops, the For variable is incremented by one. This process continues until the outer count range is exceeded, causing the ASP.NET engine to stop looping and continue with the statement that follows the next keyword at the end of the For loop. In this example, this means that the ASP.NET engine loops ten times.

Statements that you want to execute each time the For loop is looped must be placed between the For keyword and the Next keyword.

Try this example of a For loop. Here's what is happening: The visitor is prompted to enter a starting value for the counters. This is the value that is assigned to the For variable. The ASP.NET engine is then told to count by one until it reaches ten, when it stops and displays the last count on the screen.

Figure 5-5 shows the design of the web page. You'll notice that we include all the objects on the web page and then make some invisible until we need them, using the same technique as you saw used in previous examples in this chapter.

The code follows after this list. Here is what is happening in the code:

1. The ASP.NET engine displays the web page. Notice that the Visible property of the Result label and that of ResultValue text box are set to false so that they are not displayed (Figure 5-6).

2. The visitor then enters the starting number and clicks the Count button. We're assuming that the number is less then ten; otherwise, statements in the loop are not executed.

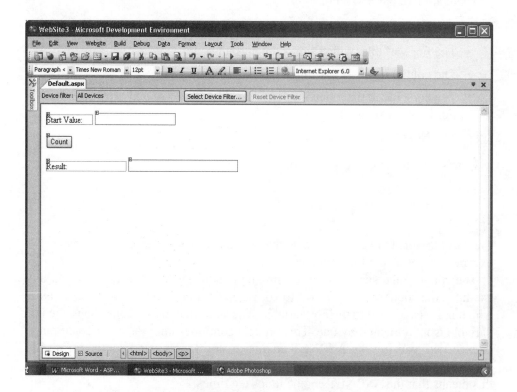

Figure 5-5   Be sure to include all these objects in your design.

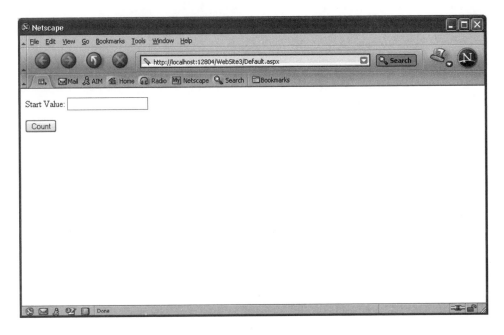

Figure 5-6 The visitor is prompted to enter a starting value for the count.

3. The ASP.NET engine then declares an Integer variable called i.

4. The For loop is then entered. The start number that the visitor entered is a string data type (see Chapter 4). The For loop requires an Integer value. Therefore, the ASP.NET engine is told to convert the start number to an integer using the CInt() conversion function that you learned about in Chapter 4.

5. The ASP.NET engine adds 1 to the variable until the value of the variable equals 10, at which time it breaks out of the For loop. Notice there is no need to insert statements within the For loop, because we're only interested in the final value of the variable.

6. The Enabled property of the StartValue text box is set to false so that the visitor cannot change this value.

7. The visible properties of the Result label and the ResultValue are set to true so that the visitor can see these objects.

8. The value of the variable is then placed into the ResultValue text box. Remember that the ResultValue text box needs a string and that the variable is an Integer. Therefore, we use the CStr() conversion function to change the Integer to a string before placing it into the text box.

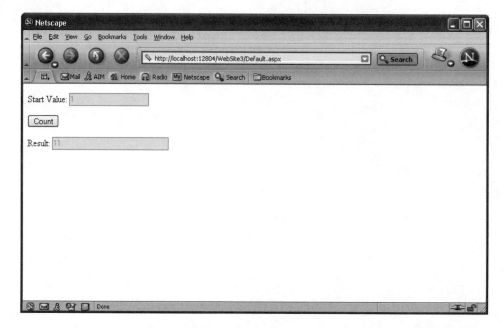

Figure 5-7   If the visitor enters 1 as the start value, the ASP.NET displays 11 as the result.

9. The Enabled property of the ResutlValue text box is set to false so that the visitor cannot change this value. Figure 5-7 shows the web page after the visitor enters 1 as the starting value.

```
<script runat="server">
Sub Count_Click(ByVal sender As Object, ByVal e As System.EventArgs)
    Dim i As Integer
    For i = CInt(StartValue.Text) To 10
    Next I
    StartValue.Enabled = False
    Result.Visible = True
    ResultValue.Visible = True
    ResultValue.Text = CStr(i)
    ResultValue.Enabled = False
End Sub
</script>
<html>
<head>
</head>
<body>
```

```
<form id="Form1" runat="server">
   <p>
      <asp:Label id="Label1" runat="server" Width="92px">Start Value:
      </asp:Label>
      <asp:TextBox id="StartValue" runat="server"></asp:TextBox>
   </p>
   <p>
      <asp:Button id="Count" onclick="Count_Click" runat="server" Text="Count">
      </asp:Button>
   </p>
   <p>
      <asp:Label id="Result" runat="server" Width="156px" Visible="False">Result:
      </asp:Label>
      <asp:TextBox id="ResultValue" runat="server" Width="210px" Visible="False">
      </asp:TextBox>
   </p>
</form>
</body>
</html>
```

A Variation of the For Loop

The For loop increments the count variable by one each time the For loop is iterated. However, you can increment or decrement the count variable by a particular value if you use the Step keyword in your For loop.

The Step keyword tells the ASP.NET engine how to increment or decrement the count variable. Let's say that you want to increment the count variable by two instead of one. Here's what you need to write:

```
For i = 1 to 10 Step 2
   'Place statements here
Next i
```

In this example, the ASP.NET engine is told to start with 1 and increment the loop counter by 2 after each loop. This means it starts by assigning 1 to variable i. After the first loop, variable i is incremented by 2, making it 3. After the second loop, variable i is again incremented by 2, making it 5. This process continues until the value of the For variable is greater than 10.

You can count backward by using a negative value to decrement the for value. Let's see how this works. The next example has an unusual count range. It begins with 10 and ends with 1. Notice that the Step value is −2. This means that after each loop, the value of the For variable is decreased by 2. This process continues until the value of the For variable is less than 1, at which time the loop ends and the ASP.NET engine executes the statement following the next keyword.

```
For i = 10 to 1 Step -2
   'Place statements here
Next i
```

The Do While Loop

The Do While loop also causes the ASP.NET engine to repeatedly execute one or more statements; however, this is done differently than using a For loop. The Do While loop is basically saying to the ASP.NET engine, "Do these statements while this condition is true." The condition is a conditional expression, which you learned about in Chapter 4.

There are four parts to a Do While loop:

- The Do While keywords
- The condition
- The code block that contains statements that are executed if the condition is true
- The Loop keyword

Here's how to structure the Do While loop:

```
Do While condition
    'Place statements that are executed if the condition is true.
Loop
```

The condition is a logical expression that evaluates to either true or false. The ASP.NET engine evaluates the expression.

If the condition is true, then statements within the Do While loop are executed and then the ASP.NET engine reevaluates the expression. Statements are executed again if the expression continues to evaluate to true.

If the condition is false when the Do While loop is first encountered, then statements within the Do While loop are skipped, causing the ASP.NET engine to execute the statement below the Loop keyword.

Try this example of the Do While loop. This is a modification of the For loop example that you saw previously in this chapter. In this example, we're still asking the visitor to enter the start value for the count. However, the ASP.NET engine uses a Do While loop to count.

Here's what is happening:

1. An Integer variable called i is declared.

2. The contents of the StartValue text box, which is a string, is converted to an Integer and assigned to the variable.

3. As long as the value of the variable is less than 10, then the ASP.NET engine adds 1 to the variable and assigns the sum to the variable.

4. The remainder of the code is the same as in the For loop.

```
Sub Count_Click(ByVal sender As Object, ByVal e As System.EventArgs)
    Dim i As Integer
    i = CInt(StartValue.Text)
    Do While i < 10
        i = i + 1
    Loop
    StartValue.Enabled = False
    Result.Visible = True
    ResultValue.Visible = True
    ResultValue.Text = CStr(i)
    ResultValue.Enabled = False
End Sub
```

The Do Loop While Loop

The Do Loop While loop is a variation of the Do While loop, except the ASP.NET engine doesn't evaluate the conditional expression until code within the Do Loop code block executes at least once.

There are four parts to a Do Loop While loop:

- The Do keyword
- The code block that contains statements that are executed at least once even if the condition is false
- The Loop While keywords
- The condition

Here's how to structure the Do Loop While loop:

```
Do
    'Place statements that are executed at least once.
Loop While condition
```

The ASP.NET engine enters the code block of the Do Loop, executes the code, and then evaluates the condition following the While keyword.

If the condition is true, then statements within the Do Loop are executed again and then the ASP.NET engine reevaluates the expression.

If the condition is false, then statements within the Do Loop are skipped the second time, causing the ASP.NET engine to execute the statement below the Loop While keyword.

Try this example of the Do Loop While. In this example, we're still asking the visitor to enter the start value for the count. However, the ASP.NET engine uses a Do Loop While to count.

Here's what is happening:

1. An Integer variable called i is declared.
2. The contents of the StartValue text box, which is a string, is converted to an Integer and assigned to the variable.
3. The ASP.NET engine adds 1 to the variable and assigns the sum to the variable.
4. The ASP.NET engine then evaluates the condition.
5. If the condition is true, then the ASP.NET reenters the code block and adds 1 to the variable and assigns the sum to the variable.
6. If the condition is false, then the ASP.NET no longer reenters the code block but instead executes statements that follow the Loop While keywords.

```
Sub Count_Click(ByVal sender As Object, ByVal e As System.EventArgs)
    Dim i As Integer
    i = CInt(StartValue.Text)
    Do
        i = i + 1
    Loop While i < 10
    StartValue.Enabled = False
    Result.Visible = True
    ResultValue.Visible = True
    ResultValue.Text = CStr(i)
    ResultValue.Enabled = False
End Sub
```

The Do Until Loop

The Do Until loop tells the ASP.NET engine to execute one or more statements until the condition is true. That is, as long as the condition is false, the ASP.NET engine executes statements within the code block of the Do Until loop.

There are four parts to a Do Until loop:

- The Do Until keyword
- The conditional expression
- The code block
- The Loop keyword

Here is the structure of the Do Until loop:

```
Do Until condition
    'Place statements that are executed if the condition is false.
Loop
```

Let's take a look at a simple example that illustrates how to use a Do Until loop. This is basically the same as the Do While example, except we are using a Do Until loop. The ASP.NET engine is told to add 1 to the value of the variable and assign the sum to the variable until the value of the variable is equal to 10.

```
Sub Count_Click(ByVal sender As Object, ByVal e As System.EventArgs)
    Dim i As Integer
    i = CInt(StartValue.Text)
    Do Until i = 10
        i = i + 1
    Loop
    StartValue.Enabled = False
    Result.Visible = True
    ResultValue.Visible = True
    ResultValue.Text = CStr(i)
    ResultValue.Enabled = False
End Sub
```

The Do Loop Until Loop

The Do Loop Until loop is a variation of the Do Until loop, except the ASP.NET engine doesn't evaluate the conditional expression until code within the Do Loop code block executes at least once.

There are four parts to a Do Loop Until loop:

- The Do keyword
- The code block that contains statements that are executed at least once even if the condition is false
- The Loop Until keywords
- The condition

Here's how to structure the Do Loop Until loop:

```
Do
    'Place statements that are executed at least once.
Loop Until condition
```

The ASP.NET engine enters the code block of the Do Loop and executes the code and then evaluates the condition following the Until keyword.

If the condition is false, then statements within the Do Loop are executed again and then the ASP.NET engine reevaluates the expression.

If the condition is true, then statements within the Do loop are skipped the second time, causing the ASP.NET engine to execute the statement below the Loop Until keywords.

Try this example of the Do Loop Until. In this example, we're still asking the visitor to enter the start value for the count. However, the ASP.NET engine uses a Do Loop Until to count.

Here's what is happening:

1. An Integer variable called i is declared.

2. The contents of the StartValue text box, which is a string, is converted to an Integer and assigned to the variable.

3. The ASP.NET engine adds 1 to the variable and assigns the sum to the variable.

4. The ASP.NET engine then evaluates the condition.

5. If the condition is false, then the ASP.NET reenters the code block and adds 1 to the variable and assigns the sum to the variable.

6. If the condition is true, then the ASP.NET no longer reenters the code block but instead executes statements that follow the Loop Until keywords.

```
Sub Count_Click(ByVal sender As Object, ByVal e As System.EventArgs)
    Dim i As Integer
    i = CInt(StartValue.Text)
    Do
        i = i + 1
    Loop Until i > 10
    StartValue.Enabled = False
    Result.Visible = True
    ResultValue.Visible = True
    ResultValue.Text = CStr(i)
    ResultValue.Enabled = False
End Sub
```

Looking Ahead

In this chapter you learned how to have the ASP.NET engine make decisions for you while processing a request from a visitor to your web site. The simplest way to do this is to use an If...Then statement, which specifies a condition that if true causes the ASP.NET engine to execute a set of statements contained within its code block. These statements are skipped if the condition isn't true.

You can have a block of code executed if a condition is false by using the If... Then...Else statement. This statement contains two blocks of code. The first block is executed if the condition is true, and the second block executes if the condition is false.

Sometimes you'll need to have the ASP.NET engine evaluate a second condition if the first condition is false. To do this, you'll need to use the If...Then...Elseif statement. The Elseif portion of this statement defines another condition. Only if this condition is true are statements within the Elseif code block executed by the ASP.NET engine.

In more complex situations, you may find yourself having to make another decision if a condition is true; for instance, if the user ID is valid, then validate the user password. This situation calls for nested If...Then statements. The outer If...Then statement determines if the user ID is valid. The inner If...Then statement determines if the user password is valid.

Processing a menu selection poses a challenge. You could use a series of If...Then statements to compare the selection to each menu option, but then you'll end up with a long list of If...Then statements that can be difficult to read. The case statement is the better choice because it enables you to efficiently compare the selection to many items.

You also learned in this chapter how to have ASP.NET continually execute the same code over and over again by using a loop. You use the For loop if you know the number of times you want the code to execute. The Do While loop is used to continue to execute code as long as a condition is true. The Do Until loop continually executes code until a condition becomes true.

Now that you know how to have the ASP.NET engine make decisions and execute code repeatedly, it is time to learn how to store a series of data efficiently in your ASP.NET application by using an array.

Think of an array as a group of valid user IDs that are stored in a long list that can be assessed by using the name of the list. You'll see how this is done in the next chapter.

Quiz

1. What loop executes statements if a condition is false?

    a. Do While loop

    b. Do Until loop

    c. Until loop

    d. None of the above

2. What loop executes statements if a condition is true?

    a. Do While loop

    b. Do Until loop

   c. Until loop

   d. None of the above

3. The counter range in the For loop is used to

   a. Increase the expression by 1.

   b. Determine the range of values used to control the iterations of the loop by the ASP.NET engine.

   c. Limit the number of statements that can be contained in the code block.

   d. Limit the output of statements within the code block.

4. A Case statement cannot have a default Case.

   a. True

   b. False

5. A For loop can skip values in the counter range.

   a. True

   b. False

6. What would you use if you want a block of statements to be executed only if a condition isn't true?

   a. If...then

   b. If...Then...Else

   c. For loop

   d. For in loop

7. The default clause is used in an If statement to set default values.

   a. True

   b. False

8. What is the purpose of Elseif in an If...Then...Elseif statement?

   a. Contains statements that are executed only if the conditional expression is true.

   b. Defines another conditional expression the ASP.NET engine evaluates if the first conditional expression is false.

   c. Contains statements that are executed only if the conditional expression is false.

   d. Is used to nest an If statement.

9. Statements within a For loop can reference the For loop variable.

   a. True

   b. False

10. A Case statement is ideal to use to evaluate a menu option selected by a visitor to your web site.

   a. True

   b. False

Answers

1. b. Do Until loop

2. a. Do While loop

3. b. Determine the range of values used to control the iterations of the loop by the ASP.NET engine.

4. b. False. The default case is defined by the Case Else construct.

5. a. True. The Step clause can cause values to be skipped.

6. b. If...Then...Else

7. b. False. It's used to execute code if none of the conditions specified are true.

8. b. Defines another conditional expression the ASP.NET engine evaluates if the first conditional expression is false.

9. a. True

10. a. True

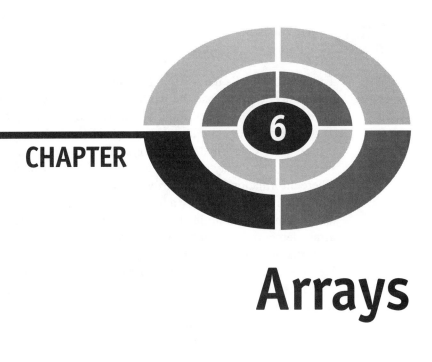
Arrays

Suppose you had to store the name of 100 products of a sales catalog in memory. As you learned in Chapter 4, you could declare 100 variables, one for each product name; however, you'd have to come up with 100 unique variable names—and remember those names each time your ASP.NET engine needs to display products on a web page.

ASP.NET developers don't use variables in such cases, as you probably surmise. Instead they use an array. An array has one name and can hold any number of product names. You'll learn about arrays and how to use them in your ASP.NET application to store and manipulate large amounts of information.

What Is an Array?

The ASP.NET sometimes needs to temporarily store information in memory just long enough to process a visitor's request. First you need to reserve space in memory by declaring a variable such as

```
Dim selection AS Integer
```

This statement tells the ASP.NET engine to reserve a place in memory and call that place selection. You use the word selection each time you want to use the value stored at that memory location. You learned this in Chapter 4.

An *array* is very similar to a variable in that an array is a place in memory that is used to store information. Unlike a variable, however, an array can have multiple variables called array elements. Each array *element* refers to a location in memory where information is temporarily stored.

An array is identified by a unique name similar to the name of a variable. Each array element is identified by using the array name followed by the number of the array element. This number is called an *index*.

Think of an array as a column of a spreadsheet (see the following table). A letter identifies the column, and a number identifies each row. In an array, the letter that identifies the column is the array name. A row is an element of the array, and the row number is the index.

We refer to the first cell of the column by combining the column name with the row number, such as A1 to refer to the first cell of the column. An array works basically the same way in that you combine the name of the array with the index to reference an array element. You'll see how this is done later in this chapter.

Row	Column A
1	
2	
3	

Declaring an Array

An array is created by writing a declaration statement, which is very similar to the way a variable is declared. There are four parts to this declaration statement:

- The first part is the Dim keyword.
- The second part is the array name, which you create.
- The third part is the number of elements of the array.
- The fourth part is the data type of the array (see Chapter 4).

Here we declare an array called products that has three array elements, all of which have a String data type.

```
Dim products(3) AS String
```

The next table shows you how this looks if it were a column of a spreadsheet. Look carefully and you'll notice that the rows are numbered beginning with 0—not 1 as in a spreadsheet. This is because the first array element is always 0, not 1.

Row	Products
0	
1	
2	

Tip: *When declaring an array, always specify the number of elements that you need. If you want one element, then specify 1 and not zero.*

Initializing an Array

As you'll recall from Chapter 4, initialization is when you assign an initial value to a variable when the variable is declared. A similar process is used to initialize an array when you declare an array. That is, you assign an initial value to each element of the array when the array is declared.

You'll probably remember that the assignment operator is used to assign a value (initialize) to a variable when declaring the variable. This is shown here:

```
Dim product AS String = "Soda"
```

The assignment operator is also used to initialize an array. Since an array usually has more than one element, you'll need to initialize an array with multiple values— one for each array element. This is done by placing these values within French braces and separating each one with a comma. The first value is assigned to the first array element. The second value is assigned to the second array element and so on (see the table that follows), as is illustrated here:

```
Dim products() AS String = {"Soda", "Water", "Pizza", "Beer"}
```

Notice that

- Each value is placed within the French braces ({ }).
- Values must be the same date type as the data type of the array.
- A comma must separate each value.
- The number of values used to initialize the array determines the number of elements of the array. If there are four initial values, then there are four array elements.

Row	Products
0	Soda
1	Water
2	Pizza
3	Beer

Array Elements

Previously in this chapter you learned that an array is like a group of variables all having the same name. Each variable in the group is referred to as an element and is identified with a number called an index. The first index is a 0. The second is 1, and so on.

Starting with 0 and not 1 is confusing, since we start counting with 1 and not 0. However, the first digit in our numbering system (decimal number system) is 0, not 1. That is, our numbering system has ten digits, 0 through 9. Don't be overly concerned about the decimal numbering system. All you have to remember is that the first element of an array is 0 and not 1.

Each element of an array is accessed by using the name of the array followed by parentheses containing the element's index. Suppose we want to refer to the first element of the products array that we declared in the previous section of this chapter. Here's how we do this:

```
Products(0)
```

Think of this array element as a variable, because you use an array element just as you use a variable in your ASP.NET web page. Anything that you can do with a variable, you can also do with an array element.

Let's create a web page that displays a product in a text box when the visitor clicks a button. Create the web page that you see in Figure 6-1 using techniques that you learned in Chapter 3. Here's what you'll need to create:

- A label whose text is Product
- A text box whose ID is ProductsTxbx
- A button whose ID is DispProd and whose value is Display Product

Next, let's create an array called products and initialize it with the list of products shown in the preceding table. Also create a variable called CurrentProduct. Assign the first product in the array to the variable and display the value of the variable in the

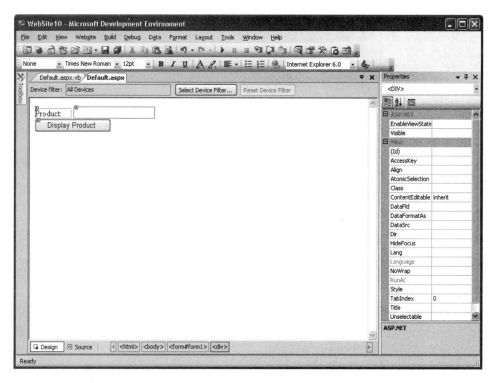

Figure 6-1 Create this ASP.NET web page to display a product contained in an array.

ProductsTxbx when the visitor clicks the Display Product button on the ASP.NET web page. Here's how this is done:

1. Double-click the Display Product button to display the empty event subroutine.

2. Enter the following code:

```
Dim CurrentProduct As String
Dim products() As String = {"Soda", "Water", "Pizza", "Beer"}
CurrentProduct = products(0)
ProductsTxbx.Value = CurrentProduct
```

Your event subroutine should look like Figure 6-2.

Select CTRL-F5 to run your ASP.NET web page and then click the Display Product button to see the Soda displayed in the text box (Figure 6-3).

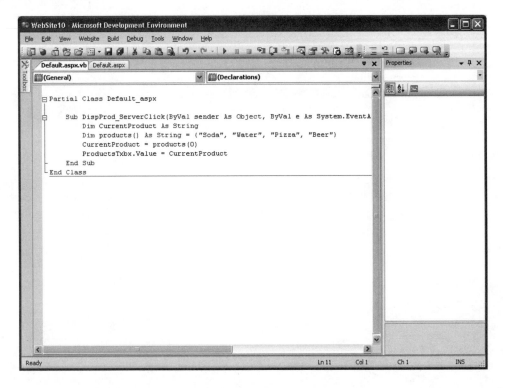

Figure 6-2 Here is the event subroutine that executes when the Display Product button is clicked.

You can also assign a value to an array element using the same technique you use to assign a value to a variable, as is illustrated in this example, where Wine is assigned as the new value to the first element of the array:

```
products = "Wine"
```

Change the value of the first array element in your code and then rerun your ASP.NET web page to see how your change affects the outcome of your program. Here's what your code should look like:

```
Dim CurrentProduct As String
Dim products() As String = {"Soda", "Water", "Pizza", "Beer"}
products(0) = "Wine"
CurrentProduct = products(0)
ProductsTxbx.Value = CurrentProduct
```

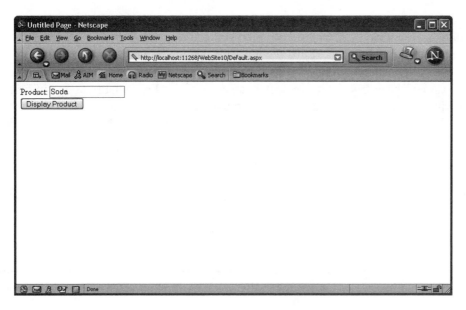

Figure 6-3   Clicking the Display Product button displays Soda in the text box.

Looping the Array

If an array element is basically the same as a variable, then what is the advantage of using an array over a variable except that you can use the same name for each array element? The magic of an array comes when you need to process each element of an array.

Suppose you needed to total the price of each product. If prices were assigned to variables, you'd need to create a formula using such variable names as

```
Dim TotalPrice AS Single
Dim SodaPrice, WaterPrice, PizzaPrice, BeerPrice AS Single
SodaPrice = 2.50
WaterPrice = 1.50
PizzaPrice = 10
BeerPrice = 5.50
TotalPrice = SodaPrice + WaterPrice + PizzaPrice + BeerPrice
```

TIP: *Remember from Chapter 4 that the Single data type is used to store mixed numbers.*

However, using an array along with a For loop (see Chapter 5) is more efficient than using a series of variables because you can step through each element of the array by using the index. You'll see how this is done in the following example.

First, we declare and initialize a variable called TotalPrice that will be assigned the sum of the prices. Next, we declare an array called ProductsPrices and initialize it with prices for each product (see the table that follows). Finally, the For loop is used to step through each array element, adding each to the value of the TotalPrice and then assigning the sum to the TotalPrice variable.

```
Dim TotalPrice AS Single = 0
Dim i as Integer
Dim ProductsPrices() AS Single = {2.50, 1.50, 10, 5.50}
for i = 0 to 3
   TotalPrice = TotalPrice + ProductsPrices(i)
next i
```

Row	ProductsPrices
0	2.50
1	1.50
2	10
3	5.50

This example might look confusing, but it really isn't. Here's what is happening.

When the ASP.NET engine enters the For loop for the first time, the value of i is 0 and the value of TotalPrice is also 0.

We use the i instead of a number as the index value for the element of the ProductsPrices array so that we can easily step through the array because the value of i is incremented by the For loop.

The ASP.NET engine is told to add the value of the ProductsPrices(i) element of the array to the TotalPrice variable and assign the sum to the TotalPrice variable. Remember that ProductsPrices[i] is really ProductsPrices[0], because the value of i is 0. And the value of ProductsPrices[0] is 2.50.

Therefore, the ASP.NET engine is told to do this:

```
TotalPrice = 0 + 2.50
```

Now the value of TotalPrice is 2.50. The ASP.NET engine returns to the top of the For loop, where it increments i, making the value of i equal to 1. As long as the value of i isn't greater than 3, the ASP.NET engine enters the For loop another time. This time, the ASP.NET engine references ProductsPrices[1], since the value of i is 1, and performs the calculation again.

```
TotalPrice = 2.50 + 1.50
```

This process continues until all four array elements are tallied.

Adding an Array Element

There will be occasions when you will need to increase the size of the array while your ASP.NET web page is running. You can do this by resetting the dimensions of the array using the ReDim keyword.

The ReDim keyword is used just as you use the Dim keyword to set the original dimensions of the array. Here's how to do this:

```
Dim ProductsPrices() AS Single = {2.50, 1.50, 10, 5.50}
ReDim ProductsPrices(5)
```

The first statement declares the ProductsPrices array as having four elements and assigns each of them an initial value, which you saw in the preceding table. The second statement resets the dimensions of this array to five array elements. In doing so, however, all the values of the original ProductsPrices array are lost. The redimensioned ProductsPrices looks like the following table.

Row	ProductsPrices
0	
1	
2	
3	
4	

You can retain values of the original array by using the Preserve keyword when you reset the dimensions of the array. This is shown in the next example. The next table shows the revised ProductsPrices array. Notice there isn't a value for the last array element.

```
Dim ProductsPrices() AS Single = {2.50, 1.50, 10, 5.50}
ReDim Preserve ProductsPrices(5)
```

Row	ProductsPrices
0	2.50
1	1.50
2	10
3	5.50
4	

TIP: *The ReDim keyword is also used to reduce the dimensions of an array, thereby freeing memory for other processing. However, doing so will lose the value of any element that is downsized even if you use the Preserve keyword in the statement.*

Multidimensional Arrays

The arrays that we've used so far in the chapter are called one-dimensional arrays, because the array has one set of elements. One-dimensional arrays are perfect for storing information that isn't associated with other information such as a product name or the name of a company.

However, one-dimensional arrays are not well suited for information that is related to other information, as is the case with a person's name, which consists of a first name and a last name. You need to create a multidimensional array to relate this information.

Think of a multidimensional array as an array where each element has its own array. Previously in this chapter you learned to declare a one-dimensional array like this:

```
Dim MyArray(5) As String
```

This statement creates a one-dimensional array that has five array elements. The next table shows what this looks like. Numbers represent the index for each array element.

First Dimension
0
1
2
3
4

A two-dimensional array creates a second dimension to the array where each array element of the first dimension has array elements. Here's how to create a two-dimensional array:

```
Dim MyArray(5,2) As String
```

Each array element of the first dimension has an array that has two array elements. The next table shows you how this looks.

First Dimension	Second Dimension
0	0
0	1
1	0
1	1
2	0
2	1
3	0
3	1
4	0
4	1

Let's return to the problem of relating first and last names of customers. You probably have a good idea how to do this by looking at the preceding table. As you can see, the second dimension has two array elements. We could store a last name in the first array element of the second dimension and the first name is the second array element of the second dimension. The results will look like the table that follows.

TIP: *You can have up to 32 dimensions, but rarely will you need to go beyond two dimensions.*

First Dimension	Second Dimension	
0	0	Smith
0	1	Mary
1	0	Jones
1	1	John
2	0	Adams
2	1	Tom
3	0	Rogers
3	1	Sue
4	0	Martin
4	1	Mary

Declaring a Multidimensional Array

A multidimensional array is declared by specifying the number of elements for each dimension within the parentheses of the array name. Each dimension must be separated from the next with a comma. Here's how to declare a two-dimensional array, which we'll use to store customer names:

```
Dim CustomerNames(5,2) AS String
```

The number of elements for each dimension is specified within parentheses. The first dimension creates five elements. The second dimension creates two elements, one for each element in the first dimension. The first element in the second dimension will be used to store the customer's last name, and the second element in the second dimension will store the customer's first name. The preceding table illustrates how this two-dimensional array looks.

Referencing a Multidimensional Array

You access elements of a multidimensional array by referencing the index of an array element, similar to how you access elements of a single-dimensional array, which you learned how to do previously in this chapter.

For example, we can store a customer's last name in the first array element by referencing the first element of the first dimension and the first element of the second dimension, such as:

```
CustomersName(0,0) = "Smith"
```

Likewise, we can assign the first name to the first array element by referencing the first element of the first dimension and the second element of the second dimension, like this:

```
CustomersName(0,1) = "Mary"
```

Practically the same technique is used to access the value of an element of a multidimensional array. You use the index of the first and second dimensions of the array. Here's how to access the last name Smith:

```
CustomersName(0,0)
```

Arrays and the Array Class

You'll recall from Chapter 2 that we see the world as objects such as a computer keyboard rather than a bunch of keys, springs, diodes, and other keyboard parts. All objects have data and actions associated with it. Data is the size and color of the

keys on the keyboard. An action is a key moving down when pressure is placed on it and up when pressure is removed.

An object is described in an application by using a class definition written using an object-oriented programming language such as Visual Basic .NET. Think of a class definition as a stencil of the letter *W*. The stencil describes a *W*, but it isn't a *W* until you place the stencil on paper and roll paint over it. You have a *W* when the stencil is removed from the paper.

A class definition is similar in concept to a stencil of the letter *W* in that a class describes the real object, but the class definition isn't the real object. The real object is called an instance of the class, just as the letter *W* on the paper is an instance of the stencil *W*.

A class definition describes both the data and the actions that are associated with the real object. Data is referred to as *property* of the class, and actions are called *methods* of the class. For example, a keyboard is an object. The class definition of the keyboard consists of the size and color of the keys as properties of the keyboard. The actions of moving the key down and then up are methods of the keyboard.

At this point, you might be wondering what all this talk about classes has to do with an array. An array is an object that is defined by the Array class. Each time you use an array in your application, you are actually using an instance of the Array class.

So what's the big deal? Well, the Array class contains properties and methods that make life easier when you work with an array. Suppose you want to known the number of elements in the array. Simply use the Length property that contains the length of the array. Suppose you want to sort values assigned to elements of the array. Simply call the Sort() method and the ASP.NET engine does all the work for you.

How Many Elements Are There in the Array?

There are a number of ways to determine the number of array elements, but the easiest and most efficient way is to use the length property of the array object. The length property of the array object contains the number of elements in the array.

Here's how to access the length property of the CustomerNames array that we declared in the previous section of this chapter:

```
Dim len AS Integer = CustomerNames.length
```

You specify the name of the array object and the name of the property (length) separated by a dot to access the length property. In this example, the length of the array is assigned to the variable len.

You don't have to assign the length property to a variable. Simply use the length property where you need to use the length of the array in an expression.

Remember that the length of an array is the actual number of array elements and not the index of the last array element. Take a look at the following array. The length of this array is four elements. Rookies tend to assume that the value of the length property is 3 because the last element in the array has an index of 3. This is a mistake; the length property is 4, since there are four elements in the array.

```
CustomerNames[0] = "Mary"
CustomerNames[1] = "John"
CustomerNames[2] = "Mike"
CustomerNames[3] = "Tom"
```

There Are Methods to Our Madness

The array class contains a number of methods that you'll find very useful when building your ASP.NET application. We'll explore many of these in this section of the chapter.

Sorting Array Elements

Sorting elements of an array is probably one of the more common tasks that you'll be required to perform. Fortunately, you don't have to reorder elements yourself, because there is a method to do this for you called the Sort() method.

The Sort() method rearranges values assigned to elements of an array in sort order, which is alphabetical order for characters and numerical order for numbers. Suppose you have the array called products shown in the next table, which is an unsorted array, and you need to have it placed in sort order.

Row	Products
0	Soda
1	Water
2	Pizza
3	Beer

Here's how to sort the products array. The third line calls the Sort() method to place the array in alphabetical order. Try replacing the code in the button event

(see the earlier section "Array Elements") with this code, and you'll see that the list of products is displayed in alphabetical order.

```
Dim i As Integer
Dim products() As String = {"Soda", "Water", "Pizza", "Beer"}
Array.Sort(products)
For i = 0 To 3
   Response.Write(products(i))
Next
```

Reversing the Order of Array Elements

Array elements can be reversed by calling the Reverse() method, which reverses the order in which values appear in the array. Let's say that you want to reverse the order of the previously sorted array. You do this by calling the Reverse() method, as shown in the following code. Try this in your button event:

```
Dim i As Integer
Dim products() As String = {"Soda", "Water", "Pizza", "Beer"}
Array.Sort(products)
Array.Reverse(products)
For i = 0 To 3
   Response.Write(products(i))
Next
```

Searching Array Elements

Searching an array for a specific value is another common task that your application will need to perform. You could use a loop to step through each element of the array until you found one that matches the search criteria, but this is the hard way to search. There are two easier and faster ways to do this by using methods of the Array class.

One of these methods is IndexOf(). The IndexOf() method requires two pieces of information in order to perform the search. These are the name of the array that is being searched and the search criterion. If the search criterion matches the value of an element of the array, then the IndexOf() method returns the index of the matching element. A negative number is returned if none of the values of the elements match the criterion.

For example suppose you wanted to locate Pizza in the array shown in the preceding table. Here's the code that you'll need to write to do this:

```
Dim result AS Integer
Dim products() AS String = {"Soda", "Water", "Pizza", "Beer"}
 result = Array.IndexOf(products, "Pizza")
If result >= 0 Then
   Response.Write("Pizza is located in array element: " + result)
Else
   Response.Write ("Pizza is not in the products array.")
End If
```

The IndexOf() method searches the products array for Pizza and assigns the results of the search to the result variable. If the value of the result variable is equal to or greater than 0, then we know that the search criterion was found, and we then proceed to display the results on the screen. If the value is less then 0—a negative number—then we know the array does not contain the search criterion, and we display the appropriate method on the screen.

An alternative to the IndexOf() method is the LastIndexOf() method. This method is called the same as the IndexOf() method, except that the index returned is that of the last array element that contains the search criterion. The IndexOf() method and the BinarySearch() method both return the index of the first array element that meets the search criterion.

Copy an Array

Values from one array can be copied to another array by calling the Copy() method. The Copy() method enables you to copy a segment of the array or the entire array by specifying the number of elements to copy.

The Copy() method requires five pieces of information in order to copy values from one array to another:

- **SourceArray**   This is the name of the array whose values are being copied to the destination array.

- **SourceIndex**   This is the index of the first element that will be copied.

- **DestinationArray**   This is the name of the array that is receiving the values from the SourceArray.

- **DestinationIndex**   This is the index of the first element in the destination index that is to receive the first value.

- **Length**   This is the number of elements that are to be copied.

Take a look at the next table. There are two arrays. Let's copy the values of the productsA array to the productsB array. We'll do this by calling the Copy() method.

Row	productsA	Row	productsB
0	Soda	0	
1	Water	1	
2	Pizza	2	
3	Beer	3	

The SourceArray is productsA and the SourceIndex is 0 because we are copying the first array element. The DestinationArray is productsB and the DestinationArray is 2 because we are copying the first array element of the ProductsA array to the third element (index 2) of the productsB array. The length is the number of elements that we're copying, which is 2. Here's the code segment that calls the Copy() method. The next table shows both arrays after values are copied to the productsB array.

```
Dim result AS Integer
Dim productsA() AS String = {"Soda", "Water", "Pizza", "Beer"}
Dim productsB(4) AS String
Array.Copy(productsA, 0, productsB, 0, 2)
```

Row	productsA	Row	productsB
0	Soda	0	Soda
1	Water	1	Water
2	Pizza	2	Pizza
3	Beer	3	Beer

Reset Values of an Array

You can reset array elements by calling the Clear() method. This is a fast way of getting rid of values that are assigned to an array without having to write code to overwrite these values. The Clear() method requires three pieces of information:

- **Array**   This is the name of the array that is being reset.
- **Index**   This is the index of the first element of the array that will be reset.
- **Length**   This is the number of elements to be reset.

Let's reset the last two elements of the productsA array shown in the preceding table by using the following code segment. The table that follows shows the result of resetting the productsA array.

```
Dim result AS Integer
Dim productsA() AS String = {"Soda", "Water", "Pizza", "Beer"}
Array.Clear(productsA, 2, 2)
```

Row	productsA	Row	productsB
0	Soda	0	
1	Water	1	
2		2	
3		3	

Array Using Different Data Types

So far in this chapter you have learned that all elements of an array must be of the same data type. That is, you cannot mix a string with an integer in the same array. However, there is a way to assign values of dissimilar data types to elements of the same array by declaring an array of objects. An *object* is a data type used to store data of different data types.

This sounds a little confusing, so let's walk through this step-by-step beginning with declaring the array. You must specify a data type when you declare an array. Since the array is going to store values that are of different data types, you declare the array as being of the Object data type as shown here:

```
Dim MyData(4) AS Object
```

An array of an Object data type can store values of any data type in its elements. So we could store a product name in one element and a product price in another element. The product name is a String data type, and the product price is a Single data type. This is shown in the following code segment. You can use these elements as you would any array element:

```
MyData(0) = "Beer"
MyData(1) = 2.50
```

The ASP.NET engine has to perform more work when using an array of an Object data type than with the other data types because it must convert the value to the proper data type before the value is used within your application.

For example, the ASP.NET engine converts MyData(1) to a Single data type it can use as its value. Likewise, MyData(0) is converted to a String data type. The extra work might have a performance impact, depending on the nature of your application.

Looking Ahead

In this chapter you learned how to group together values by using an array. An array has a name and one or more elements. Elements are used much as variables are used. Each element is identified by an index. The first element is index 0. The second element is index 1, and so on.

There are two ways in which a value can be assigned to an element: by placing values between the French braces following the array's data type when the array is declared or by using the assignment operator in a statement.

You can determine the number of elements in an array by using the length property of the array object. The length property is accessed by specifying the name of the array followed by a dot and the word length.

You can access the value of an element by specifying the name of the array followed by the index of the element within parentheses. If you need to access all elements of the array, then use a For loop; the initializer of the For loop (see Chapter 5) is used as the index for the array elements.

The array object has several methods that you can use to manipulate elements of the array. For example, the Sort() method places elements in sorted order. Reverse() is used to reverse the order of the values assigned to elements of the array. IndexOf()locates a value in an array, Copy()copies values from one array to another array, and Clear()resets the values of an array.

You now have a good working knowledge of how to store and use information within an ASP.NET application. In the next chapter, you'll learn how to divide your application into building blocks called subroutines and functions.

Quiz

1. This is the first element of the products array: products[1].

   a. True

   b. False

2. How many elements are there in Dim productsA() AS String = {"Soda", "Water", "Pizza" }?

  a. 2

  b. 3

  c. 4

  d. None

3. What method would you use to reset values of an array?

  a. Reset()

  b. Copy()

  c. Clear()

  d. Reboot()

4. What method is used to search for a value in an array?

  a. IndexOf()

  b. LastIndexOf()

  c. BinarySearch()

  d. All of the above

5. What method is used to copy a segment of an array to another array?

  a. Copy()

  b. SigCopy()

  c. PartCopy()

  d. ShortCopy()

6. What method is used to compare two arrays?

  a. Comp()

  b. CompareArray()

  c. Compare()

  d. None of the above

7. The sort() method only places text in sorted order.

  a. True

  b. False

8. The length of an array is equal to the index of the last element of the array.

    a. True

    b. False

9. An array element can be used the same way a variable is used.

    a. True

    b. False

10. An array cannot have elements of different data types.

    a. True

    b. False

Answers

1. b. False
2. b. 3
3. c. Clear()
4. d. All of the above
5. a. Copy()
6. d. None of the above
7. b. False
8. b. False
9. a. True
10. b. False

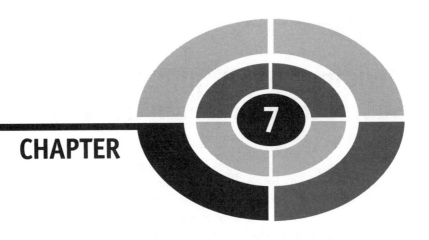

CHAPTER

7

Subroutines and Functions

In a real-life ASP.NET application snippets of code like those shown in this book are assembled to create a complex set of instructions that can respond to any request a person makes when visiting a web site. However, complex instructions are inherently difficult to write, difficult to read, and difficult to change.

In Chapter 5 you learned how to reduce the number of instructions in your ASP.NET application by having the ASP.NET engine execute instructions more than once by placing those instructions in a loop.

Another way to reduce the number of instructions in your ASP.NET application is to place instructions that perform the same functionality into a group. You can then tell the ASP.NET engine to execute the group whenever you want ASP.NET to perform the operation, such as validating a user ID and password. This group is called a subroutine or a function. And in this chapter you'll learn how to use subroutines and functions to simplify your ASP.NET application.

Dividing Your Application into Subroutines and Functions

Take a close look at your ASP.NET application, and you'll realize that you probably repeat the same lines of code in a few places within your application. This occurs naturally because you typically want the ASP.NET to perform the same task, only at different times while your application runs.

Suppose you want to give a visitor to your web site the opportunity to review his shopping cart from any web page on your site. This means you must insert the code that displays the shopping cart on each web page. However, this isn't advantageous for a number of reasons, the most obvious being that if the steps for displaying the shopping cart change, then you'll need to change every web page in your application.

ASP.NET developers avoid repeating code by carefully reviewing their application to identify places where the same task is performed multiple times. Code for those tasks is then grouped together into either a subroutine or a function that can be called from anywhere in the application. Whenever the task needs to be performed, the developer simply tells the ASP.NET engine to run the instructions contained in the group.

Thus, steps to display the shopping cart would be placed in a subroutine or function. You then tell the ASP.NET engine to run the subroutine or function each time you want the shopping cart displayed. Anytime those steps change, you only need to make those changes in one place—the subroutine or function.

Subroutine Versus Function

You've seen me use the terms subroutine and function whenever speaking about grouping instructions together to perform a task, and by now you're probably wondering how they differ. In order to appreciate the difference, you need to learn a little more about how subroutines and functions work.

Let's say that your application has a task that tells the visitor he has made an incorrect selection. This task simply displays an appropriate message on the screen. The message changes to reflect the incorrect selection.

Thus, the message might say, "Your shopping cart is empty" if the visitor tries to view the shopping cart without selecting an item. Another message might say, "You need to supply a valid credit card number" if the visitor tries checking out without giving his credit card information.

You'd write one group of steps that can display any message rather than a separate group of steps for each message. The message that is displayed is then given to the group when the task is performed. This is like saying to the ASP.NET engine, "Display a message on the web page—and here's the message that needs to be displayed."

The message is called a *parameter*, and giving the message to the group is called *passing* the parameter to a subroutine or function. You'll see how to do this later in this chapter. Both a subroutine and a function can use a parameter.

Up to this point a subroutine and a function are the same. Both are groups of instructions that can be called from elsewhere in an application and can receive a parameter (actually multiple parameters, as you'll see in the next few sections).

Now they'll go their separate ways.

Sometimes a task returns a result. For example, suppose the task calculates a 10 percent price increase. The price is passed as a parameter. The task performs the calculation and returns the result—the new price—to the statement in the application that called the task. This is called *returning a value*.

Only a function returns a value. A subroutine cannot return a value. And that's the difference between a subroutine and a function.

Creating a Subroutine

A *subroutine* is a group of instructions that perform a task and can be called from another part of your application whenever you want the ASP.NET to perform the task. However, you must create a subroutine before calling it in your application.

You create a subroutine by using the following structure:

```
Sub Name()
   'Place code here
End Sub
```

- **Sub**   This is a keyword that defines the beginning of the subroutine.
- **Name**   This is the unique name that you give to the subroutine. Good programming practice requires that the name of a subroutine reflect the nature of the task it performs. Thus, DisplayMessage might be a good name for a subroutine that warns a visitor that he made an incorrect selection.
- **()**   Parentheses identify parameters that are passed to the subroutine. Empty parentheses indicate no parameters are being passed. Later in this chapter, you'll learn how to insert parameters between the parentheses.
- **End Sub**   This is a keyword that defines the end of the subroutine.

Any statements that you want executed when the subroutine is called are placed between the Sub Name() and End Sub. Statements are executed sequentially until End Sub is reached. You can exit the subroutine before reaching End Sub by placing Exit Sub in the subroutine. Exit Sub causes the subroutine to terminate just as if the End Sub were encountered.

You place the definition of a subroutine in the code portion of your application. Here's how this is done:

1. Select the Source tab.

2. Press the right mouse button.

3. Select View Code from the pop-up menu.

Let's create a simple subroutine that displays "Hello world!" on a web page. There is no need to use parameters, since the message won't change. Enter the following code in the code portion of your application (Figure 7-1). More code will be added later:

```
Sub DisplayMessage()
   Response.Write("<b>Hello world!</b>")
End Sub
```

Calling a Subroutine

Once you define the subroutine, you can call the subroutine from anywhere in your application. You call a subroutine by simply using the subroutine name in a statement.

Here's what you need to do to call the DisplayMessage() subroutine:

```
DisplayMessage()
```

The ASP.NET engine executes all the instructions contained in the DisplayMessage() subroutine whenever the DisplayMessage() subroutine name is encountered in your application. This has the same effect as if you replaced the name of the subroutine with the code found in the definition of the subroutine.

Let's call the DisplayMessage() subroutine from a button event. Here's how to do this:

1. Select the Design tab and insert a button onto your web page (see Chapter 5).

2. Double-click the button to display the button event.

3. Enter the code in the button event as shown in Figure 7-1.

When you run your application and click the button, the DisplayMessage() subroutine displays the message on the screen as shown in Figure 7-2.

```
Default.aspx  Default.aspx.vb                                      ▽ ✕
Default_aspx                              ▼  (Declarations)          ▼

Partial Class Default_aspx

    Sub DisplayMessage()
        Response.Write("<b>Hello world!</b>")
    End Sub

    Sub Button1_Click(ByVal sender As Object, ByVal e As System.EventArgs)
        DisplayMessage()
    End Sub
End Class
```

Figure 7-1   The button event calls the DisplayMessage() subroutine to display the message on the screen.

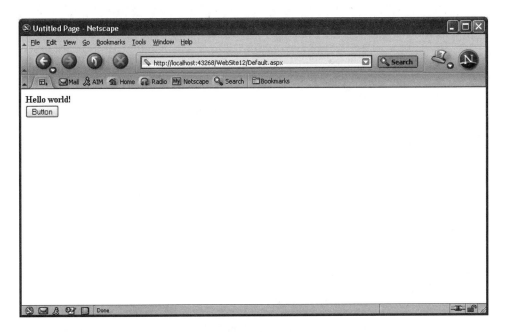

Figure 7-2   The DisplayMessage() subroutine is called when the visitor clicks the Display button.

Subroutines and Parameters

A *parameter* is an item of information that the subroutine requires in order to perform the task, such as displaying the message on the web page. A parameter is declared within the parentheses of the subroutine definition much as how you declare a variable (see Chapter 4).

Here's how you declare a parameter:

```
Sub Name(ByVal ParameterName As DataType)
    'Place code here
End Sub
```

- **ByVal**   When the subroutine is called, a copy is made of the parameter that is passed to the subroutine. This is referred to as passing the parameter by value. Another way to pass a value is by reference, noted as ByRef. A value passed by reference isn't copied. Instead, statements within the subroutine use the same value as the statement that called the subroutine.

- **ParameterName**   This is the name of the parameter passed to the subroutine and is used to reference the argument within the subroutine.

- **As**   This is the keyword that links the name of the parameter to the data type of the parameter.

- **DateType**   This is the keyword that defines the data type of the parameter. (See the section "Data Types: What kind of Data Is the Box?" in Chapter 4 for a list of data types.)

The name of the parameter used within the subroutine is called an *argument* and is used in place of the actual data that is passed to the subroutine. Think of the name of the parameter as a name of a variable. You use the parameter name just as you use the variable name.

Let's rewrite the DisplayMessage() subroutine so that the subroutine can display the message passed to it as an argument rather than displaying Hello world! Here is the revised definition:

```
Sub DisplayMessage(ByVal Mesg As String)
    Response.Write("<b>" + Mesg + "</b>")
End Sub
```

The parameter is called Mesg and is declared as a String data type. We won't know the content of the actual message until another part of the application calls the DisplayMessage() subroutine and passes it the message, as you'll see how to do in the next section.

However, the parameter name Mesg represents the message within the subroutine. The ASP.NET engine replaces Mesg with the actual message when the application runs.

Passing Parameters

An argument is passed from the statement that calls the subroutine to the subroutine by placing the value between the parentheses of the subroutine's name. For example, suppose we want the message "Shopping cart is empty." displayed on the web page. Here's how to do it (Figure 7-3):

```
DisplayMessage("Shopping cart is empty.")
```

When the DisplayMessage() subroutine is called, the message "Shopping cart is empty." is assigned to the Mesg parameter in the definition of the DisplayMessage() subroutine. The Write() function then displays this message on the screen.

The "Shopping cart is empty." message is displayed when the DisplayMessage() subroutine is called after the visitor clicks the button.

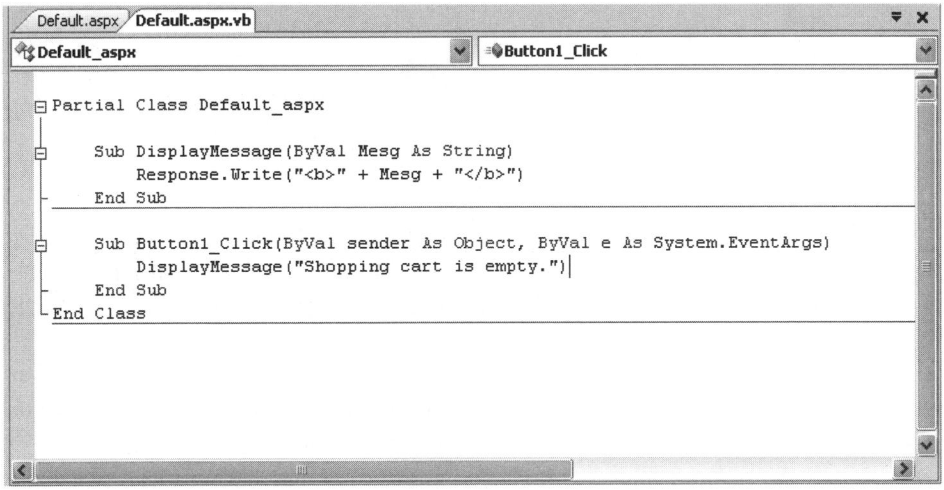

```
Default.aspx  Default.aspx.vb                                          ▼ ✕
Default_aspx                              ▼  ◈ Button1_Click              ▼

Partial Class Default_aspx

    Sub DisplayMessage(ByVal Mesg As String)
        Response.Write("<b>" + Mesg + "</b>")
    End Sub

    Sub Button1_Click(ByVal sender As Object, ByVal e As System.EventArgs)
        DisplayMessage("Shopping cart is empty.")
    End Sub
End Class
```

Figure 7-3   The message displayed by the DisplayMessage() subroutine is passed to this subroutine when the subroutine is called.

Multiple Parameters

Sometimes a subroutine requires more than one piece of information to perform a task. Therefore, you'll need to declare multiple parameters in the definition of the subroutine. Multiple parameters are declared the same way you declare a single parameter, except each is separated with a comma.

Here's how you declare multiple parameters:

```
Sub Name(ByVal ParameterName1 AS DataType, ByVal ParameterName2 AS DataType)
   'Place code here
End Sub
```

Each parameter name must be unique within the subroutine; otherwise, you'll confuse the ASP.NET engine. You can have parameters of different data types, depending upon the type of information needed by the subroutine to perform the task. For example, the first parameter might be a String, and the second parameter an Integer.

Let's rewrite the DisplayMessage() subroutine so that the subroutine displays two messages on the web page. Here's the revised subroutine:

```
Sub DisplayMessage(ByVal Mesg1 AS String, ByVal Mesg2 As String)
    Response.Write(Mesg1)
    Response.Write("<BR>")
    Response.Write(Mesg2)
End Sub
```

Passing Multiple Arguments

Multiple arguments are passed to a subroutine by placing the value of each argument within the parentheses of the statement that calls the subroutine. Each argument must be separated from the next by a comma and must correspond to the data type of the parameter declared in the subroutine definition.

Suppose MySub() has two parameters. The first parameter is a String, and the second parameter is an Integer. Therefore, when MySub() is called, the first value passed must be a String, and the second value passed must be an Integer.

Let's call the revised DisplayMessage() subroutine and pass it these two messages (Figure 7-4): "Shopping cart is empty." and "Returning you to our catalog." Figure 7-5 shows the results of calling this subroutine.

```
DisplayMessage("Shopping cart is empty.", "Returning you to our catalog.")
```

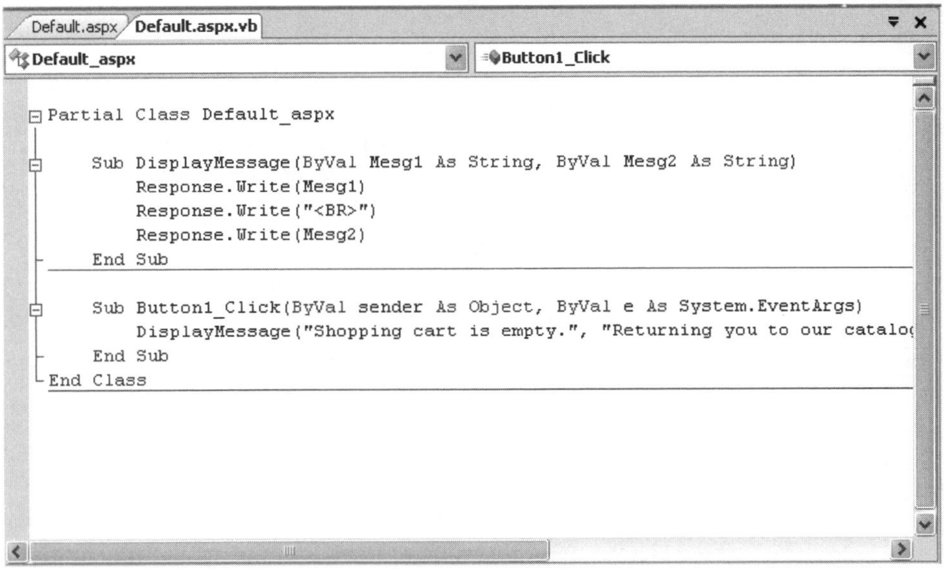

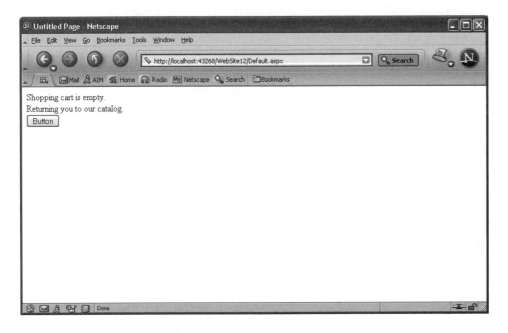

Default.aspx
Default.aspx.vb
Default_aspx
Button1_Click
Partial Class Default_aspx
Sub DisplayMessage(ByVal Mesg1 As String, ByVal Mesg2 As String)
Response.Write(Mesg1)
Response.Write("<BR>")
Response.Write(Mesg2)
End Sub
Sub Button1_Click(ByVal sender As Object, ByVal e As System.EventArgs)
DisplayMessage("Shopping cart is empty.", "Returning you to our catalo
End Sub
End Class

Figure 7-4 Two messages are passed to the DisplayMessage().

Untitled Page - Netscape
File Edit View Go Bookmarks Tools Window Help
http://localhost:43268/WebSite12/Default.aspx
Search
Mail AIM Home Radio Netscape Search Bookmarks
Shopping cart is empty.
Returning you to our catalog.
Button
Done

Figure 7-5 Two messages are passed to the DisplayMessage() subroutine when the visitor clicks the Display button.

Functions

A *function* is very similar to a subroutine in that a function is a group of instructions that perform a task and can be called from another part of your application whenever you want ASP.NET to perform the task. And, as when writing a subroutine, you must create a function before calling the function in your application.

Unlike a subroutine, a function can return a value.

A function is created in much the same way as you create a subroutine, except you use the keywords Function and End Function instead of Sub and End Sub. And, you specify the data type of the value that the function returns.

Here's how you create a function:

```
Function FunctionName() As ReturnDataType
    'Place code here
End Function
```

- **Function**   This is a keyword that defines the beginning of the function.
- **FunctionName**   This is the unique name that you give to the function. It is always a good practice to give the function a name that relates to the task that the function performs.
- **()**   Parentheses identify parameters that are passed to the function. Empty parentheses indicate no parameters are being passed.
- **As**   This is a keyword that defines the data type of the value returned by the function.
- **ReturnDataType**   This is the data type of the return value.
- **End Function**   This is a keyword that defines the end of the function.

All statements that are necessary to perform the task are placed within the body of the function.

You declare parameters that are passed to the function the same way as you do in a subroutine. There is no difference between the two when it comes to parameters.

Return Value

Unlike a subroutine, a function returns a value to the part of your application that called the function. You return a value from a function by using the Return keyword followed by the value that you want to return. You can also assign the value you want to return a name that is different from the function name.

Let's create a function that validates a user ID and password and use the Return keyword to return a value that indicates if the login information is valid or not. The user ID and password are passed as parameters to the program as shown here:

```
Function ValidateLogin
    (ByVal UserID AS String, ByVal Password As String)
    AS Boolean
    If UserID = "Bob" And Password = "BSmith" Then
        Return True
    Else
        Return False
    End If
End Function
```

The ValidateLogin() function receives the user ID and password from the portion of the application that requests the function to validate the login information. The ValidateLogin() function returns a Boolean value. You'll recall from Chapter 4 that a Boolean value is either True or False.

We purposely kept the validation process simple so as not to complicate the function by using an If...Then statement to compare the login information to one user ID and password. A real application would compare the user ID and password to valid login information that is stored in a database.

The function returns either a True if the login information matches or False if there isn't a match. It is the responsibility of the statement that called the function to do something with the return value.

Calling a Function

A function is called much the way a subroutine is called, by using the function name and passing parameters, if any parameters are required. However, a function is usually called as part of an expression, enabling the application to use the value returned by the function.

Here's how a function is called:

```
Dim Result AS Boolean
Result = ValidateLogin("Bob", "BSmith")
```

This example calls the ValidateLogin() function that is defined in the preceding section and passes the function the user ID Bob and password BSmith. Notice that this function is called within an expression. As you'll recall from Chapter 4, an expression consists of an operator and one or more operands. The assignment operator (=) is the operator in this expression, and Result and the value returned by the ValidateLogin() function are the operands.

ASP.NET 2.0 Demystified

However, you don't have to worry about operators and operands. All you really need to know is that the value returned by the ValidateLogin() function is assigned to the variable Result. Result is a Boolean variable, meaning that it can be assigned either a True or a False value. The ValidateLogin() function returns either a True or False value.

You don't have to assign the return value to a variable. Instead you can use the function call in place of the variable in an expression. For example, you could write the following code to process the value returned by the function. Notice that the return value is assigned to the variable Result, and then Result is used as the conditional expression in the If...Then statement.

Tip: *It might look strange to have just the Result variable as the conditional expression in the If statement. Remember that a condition expression resolves to either True or False. The value of the Result variable is either True or False, and therefore the Result variable can be used by itself as the conditional expression.*

```
If ValidateLogin("Bob", "BSmith")Then
   Response.Write("Approved.")
Else
   Response.Write("Disapproved.")
End If
```

Another approach is to use the function call in place of the variable, as shown in the next example. This, too, might be confusing to read. Here's what is happening: The ASP.NET engine first calls the ValidateLogin() function, which returns either True or False, depending on whether the user ID and password are valid. Next, ASP.NET evaluates the return value and determines which portion of the If...Then statement is executed.

```
If ValidateLogin("Bob", "BSmith") Then
   Response.Write("Approved.")
Else
   Response.Write("Disapproved.")
End If
```

Imbedding a function call within an expression is particularly advantageous if the return value is going to be used only once in your application, because you don't have to declare a variable to hold the return value. However, it is wise to assign the return value to a variable if the return value is going to be used in more than one expression, because you only need to call the function once.

You can call a function without retrieving its return value, in which case you don't use it as part of an expression.

```
ValidateLogin("Bob", "BSmith")
```

Passing an Array

As you learned in Chapter 6, an array is very similar to a variable in that an array is a place in memory that is used to store information. Unlike a variable, however, an array can have multiple variables called array elements. Each array element refers to a location in memory where information is temporarily stored.

You can pass an array to a subroutine or a function by including the array as a parameter, as shown in the following example. The DisplayStudents() subroutine declares a string array called StudentNames() in the parameter list. A For loop is then used to display each element of the array. The LBound() and UBound() functions are used to determine the lower and upper boundaries of the array:

```
Sub DisplayStudents(ByVal StudentNames() As String)
   Dim i As Integer
   For i = LBound(StudentNames) To UBound(StudentNames)
      Response.Write(StudentNames(i))
      Response.Write("<BR>")
   Next I
End Sub
```

You pass an array to a subroutine or function the same way you pass other values. This is illustrated in the following example. The first line declares an array and initializes it with names of students. Remember that the ASP.NET engine assumes that this array has three elements because three students are used to initialize the array. Also, the ASP.NET engine assumes this is an array of strings because the initialized values are strings.

The subroutine is then called and is passed the array.

```
Dim Students() As String = {"May", "Bob", "Joan"}
DisplayStudents(Students)
```

Returning an Array from a Function

An array can be returned by a function by specifying the array in the Return statement of the function. The following example shows how this is done. First we'll create a function called GetStudents(), which returns a list of students as elements of an array. In a real application, such a function would retrieve names of students from a database; however, we simplified this by initializing the array with the names of three students. The array is then returned to the portion of the program that called the StudentNames() function (see Figure 7-6). Notice there aren't any parameters

```
Default.aspx  Default.aspx.vb*                                        ≡ ✕
Default_aspx                              ▼  ≡● Button1_Click            ▼
⊟ Partial Class Default_aspx
 ⊟    Function GetStudents() As String()
          Dim StudentNames() As String = {"May", "Bob", "Joan"}
          Return StudentNames
 ╶    End Function


 ⊟    Sub Button1_Click(ByVal sender As Object, ByVal e As System.EventArgs)
          Dim i As Integer
          Dim Students(3) As String
          Students = GetStudents()
          For i = LBound(Students) To UBound(Students)
              Response.Write(Students(i))
              Response.Write("<BR>")
          Next i
 ╶    End Sub
◄                        ▓                                          ►
```

Figure 7-6   When the visitor clicks the button, the button event calls the GetStudents()
function to retrieve the list of students.

in this function, because the function contains all the information that it needs to
perform this task.

```
Function GetStudents() As String()
   Dim StudentNames() As String = {"May", "Bob", "Joan"}
   Return StudentNames
End Function
```

The GetStudents() function is then called as shown next. The return value, which
is the array, is assigned to another array, which is then used in a For loop to display
the names of students on the web page (Figure 7-7).

```
Dim i As Integer
Dim Students(3) As String
Students = GetStudents()
For i = LBound(Students) To UBound(Students)
   Response.Write(Students(i))
   Response.Write("<BR>")
Next I
```

Sometimes you don't know the size of the array that is being passed to the function. In this case, you can define the array without a dimension as shown here:

```
Dim Students() As String
```

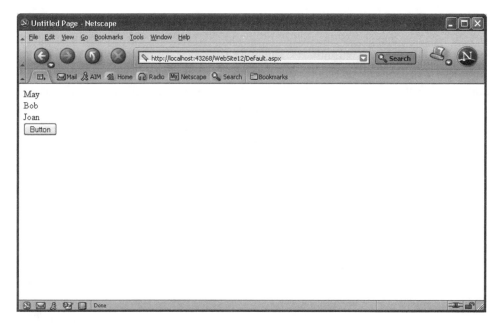

Figure 7-7   Here is what is displayed when the button is clicked.

Looking Ahead

ASP.NET applications can become complex. Developers simplify them by dividing the application into tasks and then create subroutines and functions to perform those tasks. Think of a subroutine or a function as a group that contains statements that perform a specific task within an ASP.NET application when the subroutine or function is called by another part of the application.

A subroutine must be created before it is called by using Sub...End Sub to define the subroutine and placed in the code portion of your application. Each subroutine must have a unique name followed by parentheses.

Information can be passed to a subroutine when the subroutine is called by declaring parameters. A parameter is similar to a variable that is declared within the parentheses of a subroutine and is used as a variable is used within the subroutine. Multiple parameters can be declared; however, a comma must separate each parameter from the next.

Statements that are executed when the subroutine is called are placed between the Sub and End Sub keywords in the definition of the subroutine. Any statement that can be used in an ASP.NET application can also be used in a subroutine.

A subroutine is called by using the name of the subroutine in a statement followed by parentheses. Values that correspond to the subroutine's parameters must be included within the parentheses when the subroutine is called. Each value must match the position and data type of the corresponding parameter in the subroutine's definition. Values are only necessary if parameters are defined for the subroutine; otherwise, no values need to be inserted in the parentheses and the parentheses aren't needed.

A function is similar to a subroutine in all respects except a function can return a value to the statement that calls the function, by using the Return statement within the body of the function. The data type of the return value must be specified when the function is defined. A subroutine cannot return a value.

Functions are commonly called within an expression, enabling the return value to be used by the expression without your having to declare and use a variable to store the return value.

An array can be passed to a subroutine or function by declaring the array as a ParamArray. Likewise, a function can return an array as a return value to the statement that called the function.

Now that you know how to use subroutines and functions to simplify your ASP.NET application, we'll turn our attention in the next chapter to gathering input using drop-down lists, radio buttons, check boxes, and other graphical user interface (GUI) objects.

Quiz

1. You must declare parameters for all functions.

   a. True

   b. False

2. You can return a value from a function by using

   a. Submit

   b. Apply

   c. Return

   d. Ret

3. What information should you include when declaring a parameter?

   a. The Ad keyword

   b. Parameter name

   c. Parameter data type

   d. All of the above

4. A subroutine is usually defined in the

   a. Page_Login event

   b. Code section of an application

   c. Page_Upload event

   d. Page_Download event

5. A subroutine's return value

   a. Is always assigned to a variable

   b. Is always used in an expression

   c. May or may not be used in an expression

   d. None of the above

6. All returned values must be

   a. A String data type

   b. A Boolean data type

   c. An Integer data type

   d. None of the above

7. A function must be called from an expression.

   a. True

   b. False

8. The return value from a subroutine must be assigned to a variable.

   a. True

   b. False

9. A subroutine is an older version of a function.

   a. True

   b. False

10. The data type of the return value should be specified when declaring a function that returns a value.

   a. True

   b. False

Answers

1. b. False
2. c. Return
3. d. All of the above
4. b. Code section of an application
5. d. None of the above. A subroutine does not return a value.
6. d. None of the above. It can be any data type.
7. b. False. A function can also be called just as you would a subroutine if you're not interested in its return value.
8. b. False
9. b. False
10. a. True

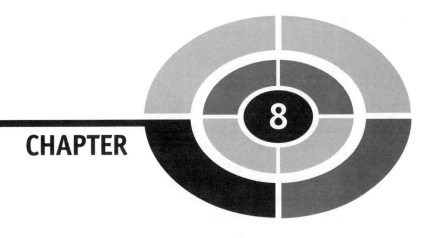

Drop-Down Lists, Radio Buttons, Check Boxes

Customers are resigned to the fact that they must fill out forms in order to do business online. However, customers don't expect to type a lot of data. Instead, they would rather pick and choose selections using a mouse.

You can meet this expectation by providing visitors to your web site with an assortment of drop-down list boxes, radio buttons, and check boxes and minimize the use of text boxes to gather information.

No doubt you're familiar with these GUI objects, since they are widely used on e-commerce web sites. In this chapter, we'll show you how to create these GUI objects on your ASP web page. You'll also learn how to retrieve values selected by visitors to your web site.

Drop-Down Lists

A *drop-down list box* resembles a text box that you learned how to create in Chapter 4, except the visitor is limited to entering text from a list of possible choices that you provide. Those choices are hidden from view until the visitor selects the down arrow that is adjacent to the drop-down list box.

A choice is made by selecting an item from the list, typically by using the mouse to point to the item and then clicking the mouse button to select the item. Alternatively, some visitors might use the UP ARROW and DOWN ARROW keys to highlight the item and then press ENTER to select the item. Regardless of the method used by the visitor, the selected item appears in the drop-down list box and then the list is automatically hidden again. Drop-down list boxes are ideal for choosing an item such as the abbreviation of a state from a set of items.

Creating a Drop-Down List Box

A drop-down list box is created by dragging and dropping the drop-down list box icon from the Toolbox onto the web page in the Design tab. Once it is in position, set the ID property or simply use the default ID. You'll be using the ID property to access the selected item from within your ASP.NET code. Your next job is to enter items onto the list. This is done by selecting the Items property found on the Properties pane.

The Items property contains the word Collection. Select the Items property and then select the three dots (…) that follow the word Collection (Figure 8-1) to display the ListItem Collection Editor dialog box. The ListItem Collection Editor is where you insert items onto the list and remove items from the list.

In this example, we'll insert three items called One, Two, and Three. The first item will be the default selection where the Selected property is set to true. Use the default values for the other properties.

Let's insert a new item onto the list (Figure 8-2).

1. Click Add. A new entry is added to the left text box in the ListItem Collection Editor.

2. Set the Selected value for the new entry. True means the new item becomes the default item for the list. The default item is automatically chosen if the visitor doesn't select an item from the list. False means the new item isn't the default item.

3. Set the Text property for the new entry. The Text property is the text of the item that is displayed on the list. This is what the visitor sees when the list opens on the screen.

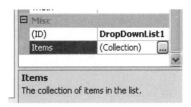

Figure 8-1   Select the three dots to open the ListItem dialog box.

4. Set the Value property. The Value property is the information that your code receives when the visitor selects the item. Some developers don't assign a value to the Value property because the value of the Text property is used as the Value property default value. This means that your code receives the text of the item if the visitor selects the item.

5. Insert additional items onto the list.

6. Reorder items on the list, if necessary, by selecting a list item and then selecting the UP ARROW and DOWN ARROW keys to reposition the item on the list.

7. Select OK.

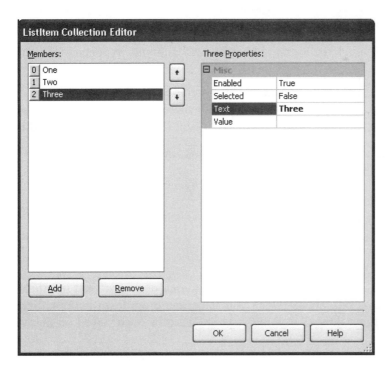

Figure 8-2   Select the Add button to insert a new item on the list.

The final step is to create a Submit button on the web page that will be used by the visitor to submit the form. You do this by dragging and dropping the button from the Toolbox onto the web page in the Design tab. Be sure to set the Text property of the button to Submit (see Chapter 4). Change the ID to SubmitButton.

Tip: *The last item selected by the user becomes the current item in the drop-down list box.*

Accessing the Selected Item from a Drop-Down List Box

The next step is for you to write code that reads the item selected from the drop-down list box by the visitor to your web site. This code is placed within the event handler for the Submit button. In order to access the selected item, you'll need to use the ID that you gave to the drop-down list box and the Value property of the selected item.

You'll recall that the Value property contains the text of the item unless you specifically set a value for the Value property when you created the drop-down list box.

Here's what you need to do to access the item selected by the visitor to your web site:

1. Double-click the Submit button in the Design tab to open the button's event handler.

2. Let's assume that you inserted three items on the list. These are called "One", "Two", and "Three". Here's the code that you need to write to response to each of these items. We'll use the default ID, which is DropDownList1.

```
Select Case DropDownList1.SelectedItem.Value
    Case "One"
        Response.Write("You select: One.")
    Case "Two"
        Response.Write("You select: Two.")
    Case "Three"
        Response.Write("You select: Three.")
End Select
```

Press CTRL-F5 to run the application. Note that items that you inserted into the ListItem dialog box appear when you select the drop-down list box. Select Two from the list and then click Submit; your selection is displayed on the web page (Figure 8-3).

Figure 8-3 Your choice of item is displayed when you click Submit.

Radio Buttons

A *radio button* is a circle that appears alongside text and must exist within a set of radio buttons. Only one radio button in the set can be selected. The text, such as Male or Female, can be selected by a visitor to your web site. The circle darkens when the visitor selects the radio button; otherwise, the circle isn't darkened.

Related radio buttons are always organized into a group. Only one radio button within the group can be selected. When a visitor selects a radio button, the circle associated with that radio button is darkened and circles for the rest of the radio buttons within the group are left lightened, indicating they are unselected.

For example, we can insert two radio buttons on the form—Male and Female—and then place them in a group called Gender. If the visitor selects Male (darken circle), then Female is automatically left unselected (light color circle). If the visitor then decides to select Female, the Male radio button is automatically unselected.

Creating a Radio Button

There are two ways to create a radio button. You could use a single radio button or a radio button list. Both are found on the Toolbox. Many ASP developers prefer to use the radio button list because radio buttons are automatically grouped together and are easy to maintain.

Let's create a radio button using the RadioButtonList control:

1. Drag and drop the RadioButtonList from the Toolbox to the Design tab.

2. Select the Items property and you'll notice three dots (...) appear alongside the word Collection. This is similar to what happens when you select the Items property for a drop-down list box.

3. Select the three dots to display the ListItem Collection Editor dialog box. This is where you enter information about the radio buttons, just as you did for the drop-down list box (Figure 8-4).

4. Click Add and then enter the text for the first radio button. Repeat these steps for each radio button. A new radio button is entered into the group each time you click Add. You can remove a radio button by selecting the button from the list and then clicking Remove. We'll create two radio buttons. The first is Male and the second is Female (Figure 8-4).

5. You can set a default value by changing the Select value from False to True. You should always make one radio button the default selection; otherwise, the application won't have a value should the visitor fail to select a radio button.

6. Click OK.

Drag and drop a Button from the Toolbox onto the Design as you did with the drop-down list box example. Be sure to set the Text property of the button to Submit. Change the ID to SubmitButton.

Accessing the Selected Radio Button

You insert code to respond to a radio button within the Submit button's event handler similar to the code that you used in the drop-down list box example.

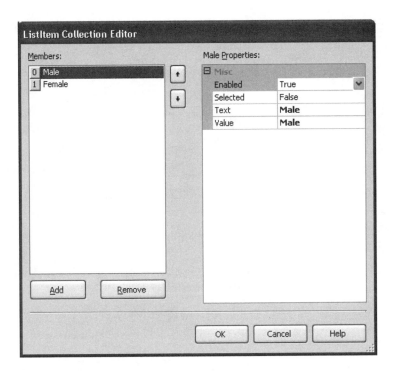

Figure 8-4 Click Add to enter information about each radio button.

Here's what you need to do:

1. Double-click the Submit button to display the event handler.
2. Enter the following code. Notice that the value of the Case statement is the text of each radio button. You'll recall from the section on the drop-down list box that the text is automatically assigned to the Value if you leave the Value blank.

```
Select Case RadioButtonList1.SelectedItem.Value
    Case "Male"
        Response.Write("You select: Male.")
    Case "Female"
        Response.Write("You select: Female.")
End Select
```

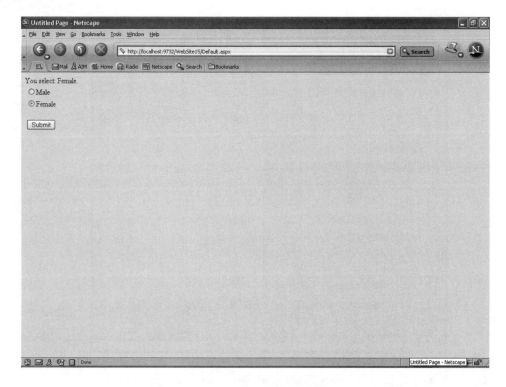

Figure 8-5 A message confirms that the Female radio button was selected.

Press CTRL-F5 to run the application. Figure 8-5 shows what you'll see when you select the Female radio button and then click Submit.

Check Boxes

A *check box* is similar to a radio button in that the visitor makes a choice by selecting a check box. However, a check box doesn't have to be within a set of check boxes. You can have one check box. And unlike with a radio button, selecting one check box has no effect on other check boxes. A check mark appears in the check box if it is selected; otherwise, the check box appears empty.

However, check boxes aren't grouped the same way as radio buttons are grouped. The status of one check box doesn't affect the statuses of the other check boxes. That is, the visitor can select two check boxes and both remain selected, as compared to a radio button, where the selection of one radio button causes other radio buttons in the group to be unselected.

Creating a Check Box

Dragging and dropping the check box icon from the Toolbox onto the Design tab creates a check box on your web page. The Text property of the check box is used to set the text that appears alongside the check box on the page.

You should position related text boxes together because this makes it easy for the visitor to make selections without looking for check boxes all around your page. Avoid using too many check boxes, since this tends to clutter your web page and confuse your visitor.

You can check the check box by setting the Checked property to True. This causes a check mark to appear in the check box when the check box is displayed. The visitor must then uncheck the box; otherwise, the application treats this check box as if the visitor checked the box.

Let's create a check box (Figure 8-6).

1. Drag and drop two check boxes from the Toolbox onto the Design tab.

2. Select the first check box.

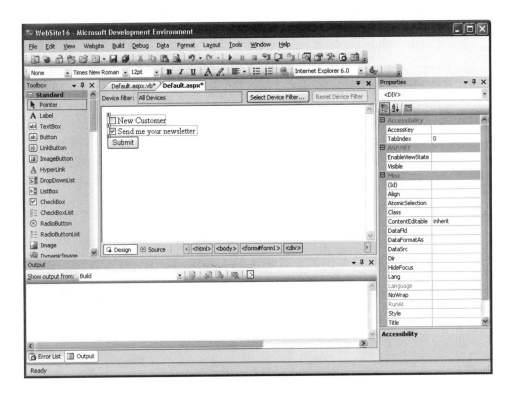

Figure 8-6   Create two check boxes and a Submit button.

3. Set the ID property to NewCustomer and the Text property to "New Customer."

4. Select the second check box.

5. Set the ID property to YesNewsletter and the Text property to "Send me your newsletter." Also, change the Checked property from False to True.

6. Drag and drop a button from the Toolbox to the Design tab and set the ID and label for the button.

Accessing a Check Box

Your application determines whether or not a check box is selected from within the Submit button event handler. You must examine the value of the Checked property for each check box that appears on the web page by using an If...Then statement. If the Checked property is true, then the check box was selected; otherwise, the visitor didn't select the check box.

Here's how to code the event handler to determine the state of a check box:

1. Double-click the Submit button to display the event handler.

2. Enter the following code.

3. Press F5 to run the application. Figure 8-7 shows what you'll see if you select the New Customer check box and then click Submit. Remember that "Send me your newsletter." is already checked by default.

```
If NewCustomer.Checked Then
    Response.Write("Welcome! We value you as a new customer.")
    Response.Write("<BR>")
End If
If YesNewsletter.Checked Then
    Response.Write("Welcome to our mailing list.")
End If
```

Selecting Check Boxes from Within Your Application

You can select or unselect a check box from within your application by changing the value of the Checked property.

Here's what you do to check the check box:

```
ID.Checked = True
```

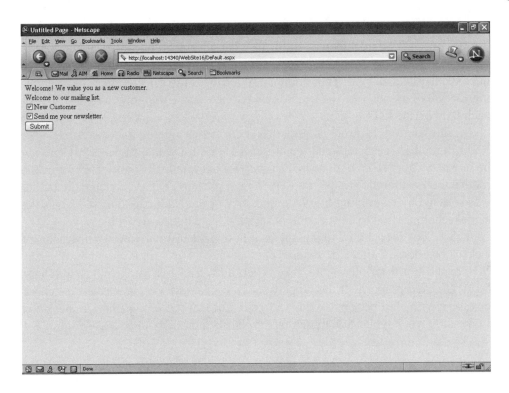

Figure 8-7 The application detects which check boxes are checked.

Here's how to uncheck the check box:

```
ID.Checked = False
```

Remember to replace the ID in the previous examples with the ID for the check box.

Looking Ahead

Designing your web page using drop-down lists, radio buttons, and check boxes is one of the most efficient ways to gather information from the visitor to your web site. Visitors can make their choices quickly with a few clicks of the mouse and not worry about typing information using the keyboard.

A drop-down list box contains two or more items that are hidden from sight (unless one has been selected) until the visitor selects the down arrow that is adjacent to the drop-down list box. The visitor then selects an item from the list once the list is displayed. Your application retrieves the selected item by examining the Value property of the drop-down list box and comparing it to the Text of each item on the list.

A radio button is grouped together with other related radio buttons in a RadioButtonList. Each radio button presents the visitor with a choice. Only one can be selected. Other radio buttons in the group are automatically unselected when one radio button within the group is chosen. Your application detects which radio button was selected by examining the Value property of the RadioButtonList. This is the same technique used to detect an item selected from a drop-down list box.

A check box is also used to present an option to the visitor. However, the status of a check box doesn't affect the statuses of other check boxes, if any, on the web page. Your application determines if the visitor checked a check box by examining the check box's Checked property. If the property is True, then the visitor selected the check box; otherwise, the check box wasn't selected. You can check or uncheck a check box from within your application by setting the Checked property in your code.

Quiz

1. You can set a default selection for a drop-down list box.

   a. True

   b. False

2. The best control to use when there is one of many options from which to select is

   a. A drop-down list box

   b. A radio button

   c. A check box

   d. None of the above

3. What is assigned to the Value property of an item in a drop-down list box if you don't assign anything to the Value property?

   a. Nothing is assigned to the Value property.

   b. The value of the ID property.

   c. The value of the Text property.

   d. You must assign a value to the Value property.

4. Unless you use the UP ARROW and DOWN ARROW keys to change the order, in what order do items appear in a drop-down list box?

    a. The order in which they are entered

    b. Alphabetical order

    c. Numerical order

    d. Random order

5. An If...ElseIf statement might be used to evaluate a check box because

    a. All check boxes within a group must be examined.

    b. All check boxes must be examined, including those outside the group.

    c. If one check box is true, you don't need to examine other radio buttons within the group.

    d. None of the above

6. What happens when the Boolean value of an item is set to true in a drop-down list box?

    a. The item is selected by default if the visitor doesn't select an item from the list.

    b. The item isn't displayed.

    c. The name of the item is set to true.

    d. The name of the item is set to false.

7. The selection of a check box affects the statuses of other check boxes.

    a. True

    b. False

8. Selecting a radio button affects the selection of every check box.

    a. True

    b. False

9. You must set the Value property of an item on the drop-down list box.

    a. True

    b. False

10. The Value property of a check box is used to identify the check box within your code.

    a. True

    b. False

Answers

1. a. True
2. a. A drop-down list box
3. c. The value of the Text property
4. a. The order in which they are entered
5. d. None of the above
6. a. The item is selected by default if the visitor doesn't select an item from the list.
7. b. False
8. b. False
9. b. False. If you don't set the Value property, it is automatically assigned the value of the item's Text property.
10. b. False. The ID property is used to identify the check box.

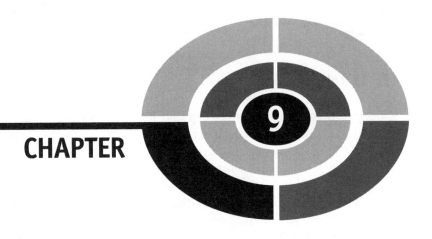

Databases

You probably access your bank account records by logging into the bank's web site. The bank's web application compares your ID and password against those stored in their database. If they match, then your account information is retrieved from a database and displayed on the screen.

This is referred to as a data-driven web application because the application centers on providing you with data that is stored in a database accessible by the ASP.NET engine. Think of a database as a sophisticated electronic filing cabinet and the ASP.NET engine as the file clerk.

There are three components to a data-driven web application: the client, the server, and the database. Throughout this book you have learned how to build the client and the server components of a web application. In this chapter you begin to learn how to build that database component. We'll start by exploring the concept of a database and how to design a database.

An Overview

Before wading knee-deep into learning about databases, it is important to clarify a common misconception about databases. You've probably read about popular database software packages such as MySQL, Microsoft Access, Oracle, DB2, and Microsoft SQL Server. Sometimes these are referred to as databases—but they're not.

As you'll learn in this chapter, a database is a collection of data organized so that it can be quickly retrieved much like a filing cabinet. A developer then writes code that inserts and removes information from the database. This is a lot of work, but fortunately much of this code is already written in the form of a database management system, which is commonly referred to as a *DBMS*.

The DBMS handles all the dirty details of how to store and retrieve information in a database. All a developer needs to do is to send the DBMS a *query* written in the Structured Query Language (SQL). Think of this as asking a file clerk to get you an invoice from the filing cabinet. You give the file clerk enough information to find the invoice, and the file clerk handles the details of locating and retrieving the invoice. Just like a file clerk, the DMBS is responsible for maintaining the information that is stored in the database and responding to your queries.

MySQL, Microsoft Access, Oracle, DB2, Microsoft SQL Server, and other popular "databases" are DBMSs—not databases.

Starting with this chapter you'll learn how to link your ASP.NET application to a DBMS and write SQL queries to communicate with the DBMS. Now that you have an overview, let's begin with a look at data.

Data, Database, and Tables

An item of data is the smallest piece of information, such as a person's first name, a person's last name, a street address, a city, a state, and a ZIP code. Notice that we didn't say a person's name or a person's address is data, because they are not the smallest piece of information. A person's name can be broken down to first name and last name—sometimes middle name. These are data. Likewise, a person's address can be subdivided into street, city, state, and ZIP code. These too are data. This subtle difference is important to keep in mind because many times you'll be responsible for identifying the data that will be used in a database.

A database is a collection of data that is identified by a unique name to distinguish the database from other databases. A collection of people's first names, last

names, street addresses, cities, states, and ZIP codes form a table in a database. A DBMS is the software you use to

- Save data
- Retrieve data
- Update data
- Manipulate data
- Delete data

The way in which a DBMS structures data in a database is called a database *model*. There are a number of different database models, ways data can be structured in a database. One of the most popular of them is the *relational* database model.

The term relational database model is a little imposing at first, but this means relating tables within a database. For example, depending on an application, data related to a person's address (street, city, state, ZIP) are similar data and are therefore placed in one group. The parts of a person's name (first name, middle name, last name) are also similar data and are placed in another group.

A group is called a table. A *table* is like a table of a spreadsheet in that both have columns and rows. A table is also given a unique name to distinguish it from other tables in the database. Each column represents a piece of data and is identified by a unique name, called a column name. For example, the table that contains a person's name will have the following columns (see Figure 9-1). Each row (or record) represents one set of data, such as a person.

Each column is defined by attributes that describe the characteristics of the data that is stored in the column. Later in this chapter we'll take a look at these attributes; however, here are three commonly defined attributes:

- **Column name**   Name of the column
- **Data type**   The kind of data that can be stored in the column
- **Size**   The number of characters that can be stored in the column

Customer Table

Customer First Name	Customer Middle Name	Customer Last Name
Bob	Allen	Smith
Mary	Alice	Jones

Figure 9-1   A table within a database

Tip: *The database name, table name, column name, and its attributes are referred to as metadata. Metadata is data that describes other data.*

Relating Tables

You might be wondering how you access information that appears in two or more tables. For example, if one table has customer information (i.e., customer name) and another table has order information, how to you link the customer information to the customer's order information?

This is done by using a column that is common to both tables. In this case, a column called customer number is the common column. Figure 9-2 shows two tables. First is the customer table, and the other is the order table.

The customer table is similar to Figure 9-1 except we inserted the customer number column. The customer number is a unique number assigned to each customer. Customer numbers are preferred over customer names to identify customers, because two customers might have the same name.

The order table consists of information that is typically associated with an order. We limited this to the order number, customer number, product number, and quantity ordered to show how tables are linked together. We'll insert additional columns in this table later in this chapter.

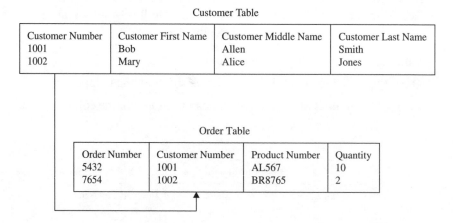

Figure 9-2 The customer table is linked to the order table using the customer number.

Only the customer table is needed if we want to look up a customer name. However, both the customer table and the order table are needed to look up an order because the order table doesn't contain the customer name. We do this by first finding the order number of the order we want in the order table. So if we wanted order 7654, we look in the order number column to find it. Next we read the customer number of that row, which is 1002. We then find customer number 1002 in the customer number column of the customer table. The row containing 1002 also contains the name of the customer who placed the order.

This process is called relating two tables and is why a database management system is called a relational database management system—it is capable of relating tables together.

Designing Your Database

One of your jobs when developing a data-driven ASP.NET application is to design its database. That is, decide on the data that will be stored in the database, the attributes of the data, and how the data is grouped. The database design is similar to the blueprint for a building. Once the design is completed, you can then build the database.

The blueprint for a database is called a database *schema*, which is a document that defines all the components of database. It shows data and its attributes. It groups data into tables and shows how tables relate to other tables.

Let's say that you are developing an e-commerce web site. In the database, you'll need to store customer information, product information, order information, vendor information, shipping information, and carrier information.

Customer information consists of the names and addresses of your customers. Product information is data about the products that you're selling, such as the product number, product name, and size. The order information is data about orders placed by customers, such as the customer number, product number, quantity purchased, and shipping instructions. Vendor information is data about the companies who sold you the products that you are reselling to your customers. Carrier information is data about the companies who deliver your products to your customers.

Your objective is to develop a database schema for this database. We'll walk you through this process, but for now take a look at Figure 9-3. This is the database schema for this example.

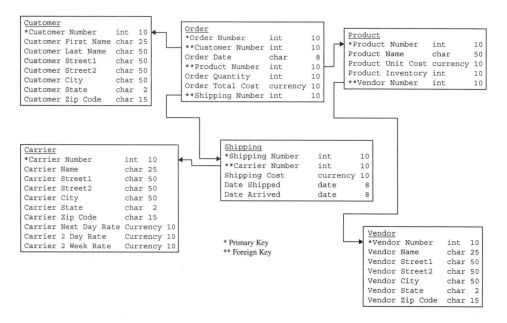

Figure 9-3 Here is the database schema for a typical e-commerce web site.

The Process

There are six steps developers perform when designing a database for their ASP.NET application:

1. Identify information that you need to store in your database. You can get this from reviewing an application that is similar to your application or simply brainstorming.

2. Change the information into data. Developers call this *decomposing*. This is where you take a customer's name and divide it into customer first name, customer middle name, and customer last name.

3. Define data. Here's where you determine the size, data type, and other attributes of the data.

4. Organize data into groups. Developers call this *normalizing* the data.

5. Identify columns that will be used to relate rows of data. Developers call this identifying primary and foreign keys.

Identifying Information

Begin by identifying all the information that you'll need for your ASP.NET application. This can be a daunting task because there is so much information that some developers have a difficult time finding the starting point.

The best way to approach this task is to think of people and things that are associated with your application. Developers call these *entities*. For example, a customer is a person associated with an e-commerce web application. Therefore, a customer is an entity. Likewise, a product, an order, and a vendor are also entities and are associated with an e-commerce web application.

It is easier to think of entities than data because you can easily identify an entity, since there are typically fewer entities than pieces of information. Entities seem to jump out at you as soon as you realize what an entity is. In addition, you can review applications that are similar to your application, and you'll probably see entities that you can use for your application.

Each entity has one or more attributes. An *attribute* is information that defines the entity. Your job is to identify attributes of each entity for your ASP.NET application. Identifying attributes is intuitive most times because you can ask yourself what information describes a customer? Likewise, what information describes an order?

Brainstorm and do a little research by reviewing similar applications and come up with a list of information for each entity. Don't expect to develop a complete list in one sitting, because it might take a professional developer weeks to flush out a thorough list of information. They write a list first and then continue to review and modify it until they feel it is complete.

Figure 9-4 shows a partial list of information that is associated with entities in our e-commerce ASP.NET application.

Don't confuse an attribute with data. An attribute is information about the entity such as a customer name. Typically an attribute can be subdivided into data such as customer first name, customer middle name, and customer last name. Other times an attribute is also data, such as a product number. Product numbers usually cannot be subdivided, and therefore it is data, too.

Change Information into Data

Now that you've identified attributes for your entities, you need to transform the attributes to data. Developers call this process decomposing attributes.

This process is also intuitive because you can easily recognize whether or not an attribute can be subdivided. Look at each attribute. Ask yourself, can this attribute be subdivided into data? If so, then write the data. If not, then use the attribute as the data.

For example, customer address is an attribute of the customer entity. Can customer address be subdivided into data? Sure it can, because an address is composed

```
Customer                 Order Form               Product
Customer Name            Customer Name            Product Name
Customer Address         Customer Address         Unit Cost
                         Date                     Inventory
                         Product                  Vendor Name
                         Quantity                 Vendor Address
                         Total Cost


Shipping Form            Carrier                  Vendor
Customer Name            Carrier Name             Vendor Name
Customer Address         Carrier Address          Vendor Address
Carrier Name             Next Day Rate            Product Name
Carrier Address          2 Day Rate
Product Name             2 Week Rate
Cost
Date Shipped
Date Arrived
```

Figure 9-4   Here is a list of entities and their attributes for an e-commerce web site.

of street, city, state, and ZIP code. Therefore, you'll need to make a list of the data associated with the attribute.

A product number is an attribute of the product entity. Can a product number be subdivided into data? It depends on the nature of the product number. However, many product numbers cannot be subdivided into meaningful data. Therefore, product number is also data.

Define Data

Once you identify data for each entity, you must define the data. The definition of data, which you'll later use when you build the database, describes the data. The most common ways to define data are by name, data type, size, range, default value, acceptable values, where a value is, format, and source of the data.

- **Name**   The name of the data, commonly called a column name, uniquely identifies the attribute from other data of the same entity. Duplicate data names within the same entity are prohibited.

- **Data type**   A data type specifies the kind of values that are associated with the data.

- **Maximum data size**   The data size describes the maximum number of characters associated with the data. Suppose 10 characters are used to represent every product number. The maximum size is 10 characters.

- **Minimum data size**   The data size describes the minimum number of characters associated with the data. Let's say that the product number cannot be less than 10 characters, so then the minimum size of the product number is 10 characters.

- **Data range**   The data range is the range of values that are associated with the data. These are specified as a minimum value and maximum value. For example, a product number might be from 10000 to 99999. Therefore, the minimum value of the data is 10000 and the maximum value is 99999. Values outside of this range are invalid.

- **Data default value**   The data default value is the value that is automatically assigned to the data if no value is explicitly assigned to the data. Let's say that an order entity has order date as one of its data elements. The default value for the order date is today's date. If an order is placed without an order date, then the value of the order date defaults to today's date.

- **Acceptable values**   An acceptable value for a data element is one of a set of values. For example, the order entity has a product number as a data element of the order. The product number must be one of a valid set of product numbers. This is different than a range of product numbers because some product numbers in the range may not have been assigned to products as yet. Therefore, they wouldn't be in the set of value product numbers.

- **Required value**   A data value may be required. For example, you cannot have an order without a product number. Therefore, product number is required. However, you might have a customer who doesn't have a middle name. Therefore, customer middle name is not required.

- **Data format**   Some data must appear in a particular format, such as mm-dd-yyyy for a date. You'll need to specify the format if the data requires one; otherwise, you don't need to describe the format.

- **Date source**   The data source is the origin of the data. Some data is provided during data entry, while other data is provided by a database or from another system. Practically all the data for your application will come from data entry.

Figure 9-5 shows the type of data that you can derive from the customer, order, product, shipping, vendor, and carrier entities for an e-commerce web site. It is all right if you come up with a different set of data and a different data definition because the actual data and data definitions used in a database schema are dependent on the particular ASP.NET application that you're building.

```
Shipping Form
Customer Number      num      10 required
Customer First Name  char     35 required
Customer Middle Name char     35
Customer Last Name   char     75 required
Customer Street      char     75 required
Customer City        char     75 required
Customer State       char      2 required
Customer Zip         char     10 required
Order Number         char     10 required
Carrier Number       char     10 required
Carrier Name         char     75 required
Carrier Street       char     75 required
Carrier City         char     75 required
Carrier State        char      2 required
Carrier Zip          char     10 required
Product Name         char     25 required
Product Number       char     10 required
Cost                 currency 10 required Not Zero
Date Shipped         date      8 required mm-dd-yyyy
Date Arrived         date      8 optional mm-dd-yyyy
```

```
Product
Product Number char     10 required
Product Name   char     50 required
Unit Cost      currency 10 required Not Zero
Vendor Number  char     10 required
Vendor Name    char     25 required
Vendor Street  char     75 required
Vendor City    char     75 required
Vendor State   char      2 required
Vendor Zip     char     10 required
```

```
Vendor
Vendor Number  char 10 required
Vendor Name    char 50 required
Vendor Street  char 75 required
Vendor City    char 75 required
Vendor State   char  2 required
Vendor Zip     char 10 required
Product Name   char 25 required
Product Number char 10 required
```

```
Order Form
Customer Number      num      10 required
Customer First Name  char     35 required
Customer Middle Name char     35
Customer Last Name   char     75 required
Customer Street      char     75 required
Customer City        char     75 required
Customer State       char      2 required
Customer Zip         char     10 required
Order Number         char     10 required
Order Date           date      8 required mm-dd-yyyy Default Today
Product Number       char     10 required
Product Name         char     25 required
Quantity             number   10 required Minimum 1
Total Cost           currency 10 required
```

```
Carrier
Carrier Number char   10 required
Carrier Name   char   75 required
Carrier Street char   75 required
Carrier City   char   75 required
Carrier State  char    2 required
Carrier Zip    char   10 required
Next Day Rate  number 10 optional
2 Day Rate     number 10 optional
2 Week Rate    number 10 optional
```

```
Customer
Customer Number      num  10 required
Customer First Name  char 35 required
Customer Middle Name char 35
Customer Last Name   char 75 required
Customer Street      char 75 required
Customer City        char 75 required
Customer State       char  2 required
Customer Zip         char 10 required
```

Figure 9-5   Here's a sample of the data and data definitions that are used in entities of an e-commerce web site.

Organize Data into Groups

Grouping data into tables is referred to as *normalizing* the data. The purpose of normalizing data is to remove duplicate data from the database. Take a look at Figure 9-5 and you'll notice that customer name and customer address appear in the customer entity, the order entity, and shipping entity. This is fine because the customer name and address need to appear in all three entities. However, the duplication causes problems when the data is stored in the database.

The first problem occurs if you need to change the customer name or address after they are stored in the database. You'll need to locate each occurrence in all the entities and then make the change. There is always the possibility that you'll miss changing one or more of them—the data becomes unreliable.

Another problem is wasted storage space, although today the cost of storage (hard disk and CD) isn't too high. Collectively, the customer name and address requires 307 characters. However, 921 characters are stored for each customer, since the customer name and address appears three times in the database.

Suppose that you have 5,000 customers and each customer places five orders a month. This results in 5,000 occurrences of the customer name and address in the customer entity; 25,000 occurrence each month (300,000 per year) in the order entity; and 25,000 occurrences each month (300,000 per year) in the shipping entity. The total number of characters that need to be stored per year is 905,000 characters.

The normalizing process can reduce this number of characters from 905,000 characters to 5,000 characters.

How to Group Data

The normalization process follows strict rules called *normal form*, but you don't need to be concerned about them. When you need to focus on is placing related data into groups, removing duplicate data, and then designating data that can be used to link together tables.

Let's begin by grouping the data. The data is pretty much grouped by now if you used entities to identify the data, because customer data is associated with the customer entity; order data is associated with the order entity; and so on, as is illustrated in Figure 9-5.

Next, we need to remove duplicate data. This might seem like a tricky process. It makes sense that a customer name and address remain in the customer entity because all customer information needs to be in the same group. The same can be said about vendor name and address being in the vendor entity and the carrier's name and address being in the carrier entity. Likewise, the product name needs to be in the product entity. Take a close look at Figure 9-5, and you'll notice that these data elements also appear outside their logical entities.

For example, customer name and address appear in the shipping entity and in the order entity, too. These entities need to reference the customer name and address. That is, the order needs to contain the customer name and address and the shipper also needs the customer name and address. However, we can point to the customer name and address in the customer entity rather than duplicating the customer name and address in the order entity and the shipping entity.

Notice that each customer has a customer number. We can remove the customer name and address from the order entity and shipping entity and use the customer number, which remains in these entities, to point to the customer name and address in the customer entity. We can also use the product number, the order number, and the carrier number to reference a product, an order, and a carrier.

Figure 9-6 shows the normalized database schema. Each group will become a table in the database.

```
Product
Product Number  char     10 required
Product Name    char     50 required
Unit Cost       currency 10 required Not Zero
Vendor Number   char     10 required
```

```
Shipping Form
Customer Number  num   10 required
Order Number     char  10 required
Carrier Number   char  10 required
Date Shipped     date   8 required mm-dd-yyyy
Date Arrived     date   8 optional mm-dd-yyyy
```

```
Vendor
Vendor Number   char  10 required
Vendor Name     char  50 required
Vendor Street   char  75 required
Vendor City     char  75 required
Vendor State    char   2 required
Vendor Zip      char  10 required
Product Name    char  25 required
```

```
Order Form
Customer Number  num       10 required
Order Number     char      10 required
Order Date       date       8 required mm-dd-yyyy Default Today
Product Number   char      10 required
Quantity         number    10 required Minimum 1
Total Cost       currency  10 required
```

```
Carrier
Carrier Number  char    10 required
Carrier Name    char    75 required
Carrier Street  char    75 required
Carrier City    char    75 required
Carrier State   char     2 required
Carrier Zip     char    10 required
Next Day Rate   number  10 optional
2 Day Rate      number  10 optional
2 Week Rate     number  10 optional
```

```
Customer
Customer Number       num   10 required
Customer First Name   char  35 required
Customer Middle Name  char  35
Customer Last Name    char  75 required
Customer Street       char  75 required
Customer City         char  75 required
Customer State        char   2 required
Customer Zip          char  10 required
```

Figure 9-6   The normalized version of the database schema

Identify Columns Used to Identify a Row of Data

The database is organized so that we can easily assemble data to fill requests from the ASP.NET application. Let's say that the request is for the name and address for the customer whose customer number is 0123456789. We look for customer number 0123456789 in the customer number column of the customer table. Once it is found, we then read the customer's name and address from the row of the table that contains that customer number.

Suppose we want to know the name and address of the customer who placed the order 9876543210. First, we'd look for the 9876543210 in the order number column of the order table. However, there's a problem. The customer name and address aren't in the order table (see Figure 9-6). The order table does contain the customer number of the customer who placed the order. We read the customer number that is associated with order 9876543210 and look up the customer number in the customer table to find the customer name and address.

The process of using a value in one table to find a corresponding row in another table is called *joining* tables. In order to relate tables, you must designate a column in both tables that can be used to join the tables. These columns are referred to as a primary key and a foreign key.

A *primary* key is a column of a table used to uniquely identify a row of the table. Customer number is the primary key of the customer table because no two customers

have the same customer number. Likewise, order number is the primary key of the order table because no two orders can have the same order number.

A *foreign* key is a column of a table that is the primary key of another table. Notice in Figure 9-6 that the order table contains a customer number column. The customer number column is a foreign key to the order table and a primary key to the customer table.

The foreign key is used to join two tables. That is, the customer number column in the order table (foreign key) is used to find a corresponding customer number in the customer table (primary key).

Figure 9-7 shows the primary keys and foreign keys used to join together tables in our database.

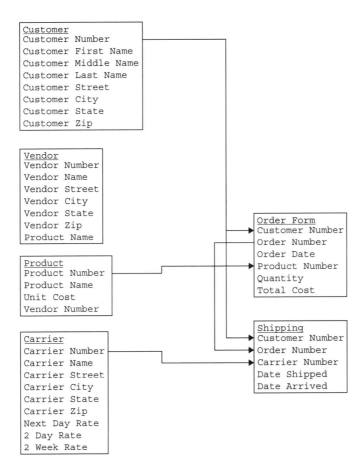

Figure 9-7   The primary key of each table can be used as the foreign key of another table. Together they are used to join together tables.

Indexes

You have two choices to find information in a book. You could scan every page or look in the index. The index has keywords and the number of the page where the keyword appears in the book.

The same concept is used in a table. You could look up each row of a table to find the keyword you need, or you can look up the keyword in an index. The index contains the keyword and the row number where the keyword is found in the table.

You need to specify indexes that you'll use as part of you database schema. Decide which data will be likely used to search for a row in a table. This is somewhat intuitive because of the way you use the application. For example, you should be able to look up customer information by a combination of last name and first name if the customer name is known, but not the customer number.

Don't create too many indexes, because each index must be updated whenever a row is inserted or deleted from a table and sometimes when the column that is indexed is modified. This maintenance requires processing time, which could in some cases decrease the performance of the database management system.

An index can be built using a single column such as ZIP code or using multiple columns, in which case it is called a *clustered* index. An index that uses the customer last name and customer first name is a clustered index.

You'll learn how to create an index in the next chapter.

Looking Ahead

Many of the products that are called databases are really database management systems (DBMSs), software packages that handle the details of storing and retrieving information in a database. A DBMS responds to requests from your application called queries that are written in the Structured Query Language (SQL).

Data is the smallest piece of information, such as a customer's first name. A database is a collection of data. The way in which data is organized within a database is called a database model. One of the most popular of these is the relational database model, which relates one group of data within the database with another group of data.

A group of data within the database is called a table. A table is similar to a spreadsheet in that both have rows and columns. Each column is a data element. A column is characterized by attributes that include a name, a data type, and a size.

The blueprint for the design of a database is called a database schema. You create a database schema by identifying information that needs to be stored in the database; define the data; organize the data into groups; and identify columns that will

be used as indexes for the table. An index is similar to an index of a book; it contains keywords and the row number of the table that contains the keyword.

Now that you have a good idea of how to design a database for your ASP.NET application, we'll turn our attention in the next chapter to how to connect to a DBMS from your ASP.NET web application. We'll continue to explore databases in Chapter 11, where you'll learn how to create queries using SQL.

Quiz

1. Microsoft Access is a database.

   a. True

   b. False

2. A database is subdivided into groups called

   a. Tables

   b. Data

   c. Subdatabases

   d. None of the above

3. An index is used to

   a. Quickly find information in another index.

   b. Quickly find information in a database.

   c. Quickly find information in a table.

   d. Quickly find information in one column.

4. Another name for relating tables together is

   a. Joining

   b. Merging

   c. Combining

   d. Gluing

5. The design of a database is called the

   a. Database layout

   b. Database blueprint

   c. Database schema

   d. None of the above

6. The first step in designing a database is to

   a. Change the information into data.

   b. Organize data into groups.

   c. Define data.

   d. Identify information that you need to store in your database.

7. Normalizing a database removes most redundant data.

   a. True

   b. False

8. A foreign key is a primary key of a different table.

   a. True

   b. False

9. A primary key uniquely identifies rows of a table.

   a. True

   b. False

10. A clustered index contains only one column.

    a. True

    b. False

Answers

1. b. False. Microsoft Access is a database management system.

2. a. Tables

3. c. Quickly find information in a table.

4. a. Joining

5. c. Database schema

6. d. Identify information that you need to store in your database.

7. a. True

8. a. True

9. a. True

10. b. False

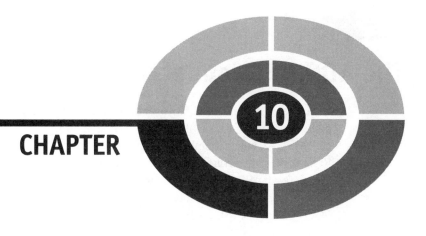

Interacting with Databases

Whenever you log into your favorite e-commerce web site, you set off a series of routines behind the scenes that, among other things, links the web site with a database that contains product information and probably information about you.

You too can link your ASP.NET web pages with your own database by using the ADO.NET connection. Think of ADO.NET as your pipeline into popular commercial database management software (DBMS) such as Microsoft SQL Server, the Oracle database server, and Microsoft Access.

In this chapter you'll learn how to make this connection and how to write SQL statements in a query that direct the DBMS to perform tasks that are commonly used in many commercial web sites.

The ADO.NET Connection

Customer data and other information that is typically used by an ASP.NET web page are stored in a database that is managed by database management software (DBMS). As you remember from the preceding chapter, a DBMS such as Microsoft SQL Server, the Oracle database server, or Microsoft Access is a filing cabinet and file clerk all rolled up into one and maintains and accesses data as requested.

Your application interacts with a DBMS by sending it queries using the Structured Query Language (SQL). For example, if you wanted to retrieve a customer's account information, you'd write an SQL query and send it to the DBMS. The DBMS locates and returns the account information to your application.

However, before you can send the query, you need to connect your application to the DBMS. You do this by using classes provided by ADO.NET. ADO.NET is part of the .NET framework. Although this sounds imposing, it really isn't.

As you'll recall from Chapter 2, an object is a real thing that is described by a class definition. In the case of ADO.NET, these objects are database-related "things" such as rows, columns, tables, and databases. ADO.NET contains class definitions that are used to access a database. Remember that a class contains functions and attributes. A function is a block of code that is executed by calling the name of the function. An attribute is data associated with the class.

Therefore, ADO.NET contains code that you call within your application to connect your application to a DBMS and enables your application to send queries to and receive data from a DBMS.

Namespaces and Classes

ADO.NET contains sets of classes designed to interact with a specific DBMS. Each set is identified by a namespace. A *namespace* organizes classes in a hierarchy of classes to prevent naming conflicts. This sounds a little strange, but you won't give the term namespace a second thought once you begin to use it in your application.

The most important point to understand is that you must import into your application the namespace that corresponds to the DBMS that is accessed by your application. Here are commonly used namespaces:

- **System.Data.SqlClient**   Used for Microsoft SQL Server version 7.0 or higher
- **System.Data.OleDb**   Used for OLE DB DMBSs such as Microsoft Access
- **System.Data.Odbc**   Used for ODBC driver-based DBMSs. ODBC is used in Windows to connect to many popular DBMSs.
- **System.Data.OracleClient**   Used for the Oracle database server

Throughout this chapter, we'll be showing examples that use System.Data .SqlClient to interact with the Microsoft SQL Server and System.Data.OleDb used to interact with Microsoft Access. Techniques used in these examples are similar to the way you use the other namespaces to interact with other DBMSs.

Although each namespace refers to different classes, there are similarities among them. For example, SqlConnection is used to open a DBMS connection using the System.Data.SqlClient namespace. OleDbConnection performs the same task when using the System.Data.OleDb namespace.

Likewise, SqlCommand is used to send a query to the DBMS in the System .Data.SqlClient namespace. OleDbCommand does the same using the System.Data .OleDb namespace.

Opening a Connection to a DBMS

Your application must open a connection to the DBMS before sending or requesting data from the DBMS. Think of a DBMS connection as the same as a telephone connection. Before you can talk to your friend, you must dial your friend's telephone number and wait for her to answer. You talk as long as you want once the connection is made, and you close the connection after you are through, enabling someone else to connect to your friend.

To create a connection to the DBMS, follow these steps:

1. **Import the namespace**   This identifies the set of classes that you'll be using within your application to interact with the database. Developers import the namespace so that they don't have to write the fully qualified class name, which is much longer than if the namespace is imported.

2. **Create an instance of the connection class**   Remember from Chapter 2 that a class definition describes a class much as a stencil describes a letter of the alphabet. You create a real object described by the class by creating an instance of the class. This is similar to using the stencil to create a real letter of the alphabet.

3. **Open the connection**   You do this by calling an appropriate instance function of the instance of the class.

Let's see how this is done by creating a connection to Microsoft SQL Server. The initial step is to import that namespace. The namespace for Microsoft SQL Server is System.Data.SqlClient. We import that namespace by using the following page directive at the beginning of the ASP.NET web page.

```
<%@ Import Namespace="System.Data.SqlClient" %>
```

The next step is to create an instance of the connection class. First, declare a variable that references the instance, and second, create the instance and assign it to the variable as shown here:

```
Dim conMyDb As SqlConnection
conMyDb = New SqlConnection("Server=localhost;uid=myID;pwd=mypassword;
database=mydatabase")
```

We need to create an instance of the SqlConnection class and pass the constructor of the SqlConnection class information it needs to link to the DBMS. The constructor creates the instance of a class. There are three pieces of information that you must provide.

The first is the location of the server that contains the DBMS. This is the URL of the server or localhost if the DBMS resides on your computer. For this example, we're assuming that you have the database on your local computer.

The next two pieces of information are needed to log onto the DBMS. These are user ID (uid) and the password (pwd). These are assigned by directly interacting with the DBMS. In a business environment, the database administrator is the person who assigns logon information to everyone.

The last piece of information is the name of the database. You'll remember from Chapter 2 that the DBMS maintains many databases, each having its own unique name. You must identify the database that you want to link to by assigning the database name to the database parameter when you create an instance of the SqlConnection class.

The SqlConnection constructor returns a reference to the instance to the variable. You then use the variable to access functions and attributes of the class. One of the first of these is called the Open() function, which opens the database connection as shown here:

```
conMyDb.Open()
```

Now let's put these statements together to create an ASP.NET web page that accesses the customer database. We'll show two examples. The first is for Microsoft SQL Server, and the second is for Microsoft Access. Notice that the connection to the database is made in the Page_Load subroutine. Each time the page is loaded, the ASP.NET engine establishes a connection with the database.

```
<%@ Import Namespace="System.Data.SqlClient" %>
<Script Runat="Server">
    Sub Page_Load
        Dim custDb As SqlConnection
        custDb = New SqlConnection("Server=localhost;uid=myID;pwd=mypassword;
database=customer")
        custDb.Open()
    End Sub
</Script>
```

Here is the example for linking to Microsoft Access. You'll notice a few differences between this example and the preceding example. The first is that we're importing the SystemData.OleDb namespace, which enables us to use the OleDb classes that are needed to interact with Microsoft Access.

Another difference is in the OleDbConnection constructor. Notice that there are two parameters. The first is Provider, which is the name of the DBMS. OleDB is the provider of Microsoft.Jet.OLEDB.4.0, which Microsoft Access is associated with. The second parameter is DataSource, which is the location and name of the database. In this example the database is located on the C: drive and is called cust.mdb.

The other parts of the example are identical to the preceding example.

```
<%@ Import Namespace="System.Data.OleDb" %>
<Script Runat="Server">
    Sub Page_Load ( s As Object, e As EventArgs )
        Dim custDb as OleDbConnection
        custDb = New
OleDbConnection("Provider=Microsoft.Jet.OLEDB.4.0;DataSource=c:cust.mdb" )
        custDb.Open()
    End Sub
</Script>
```

Creating a Database and Tables

Before continuing, it is important to create a database and at least one table in order to work through examples in this chapter. You should install a DBMS (see Chapter 9). It is beyond the scope of this book to explain how to install a DBMS.

Most DBMSs have a user interface that you can use to create a database and tables. In the next chapter we'll show you how to create these using a query from within your application. For now, you'll need to create a database. You can call it MyBusiness. And then create the following table and call it custContact. Here are the column definitions:

- custNumber CHAR(4)
- custFirstName CHAR(30)
- custLastName CHAR(30)

Insert these rows so that you'll be able to retrieve them when you send a query to the DBMS in examples throughout this chapter.

custNumber	custFirstName	custLastName
1234	Bob	Smith
5678	Mary	Jones

Sending a Query to the DBMS

In order to retrieve information stored in the database, you need to create a query using SQL and then send the query to the DBMS over an open database connection. A query can be as simple as asking for the number of orders placed by a particular customer—or as complex as asking for the number of times a customer ordered each product and the dates of the orders.

We'll use simple queries in this chapter so that you can focus on how to interact with the database using your application. You'll learn how to create more complex queries in the next chapter, which focuses on SQL.

Let's get started by requesting the names of all our customers and displaying them on the web page. Here are the steps you need to perform:

1. Create a database connection and open the connection.

2. Create a query.

3. Send the query to the DBMS.

4. Read the rows returned by the DBMS and display them on the screen.

You already learned how to perform the first step in the preceding section of this chapter. The second step requires you to create a query. There are two tasks involved here. The first is writing the query using SQL, and the next is to assign the query to an instance of the command class.

You must provide the DBMS with two pieces of information. The first is the name of the columns that you want returned from the database. The second is the name of the table that contains these columns.

We want two columns returned. These are custFirstName and custLastName, which are part of the custContact table. We tell the DBMS the columns that we want returned by using the Select statement. The Select statement is another way of saying, "This is the information I want returned." The From clause is used to identify the table that contains these columns.

Here is the query written in SQL:

```
Select custFirstName, custLastName
From custContact
```

Now we need to create an instance of the command class and initialize it with the query and reference to the opened database connection. Here's how this is done using Microsoft SQL Server. First we declare a variable that will be assigned a reference to the instance of the SqlCommand class, and then we create an instance of SqlCommand. Notice that we pass it the query as the first parameter. The second parameter is the variable that references the database connection. This is like saying to the instance of the SqlCommand, there is my query. Send it over the custDb connection.

```
Dim cmdSelectCustomers As SqlCommand
cmdSelectCustomers = New SqlCommand("Select custFirstName, custLastName From
custContact", custDb)
```

We need to create an instance of SqlDataReader class in order to read the information returned to us by the DBMS. The SqlDataReader class contains functions that you call to access information returned by the DBMS.

There are two steps needed to create a reader. First, you need to declare a variable that will be assigned a reference to the instance of the reader. Next, you need to create an instance of the SqlDataReader class. Here's how this is done:

```
Dim dtrCustomers As SqlDataReader
dtrCustomers = cmdSelectCustomers.ExecuteReader()
```

The instance of the reader is returned by calling the ExecuteReader() function from the SqlCommand class. This function returns the instance of the reader, which is assigned to the variable. You then refer to the variable (dtrCustomers) each time you need to access the reader.

In response to a query, the DBMS can return no information, a single piece of information, or multiple pieces of information, depending on your query and the number of rows that match your query. This information is returned as a list that you step through from within your application.

You do this by using a While loop as shown here. Notice that we call the Read() function of the SqlDataReader class. The Read() function can return a true or a false. A true value means there is at least a current row of information. A false value means there isn't a row. That is, no data exists that corresponds to your query.

You retrieve information returned by the DBMS by using the column name of the information. The following example illustrates how to access the custFirstName and custLastName, which are then displayed on the web page. The second statement within the While loop causes the cursor to be moved to the next line. The application exits the While loop when there are no more rows to read. The Reader is then closed by calling its Close() method.

```
While dtrCustomers.Read()
Response.Write(CStr(dtrCustomers.Item("custFirstName")) & " " & _
    CStr(dtrCustomers.Item("custLastName")))

 Response.Write("<BR>")
End While
```

Here is the full example of how to query the DBMS and read the information returned by the DBMS. Remember that this example is used to access data that is managed by Microsoft SQL Server:

```
<% Import Namespace="System.Data.SqlClient" %>
<%
   Dim custDb As SqlConnection
   Dim cmdSelectCustomers As SqlCommand
```

```
    Dim dtrCustomers As SqlDataReader
    custDb = New SqlConnection("Server=localhost;uid=myID;pwd=mypassword;
database=customer")
    custDb.Open()
    cmdSelectCustomers = New SqlCommand( "Select custFirstName, custLastName From
custContact", custDb)
    dtrCustomers = cmdSelectCustomers.ExecuteReader()
    While dtrCustomers.Read()
       Response.Write(CStr(dtrCustomers.Item("custFirstName")) & " " & _
                    CStr(dtrCustomers.Item("custLastName")))
       Response.Write("<BR>")
    End While
    dtrCustomers.Close()
    custDb.Close()
%>
```

Here's how to do this with Microsoft Access:

```
<% Import Namespace="System.Data.OleDb" %>
<%
    Dim custDb As OleDbConnection
    Dim cmdSelectCustomers As OleDbCommand
    Dim dtrCustomers As OleDbDataReader
    custDb = New OleDbConnection( "PROVIDER=Microsoft.Jet.OLEDB.4.0;Data Source=c:
cust.mdb")
    custDb.Open()
    cmdSelectCustomers = New OleDbCommand( "Select custFirstName, custLastName From
custContact", custDb)
    dtrCustomers = cmdSelectCustomers.ExecuteReader()
    While dtrCustomers.Read()
       Response.Write(CStr(dtrCustomers.Item("custFirstName")) & " " & _
                    CStr(dtrCustomers.Item("custLastName")))
       Response.Write("<BR>")
    End While
    dtrCustomers.Close()
    custDb.Close()
%>
```

Were Any Rows Returned?

The question that your application needs to answer after sending a query to a DBMS is whether or not the DBMS found any information that matches your query. The easiest way to answer this question is to examine the HasRows property of the DataReader class.

The value of the HasRows property determines if any records were returned by the DBMS. It is true if records are returned; otherwise, the value of the HasRows property is false. It is important to remember that the HasRows property does not tell you the number of records that are returned. Instead, it simply states if any are returned.

Let's modify the previous examples to include the HasRows property. We'll begin with the Microsoft SQL Server example.

```
<% Import Namespace="System.Data.SqlClient" %>
<%
   Dim custDb As SqlConnection
   Dim cmdSelectCustomers As SqlCommand
   Dim dtrCustomers As SqlDataReader
   custDb = New SqlConnection("Server=localhost;uid=myID;pwd=mypassword;
database=customer")
   custDb.Open()
   cmdSelectCustomers = New SqlCommand( "Select custFirstName, custLastName From
custContact", custDb)
   dtrCustomers = cmdSelectCustomers.ExecuteReader()
   If dtrCustomers.HasRows Then
      While dtrCustomers.Read()
 Response.Write(CStr(dtrCustomers.Item("custFirstName")) & " " & _
                    CStr(dtrCustomers.Item("custLastName")))
Response.Write("<BR>")
      End While
   Else
      Response.Write("There are no customers.")
   End If
   dtrCustomers.Close()
   custDb.Close()
%>
```

Here's how to do this with Microsoft Access:

```
<% Import Namespace="System.Data.OleDb" %>
<%
   Dim custDb As OleDbConnection
   Dim cmdSelectCustomers As OleDbCommand
   Dim dtrCustomers As OleDbDataReader
   custDb = New OleDbConnection( "PROVIDER=Microsoft.Jet.OLEDB.4.0;Data Source=c:
ust.mdb")
   custDb.Open()
   cmdSelectCustomers = New OleDbCommand( "Select custFirstName, custLastName From
custContact", custDb)
   dtrCustomers = cmdSelectCustomers.ExecuteReader()
   If dtrCustomers.HasRows Then
      While dtrCustomers.Read()
Response.Write(CStr(dtrCustomers.Item("custFirstName")) & " " & _
                    CStr(dtrCustomers.Item("custLastName")))
         Response.Write("<BR>")
      End While
   Else
      Response.Write("There are no customers.")
   End If
   dtrCustomers.Close()
   custDb.Close()
%>
```

Retrieving a Specific Row

It is very common that you'll need to look for particular information stored in a database such as a customer number. To do this, you'll need to include a Where clause in your query. The Where clause requires two pieces of information: a search value and the column that contains the search value.

Let's say that you want to retrieve the customer number and customer name for customer number 1234. Here's the query that you'll need to write:

```
Select custNumber, custFirstName, custLastName
From custContact
Where custNumber = '1234'
```

The Select statement is nearly identical to the query you wrote earlier in this chapter, except we've included the custNumber column. Remember that columns that appear in the Select statement are returned by the DBMS.

The From clause is the same as in other queries in that it tells the DBMS to use the custContact table.

The Where clause is new to the query. It tells the DBMS to search for 1234 in the custNumber column. Only rows that have 1234 in the custNumber column are returned by the DBMS. There is only one row in our example that has 1234 as a customer number, so only that row is returned.

Replace the query in the previous examples with this query and run the application to retrieve customer Bob Smith from the DBMS.

Query Parameters

In the preceding example, the value of the search criterion was inserted into the WHERE clause of the query. In the real world, however, the visitor to your web site usually enters the search value into a web form. Therefore, you need to have a placeholder for the search criterion in the query that is replaced by the actual value that the visitor enters when your application runs.

The placeholder is referred to as a *parameter*, which is similar to parameters used for functions (see Chapter 7). You then use the parameter in the query as if the parameter were the actual value. The value replaces the parameter once the value is received from the visitor to your web site.

Parameters are represented by a parameter class. You define a parameter by calling the AddWithValue() method of the Parameters class as illustrated here:

```
cmdSelect.Parameters.AddWithValue( "@CustFirstName", txtCustFirstName.Text)
```

The cmdSelect is used to call the AddWithValue() method of the Parameters class, passing it two parameters. The first parameter is the name of the parameter that you are adding to the parameter collection. The second parameter is the value that is associated with the parameter. In the preceding example, the value called txtCustFirstName.Text is the text of the txtCustFirstName textbox that appears on your web page. You use @CustFirstName in your query just as if @CustFirstName were an explicit value.

You can specify the data type and maximum number of characters that can be accepted by the system by modifying the call to AddWithValue(). Here's how this is done:

```
cmdSelectCustomers.Parameters.AddWithValue ( "@CustFirstName ", SqlDbType.Varchar, 25
).Value = txtCustFirstName.Text
```

You'll notice that the AddWithValue() method takes on a slightly different form than the preceding example. The first argument is the name of the parameter.

The second argument is the data type of the parameter. The data type is automatically chosen for you if you exclude the data type as was done in the preceding example. The data type must reflect the namespace that is associated with the DBMS. SqlDbType is used for the SqlDb namespace, which is for Microsoft SQL Server. The OleDbType is used for Microsoft Access. Namespaces for other DBMSs have similar data type names.

The third argument is the maximum number of characters that can be assigned to the parameter. In this example the customer first name can have up to 25 characters. If you exclude the size parameter, then the maximum size is automatically determined by the value of the parameter.

Here's the full code for Microsoft SQL Server:

```
<%@ Import Namespace="System.Data" %>
<%@ Import Namespace="System.Data.SqlClient" %>
<Script Runat="Server">
    Sub Button_Click( s As Object, e As EventArgs )
        Dim custDb As SqlConnection
        Dim cmdSelectCustomers As SqlCommand
        Dim dtrCustomers As SqlDataReader
        custDb = New SqlConnection("Server=localhost;uid=myID;pwd=mypassword;
database=customer")
        cmdSelectCustomers = New SqlCommand("Select custFirstName, custLastName From
custContact Where custNumber=@CustNumber", custDb)
        cmdSelectCustomers.Parameters.AddWithValue ( "@CustNumber", txtCustNumber.Text )
        custDb.Open()
            dtrCustomers = cmdSelectCustomers.ExecuteReader()
                While dtrCustomers.Read()
                    txtCustFirstName.text = dtrCustomers( "custFirstName" )
                    txtCustLastName.text = dtrCustomers( "custLastName" )
                End While
            dtrCustomers.Close()
        custDb.Close()
    End Sub
</Script>
```

```
<html>
    <head><title>Customer Locator</title></head>
    <body>
        <form Runat="Server">
            <b>Customer Number:</b>
            <br>
            <asp:TextBox ID="txtCustNumber" Runat="Server" />
            <p>
              <asp:Button Text="Locate" OnClick="Button_Click" Runat="Server" />
            <p>
              <b>Customer First Name:</b>
              <br>
              <asp:TextBox ID="txtCustFirstName" Runat="Server" />
            <p>
              <b>Customer Last Name:</b>
              <br>
              <asp:TextBox ID="txtCustLastName" Runat="Server" />
            <p>
        </form>
    </body>
</html>
```

This code prompts the web site visitor to enter a customer number into a textbox and select the Locate button to search the database for the name that is associated with the customer number. Once the customer number is located, the DBMS returns the customer first name and customer last name, which are then displayed in textboxes on the form.

The code begins by defining a button click event handler for the Locate button. You'll notice that the event handler contains nearly the same code that we discussed previously in this chapter.

However, there is one difference, in that we define and use the @CustNumber parameter. The @CustNumber parameter has the text value that the visitor entered into the txtCustNumber textbox and is compared with the value of custNumber column of the table in the Where clause of the query. After the query executes, the code copies the value of the custFirstName and custLastName columns to the corresponding textboxes that appear on the form.

The web page itself displays three textboxes, for the customer number and customer first and last names, as well as the Locate button.

Here is the Microsoft Access version of this application:

```
<%@ Import Namespace="System.Data" %>
<%@ Import Namespace="System.Data.OleDb " %>
<Script Runat="Server">
    Sub Button_Click( s As Object, e As EventArgs )
        Dim custDb As OleDbConnection
        Dim cmdSelectCustomers As OleDbCommand
        Dim dtrCustomers As OleDbDataReader
        custDb = New OleDbConnection( "PROVIDER=Microsoft.Jet.OLEDB.4.0;Data Source=c:
cust.mdb")
        cmdSelectCustomers = New OleDbCommand("Select custFirstName, custLastName From
custContact Where custNumber=@CustNumber", custDb)
        cmdSelectCustomers.Parameters.AddWithValue ( "@CustNumber", txtCustNumber.Text )
```

```
        custDb.Open()
            dtrCustomers = cmdSelectCustomers.ExecuteReader()
                While dtrCustomers.Read()
                    txtCustFirstName.text = dtrCustomers( "custFirstName" )
                    txtCustLastName.text = dtrCustomers( "custLastName" )
                End While
            dtrCustomers.Close()
        custDb.Close()
End Sub
</Script>
<html>
    <head><title>Customer Locator</title></head>
    <body>
        <form Runat="Server">
            <b>Customer Number:</b>
            <br>
            <asp:TextBox ID="txtCustNumber" Runat="Server" />
            <p>
              <asp:Button Text="Locate" OnClick="Button_Click" Runat="Server" />
            <p>
              <b>Customer First Name:</b>
              <br>
              <asp:TextBox ID="txtCustFirstName" Runat="Server" />
            <p>
              <b>Customer Last Name:</b>
              <br>
              <asp:TextBox ID="txtCustLastName" Runat="Server" />
            <p>
        </form>
    </body>
</html>
```

Inserting a Row

You can insert new information into a database by using the insert statement in a query. The insert statement inserts a new row and places data into one or more columns of the row, depending on the nature of your application.

The insert statement requires the table name, the column names, and a value for each column. Here's the insert statement:

```
Insert Into custContact (custNumber, custFirstName, custLastName) Values ('0987', 'Mike',
'Jones')
```

This statement inserts a new row that contains three columns of the custContact table. The names of the columns are specified within the first set of parentheses, each separated from the next by a comma. The second set of parentheses contains the values that are to be placed in each column. Notice that the values are in the same order as the column names. That is, the customer number is placed in the custNumber column, the customer first name is placed in the custFirstName column, and so on.

It is important to remember that the logon used to access the database must have proper permission to insert data into the table. Likewise, you must be sure that the data being inserted into a column is of a compatible data type with the column. For example, a numeric value must be placed into a column that has a numeric data type.

The following is the complete code that you need to insert a new row into a Microsoft SQL Server database:

```
<%@ Import Namespace="System.Data.SqlClient" %>
<%
Dim custDb As SqlConnection
Dim cmdInsertCustomers As SqlCommand
custDb = New SqlConnection("Server=localhost;uid=myID;pwd=mypassword; database=customer")
cmdInsertCustomers = New SqlCommand("Insert Into custContact (custNumber, custFirstName,
custLastName) Values ('0987', 'Mike', 'Jones')", custDb)
custDb.Open()
    cmdInsertCustomers.ExecuteNonQuery()
custDb.Close()
%>
```

Here is the same code for Microsoft Access:

```
<%@ Import Namespace="System.Data.OleDb" %>
<%
Dim custDb As OleDbConnection
Dim cmdInsertCustomers As OleDbCommand
custDb = New OleDbConnection( "PROVIDER=Microsoft.Jet.OLEDB.4.0;Data Source=c: cust.mdb")
cmdInsertCustomers = New OleDbCommand("Insert Into custContact (custNumber,
custFirstName, custLastName) Values ('0987', 'Mike', 'Jones')", custDb)
custDb.Open()
cmdInsertCustomers.ExecuteNonQuery()
custDb.Close()
%>
```

Let's incorporate the code into a form so that you can enter information directly from your web page. This form is very similar to the preceding form example. Here is the Microsoft SQL Server version:

```
<%@ Import Namespace="System.Data" %>
<%@ Import Namespace="System.Data.SqlClient" %>
<Script Runat="Server">
   Sub Button_Click( s As Object, e As EventArgs )
       Dim custDb As SqlConnection
       Dim cmdInsertCustomers As SqlCommand
       custDb = New SqlConnection("Server=localhost;uid=myID;pwd=mypassword;
database=customer")
       cmdInsertCustomers = New SqlCommand("Insert Into custContact (CustNumber,
CustFirstName, CustLastName) Values (txtCustNumber.Text, txtCustFirstName.text,
txtCustLastName.text)", custDb)
           cmdInsertCustomers.Parameters.AddWithValue( "@CustNumber", txtCustNumber.Text )
           cmdInsertCustomers.Parameters.AddWithValue( "@CustFirstName", txtCustFirstName.Text
)
           cmdInsertCustomers.Parameters.AddWithValue( "@CustLastName", txtCustLastName.Text )
           custDb.Open()
              cmdInsertCustomers.ExecuteNonQuery()
           custDb.Close()
```

```
End Sub
</Script>
<html>
    <head><title>New Customer</title></head>
    <body>
        <form Runat="Server">
            <b>Customer Number:</b>
            <br>
            <asp:TextBox ID="txtCustNumber" Runat="Server" />
              <b>Customer First Name:</b>
              <br>
              <asp:TextBox ID="txtCustFirstName" Runat="Server" />
            <p>
              <br />
              <b>Customer Last Name:</b>
              <br>
              <asp:TextBox ID="txtCustLastName" Runat="Server" />
            <p>
            <p>
              <asp:Button Text="Add Customer" OnClick="Button_Click" Runat="Server" />
            <p>
        </form>
    </body>
</html>
```

Here is the Microsoft Access version:

```
<%@ Import Namespace="System.Data" %>
<%@ Import Namespace="System.Data.OleDb " %>
<Script Runat="Server">
    Sub Button_Click( s As Object, e As EventArgs )
        Dim custDb As OleDbConnection
        Dim cmdInsertCustomers As OleDbCommand
        custDb = New OleDbConnection( "PROVIDER=Microsoft.Jet.OLEDB.4.0;Data Source=c:
cust.mdb")
        cmdInsertCustomers = New OleDbCommand("Insert Into custContact (CustNumber,
CustFirstName, CustLastName) Values (txtCustNumber.Text, txtCustFirstName.text,
txtCustLastName.text)", custDb)
        cmdInsertCustomers.Parameters.AddWithValue( "@CustNumber", txtCustNumber.Text )
        cmdInsertCustomers.Parameters.AddWithValue( "@CustFirstName", txtCustFirstName.Text
)
        cmdInsertCustomers.Parameters.AddWithValue( "@CustLastName", txtCustLastName.Text )
        custDb.Open()
            cmdInsertCustomers.ExecuteNonQuery()
        custDb.Close()
End Sub
</Script>
<html>
    <head><title>New Customer</title></head>
    <body>
        <form Runat="Server">
            <b>Customer Number:</b>
            <br>
            <asp:TextBox ID="txtCustNumber" Runat="Server" />
              <br />
              <b>Customer First Name:</b>
              <br>
              <asp:TextBox ID="txtCustFirstName" Runat="Server" />
            <p>
```

```
            <b>Customer Last Name:</b>
            <br>
            <asp:TextBox ID="txtCustLastName" Runat="Server" />
        <p>
        <p>
          <asp:Button Text="Add Customer" OnClick="Button_Click" Runat="Server" />
        <p>
      </form>
    </body>
</html>
```

Updating a Row

You can change data already in a database from within your application by creating an update query. An update query replaces the existing value in a column with the value that you specify in the query.

The update query must contain four pieces of information. These are:

- **Table name**   Name of the table that contains the rows that are being updated
- **Column name(s)**   Name(s) of the columns that are being updated
- **Value(s)**   The value(s) that is replacing the current value of the column(s)
- **Selection criteria**   Identify the row(s) that you want updated

Here is the update query. We are telling the DBMS to find the row in the cust-Contact table where the custNumber is 1234. Once it is found, replace the content of the custFirstName with Bobby.

```
Update custContact SET custFirstName = 'Bobby'
Where custNumber = "1234"
```

Here is how to update a row in Microsoft SQL Server by using a customer number and customer first name. This example is very similar to the preceding form example in this chapter except that the query is different.

```
<%@ Import Namespace="System.Data" %>
<%@ Import Namespace="System.Data.SqlClient" %>
<Script Runat="Server">
    Sub Button_Click( s As Object, e As EventArgs )
        Dim custDb As SqlConnection
        Dim cmdUpdateCustomers As SqlCommand
        custDb = New SqlConnection("Server=localhost;uid=myID;pwd=mypassword;
database=customer")
        cmdUpdateCustomers = New SqlCommand("Update custContact SET custFirstName =
txtCustFirstName.Text Where custNumber = @CustNumber", custDb)
        cmdUpdateCustomers.Parameters.AddWithValue( "@CustNumber", txtCustNumber.Text )
        cmdUpdateCustomers.Parameters.AddWithValue( "@CustFirstName", txtCustFirstName.Text
)
```

```
            cmdUpdateCustomers.Parameters.AddWithValue( "@CustLastName", txtCustLastName.Text )
            custDb.Open()
                cmdUpdateCustomers.ExecuteNonQuery()
            custDb.Close()
    End Sub
    </Script>
    <html>
        <head><title>New Customer</title></head>
        <body>
            <form Runat="Server">
                <b>Customer Number:</b>
                <br>
                <asp:TextBox ID="txtCustNumber" Runat="Server" />
                <BR />
                <b>Customer First Name:</b>
                <br>
                <asp:TextBox ID="txtCustFirstName" Runat="Server" />
                <p>
                    <asp:Button Text="Update Customer" OnClick="Button_Click" Runat="Server" />
                <p>
            </form>
        </body>
    </html>
```

Here is the Microsoft Access version:

```
<%@ Import Namespace="System.Data" %>
<%@ Import Namespace="System.Data.OleDb " %>
<Script Runat="Server">
    Sub Button_Click( s As Object, e As EventArgs )
        Dim custDb As OleDbConnection
        Dim cmdUpdateCustomers As OleDbCommand
        custDb = New OleDbConnection( "PROVIDER=Microsoft.Jet.OLEDB.4.0;Data Source=c:
cust.mdb")
        cmdUpdateCustomers = New OleDbCommand("Update custContact SET custFirstName =
txtCustFirstName.Text Where custNumber = @CustNumber", custDb)
        cmdUpdateCustomers.Parameters.AddWithValue( "@CustNumber", txtCustNumber.Text )
        cmdUpdateCustomers.Parameters.AddWithValue( "@CustFirstName", txtCustFirstName.Text
)
        cmdUpdateCustomers.Parameters.AddWithValue( "@CustLastName", txtCustLastName.Text )
        custDb.Open()
            cmdUpdateCustomers.ExecuteNonQuery()
        custDb.Close()
    End Sub
    </Script>
    <html>
        <head><title>New Customer</title></head>
        <body>
            <form Runat="Server">
                <b>Customer Number:</b>
                <br>
                <asp:TextBox ID="txtCustNumber" Runat="Server" />
                <br />
                    <b>Customer First Name:</b>
                    <br>
                    <asp:TextBox ID="txtCustFirstName" Runat="Server" />
```

```
    <p>
        <b>Customer Last Name:</b>
        <br>
        <asp:TextBox ID="txtCustLastName" Runat="Server" />
    <p>
        <asp:Button Text="Update Customer" OnClick="Button_Click" Runat="Server" />
    <p>
    </form>
  </body>
</html>
```

Deleting a Row

One or more rows can be removed from a table by using the Delete statement in a query. The Delete statement requires the name of the table and a Where clause that identifies the row or rows that are to be deleted.

Let's say that we want to delete the record for customer 1234. Here's the Delete statement that we'll send to the DBMS:

```
Delete custContact Where custNumber = "1234"
```

This statement tells the DBMS to find the row in the custContact table that has 1234 in its custNumber column and then delete the row. Nothing happens if the row isn't found. Keep in mind that the login used to contact to the DBMS must be authorized to delete the row; otherwise, the row will not be deleted.

Here's how to use a form to delete a row in Microsoft SQL Server:

```
<%@ Import Namespace="System.Data" %>
<%@ Import Namespace="System.Data.SqlClient" %>
<Script Runat="Server">
   Sub Button_Click( s As Object, e As EventArgs )
      Dim custDb As SqlConnection
      Dim cmdDeleteCustomers As SqlCommand
      custDb = New SqlConnection("Server=localhost;uid=myID;pwd=mypassword;
database=customer")
      cmdDeleteCustomers = New SqlCommand("Delete custContact Where custNumber =
@CustNumber", custDb)
      cmdDeleteCustomers.Parameters.AddWithValue( "@CustNumber", txtCustNumber.Text )
      custDb.Open()
         cmdDeleteCustomers.ExecuteNonQuery()
      custDb.Close()
End Sub
</Script>
<html>
   <head><title>New Customer</title></head>
   <body>
      <form Runat="Server">
         <b>Customer Number:</b>
         <br>
         <asp:TextBox ID="txtCustNumber" Runat="Server" />
```

```
        <p>
           <asp:Button Text="Delete Customer" OnClick="Button_Click" Runat="Server" />
        <p>

     </form>
   </body>
</html>
```

Here is the Microsoft Access version:

```
<%@ Import Namespace="System.Data" %>
<%@ Import Namespace="System.Data.OleDb " %>
<Script Runat="Server">
   Sub Button_Click( s As Object, e As EventArgs )
      Dim custDb As OleDbConnection
      Dim cmdDeleteCustomers As OleDbCommand
      custDb = New OleDbConnection( "PROVIDER=Microsoft.Jet.OLEDB.4.0;Data Source=c:
cust.mdb")
         cmdDeleteCustomers = New OleDbCommand("Insert custContact SET custFirstName =
txtCustFirstName.Text Where custNumber = @CustNumber", custDb)
      cmdDeleteCustomers.Parameters.AddWithValue( "@CustNumber", txtCustNumber.Text )
      custDb.Open()
         cmdDeleteCustomers.ExecuteNonQuery()
      custDb.Close()
End Sub
</Script>
<html>
   <head><title>New Customer</title></head>
   <body>
      <form Runat="Server">
         <b>Customer Number:</b>
         <br>
         <asp:TextBox ID="txtCustNumber" Runat="Server" />
         <p>
           <asp:Button Text="Delete Customer" OnClick="Button_Click" Runat="Server" />
         <p>
      </form>
   </body>
</html>
```

Stored Procedures

Throughout this chapter you learned how to create simple queries to perform operations that are common to commercial web sites. These queries are created in the event handler in your web page and are sent to the DBMS for processing.

Commercial web sites typically use complex queries that perform multiple operations such as updating two or more tables whenever a new customer is added to the database.

Complex queries can become rather long, and sending them from the web page to the DBMS is time-consuming. Although the time it takes to send the query from the web page to the DBMS might seem fast to us, it can actually slow down processing if you consider that a commercial web site might need to process many requests each second.

A common way to increase speed is by using a stored procedure. A *stored procedure* is a query that resides in the DBMS and can be called from your web page. Think of a stored procedure as a function or procedure (see Chapter 7) that is stored in the DBMS.

Creating a Stored Procedure

A stored procedure is defined in a query using the Create Procedure statement. You can enter the query directly into an interactive software tool provided by the DBMS such as the Microsoft SQL Server Enterprise Manager or Query Analyzer. Alternatively, you can execute the query from your application by using the ExecuteNonQuery() function, which is illustrated in examples throughout this chapter. It is important to understand that not all DBMSs support stored procedures, and therefore, you'll need to check with the DBMS manufacturer before incorporating stored procedures in your application.

The Create Procedure statement requires a unique name, SQL statements that are to execute when the stored procedure is called, and a return value if required by your application. You'll find that some stored procedures, such as those used to insert a new row into the database, don't require a return value, while others, such as procedures for counting the number of customers, do require one.

Let's take a look at a simple stored procedure that will count the number of customers there are in the custContact table. We'll call this HowManyCustomers:

```
Create Procedure HowManyCustomers
As
Dim intNumCustomers As Integer
intNumCustomers = Select Count (*) From custContact
Return (iIntNumCustomers)
```

Statements below the As keyword form the query that you would otherwise run from your application. In this example, we declared a variable called intNumCustomers, which then receives the results from the query.

The Select statement in the query uses the SQL Count() function, which you'll learn more about in the next chapter. An asterisk is placed within the parentheses. This is a wildcard character that tells the DMBS to use any column to count the number of rows in the table. As you'll see in the next chapter, you can replace the asterisk with a column name. As you'll remember from other examples, the From clause specifies the name of the table. Return is used to specify the value that is returned to the SQL statement in the web page that called the stored procedure.

Calling a Stored Procedure

You call a stored procedure from your web page by using the name of the stored procedure. This is illustrated in the next example, which calls the HowManyCustomers stored procedure that is defined in the preceding section of this chapter.

This example is similar to others you wrote in this chapter. However, there are two new twists that you'll need to learn. The first is calling the stored procedure, and the other is using the value that the stored procedure returns to your web page.

Here's how to call the stored procedure. Notice that the query is simply the name of the stored procedure:

```
Dim cmdTotalCustomers As SqlCommand
cmdTotalCustomers = New SqlCommand("HowManyCustomers", custDb)
```

Accessing the return value requires a few steps as shown here. First you need to declare a variable as parameter. We call this parmTotalCustomers. Next you must add a parameter using the Add function, which you learned previously in this chapter. We call the parameter ReturnValue and declare it as an Int data type.

```
Dim parmTotalCustomers As SqlParameter
parmTotalCustomers = cmdTotalCustomers.Parameters.Add("ReturnValue", SqlDbType.Int )
```

Next we need to retrieve the return value. The initial step is to declare a variable that will hold the return value. We called this intTotalCustomers. Next, we associate the return value with the parameter that we previously created. The value returned from the stored procedures is assigned to the parameter. We then need to assign the value of the parameter to the variable. The variable is then used within the web page.

```
Dim intTotalCustomers As Integer
parmTotalCustomers.Direction = ParameterDirection.ReturnValue
intTotalCustomers = cmdTotalCustomers.Parameters( "ReturnValue" ).Value
Response.Write("Total Number of Customers: <%=intTotalCustomers%>")
```

Here is the complete code:

```
<%@ Import Namespace="System.Data" %>
<%@ Import Namespace="System.Data.SqlClient" %>
<%
Dim custDb As SqlConnection
Dim cmdTotalCustomers As SqlCommand
Dim parmTotalCustomers As SqlParameter
Dim intTotalCustomers As Integer
custDb = New SqlConnection("Server=localhost;uid=myID;pwd=mypassword; database=customer")
cmdTotalCustomers = New SqlCommand( "HowManyCustomers", custDb)
```

```
cmdTotalCustomers.CommandType = CommandType.StoredProcedure
parmTotalCustomers = cmdTotalCustomers.Parameters.Add( "ReturnValue", SqlDbType.Int )
parmTotalCustomers.Direction = ParameterDirection.ReturnValue
custDb.Open()
cmdTotalCustomers.ExecuteNonQuery()
intTotalCustomers = cmdTotalCustomers.Parameters( "ReturnValue" ).Value
custDb.Close()
%>
Response.Write("Total Number of Customers: <%=intTotalCustomers%>")
```

Passing Parameters to a Stored Procedure

Many times you'll need to provide a stored procedure information so that the DBMS can process the stored procedure; for instance, you must provide customer information to a stored procedure that inserts a new customer into the customer contact table.

Information is passed to a stored procedure by way of a parameter. Each parameter must have a unique name and a data type. A parameter is then used within the stored procedure.

Let's create a stored procedure called AddCustomer and declare three parameters to hold a customer number and a customer name. Parameters are declared within the French braces between the name of the stored procedure and the As keyword, as shown in the following example. You'll notice that the Insert statement in this example is nearly identical to the Insert example that you previously created in this chapter, except that the parameter names are used as values. That is, values that are passed to the stored procedure are assigned to the parameters, and the parameters are used as the values that are inserted into the table.

```
Create Procedure AddCustomer
{
    @CustNumber varchar(5), @CustFirstName varchar(30), @CustLastName varchar(30)
}
As
Insert custContact (custNumber, custFirstName, custLastName) Values (@CustNumber,
@CustFirstName, @CustLastName)
```

The next example shows how to pass parameters to the AddCustomer stored procedure. Notice that the stored procedure is called the same way you call a stored procedure that doesn't have parameters. However, we use the Add() function to create the three parameters required by the stored procedure. Here is where we insert the actual values that will be inserted into the table.

```
<%@ Import Namespace="System.Data" %>
<%@ Import Namespace="System.Data.SqlClient" %>
<%
Dim custDb As SqlConnection
Dim strInsert As String
Dim cmdInsertCustomers As SqlCommand
```

```
custDb = New SqlConnection("Server=localhost;uid=myID;pwd=mypassword; database=customer")
cmdInsertCustomers = New SqlCommand( "AddCustomer", custDb)
cmdInsertCustomers.CommandType = CommandType.StoredProcedure
cmdInsertCustomers.Parameters.AddWithValue( "@CustNumber", "45678")
cmdInsertCustomers.Parameters.AddWithValue( "@CustFirstName", "Mary" )
cmdInsertCustomers.Parameters.AddWithValue( "@CustLastName ", "Roberts")
custDb.Open()
   cmdInsertCustomers.ExecuteNonQuery()
custDb.Close()
%>
```

Looking Ahead

You can link your web page to a DBMS by using ADO.NET. ADO.NET is a component of .NET. ActiveX Data Objects have functions and properties that you can use in your application to interact with a DBMS.

There are many popular DBMSs on the market, each requiring a unique ActiveX Data Object. You let the ASP.NET engine know which ActiveX Data Object you want to use by importing the namespace that corresponds to the DBMS. A namespace organizes classes in a hierarchy of classes to prevent naming conflicts.

In order to interact with a DBMS, you import the namespace, create an instance of the connection class, and then open the connection to the DBMS. Once the connection is open, you can prepare and then send a query.

A query is a set of instructions written using SQL that direct the DBMS to do something. You use a query to request information from the database, insert new information into the database, modify existing information, and delete information. You can perform any of these tasks as long as the login used by your application has authorization to perform them.

You use a reader function to access information returned by the DBMS. The reader enables you to access the columns that you requested from the DBMS.

Each time you execute a query from your web page, the SQL statements that compose the query are sent to the DBMS for processing. This is inefficient, especially if many queries are being sent each second to the DBMS, as in the case of a popular e-commerce web site.

A more efficient method of executing queries is to store the query in the DBMS as a stored procedure, and then send the DBMS the name of that procedure each time you want the procedure executed.

In this chapter you learned how to interact with a DBMS using simple queries. However, real-world applications require more complex queries than those you learned about in this chapter. Therefore, we'll focus on how to create more complex queries in the next chapter.

Quiz

1. A namespace organizes classes in a hierarchy of classes to prevent naming conflicts.

   a. True

   b. False

2. You open a connection to a database by using

   a. ConnectDB

   b. DBConnection

   c. DBConnect

   d. None of the above

3. The best place to open a connection to a database is

   a. The On_Click event handle

   b. The Page_Load subroutine

   c. In the SQL query

   d. In the query

4. Which SQL statement specifies the information you want returned to your application?

   a. Return

   b. Where

   c. From

   d. Select

5. Which SQL statement sets the search criteria for rows that contain information you want returned to your application?

   a. Return

   b. Where

   c. From

   d. Select

6. What statement identifies the database that contains information you want returned to your application?

   a. Where

   b. From

    c. Select

    d. None of the above

7. A stored procedure is sent from your web page to the DBMS each time you execute a query.

    a. True

    b. False

8. You cannot pass information to a stored procedure.

    a. True

    b. False

9. Your application cannot determine the number of rows that were returned by the DBMS.

    a. True

    b. False

10. A query parameter is assigned values that visitors enter into a form on your web site.

    a. True

    b. False

Answers

1. a. True

2. d. None of the above. You use the Connection object available for your database type. For SQL Server, it is SqlConnect; for Access, OleDbConect; etc.

3. b. The Page_Load subroutine

4. d. Select

5. b. Where

6. d. None of the above

7. b. False

8. b. False

9. b. False

10. a. True

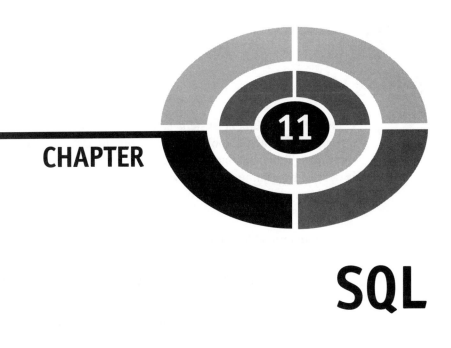

SQL

Today's ASP.NET web applications interact with information stored in a database. In the last chapter you learned how to connect your application to database management software. You also learned how to request and store data in a database by writing simple queries written in SQL.

Real-world ASP.NET web applications require more sophisticated queries than those you learned about in Chapter 10. These queries retrieve information from multiple tables, perform complex calculations, and efficiently organize information so that it can be displayed on your web page.

This chapter focuses on writing those sophisticated queries. You'll learn how to create queries that perform commonly used tasks in a typical application. In order to run these queries, insert them into the code you wrote in the previous chapter.

Tables

Database management system (DBMS) software enables you to create a table through an interactive tool that comes with the DBMS or by a query. The query uses the Create Table statement to name the table and define its columns. Each column is defined by a name and data type.

Let's say that you want to create a table called CustomerAddress that has the following six columns:

- **CustomerNumber**   The customer number is a string of a maximum of 30 characters.

- **CustomerStreet**   The customer street is a string of a maximum of 30 characters.

- **CustomerCity**   The customer city is a string of a maximum of 30 characters.

- **CustomerState**   The customer state is a string of a maximum of 2 characters.

- **CustomerZip**   The customer ZIP code is a string of a maximum of 10 characters.

- **CustomerCtry**   The customer country code is a string of a maximum of 5 characters.

Here's the query that creates this table:

```
CREATE TABLE CustomerAddress (
CustomerNumber CHAR(30),
CustomerStreet CHAR(30),
CustomerCity CHAR(30),
Customerstate CHAR(2),
CustomerZip CHAR(10),
CustomerCtry CHAR(5))
```

You'll probably want to make sure that each new row has a customer number; otherwise, you won't be able to identify the customer. The easiest way to ensure that each row has a customer number is to make the customer number column required. You do this by specifying that the CustomerNumber column is NOT NULL when you create the table. The DBMS prevents a new row from being inserted into the table unless there is a customer number.

Here's how this is done:

```
CREATE TABLE CustomerAddress (
CustomerNumber CHAR(30) NOT NULL,
CustomerStreet CHAR(30),
CustomerCity CHAR(30),
Customerstate CHAR(2),
CustomerZip CHAR(10),
CustomerCtry CHAR(5))
```

There will be times when you want to set a default value for a column. A default value is a value that the DMBS enters into a column if the new row doesn't have a value for the column. A good example is the customer country code. Suppose that nearly all your customers are based in the United States. It therefore makes sense to make the USA country code the default value for the customer country code column.

Here's how you do this:

```
CREATE TABLE CustomerAddress (
CustomerNumber CHAR(30) NOT NULL,
CustomerStreet CHAR(30),
CustomerCity CHAR(30),
Customerstate CHAR(2),
CustomerZip CHAR(10),
CustomerCtry CHAR(5) DEFAULT 'USA')
```

As you'll recall from the preceding chapter, a primary key is used to uniquely identify each row of a table. You can designate a primary key for your table by using the Constraint clause as shown in the following example. The Constraint clause requires that you give it a name and designate a column as the primary key. In this example, the CustomerNumber column is the primary key and we call it CustAddr_PK.

```
CREATE TABLE CustomerAddress (
CustomerNumber CHAR(30) NOT NULL,
CustomerStreet CHAR(30),
CustomerCity CHAR(30),
Customerstate CHAR(2),
CustomerZip CHAR(10),
CustomerCtry CHAR(5) DEFAULT 'USA',
CONSTRAINT CustAddr_PK PRIMARY KEY (CustomerNumber))
```

During development of your application, you'll probably find yourself experimenting by creating tables that eventually do not end up in the database of your finished application. You can get rid of those unwanted tables by sending a query telling the DBMS to drop the tables.

The decision to drop a table shouldn't be made lightly, because once a table is dropped, you cannot recover the table. Instead, the table must be re-created and the data must be reinserted into the table. In addition to losing data elements stored in the table, dropping a table may also affect the integrity of the database and tables that relate to values in the dropped table.

You remove a table from a database by using the Drop Table statement with the name of the table that you want dropped from the database, as shown here:

```
DROP TABLE CustomerAddress
```

Indexing

An *index* is used to speed searches through a table much as you use an index of a book to find the page that contains a keyword. However, instead of finding a page, an index for a table presents an ordered view of the table, enabling you to find the row that contains the keyword.

You can create a secondary index, or a clustered index. A secondary index uses a column other than the primary key for the index. A clustered index uses two or more columns as the key of the index.

You create both types of index by using a Create Index statement in a query, as shown here. You must give the index a name and then designate the column(s) that will be indexed. This example creates a secondary index called CustZip that indexes the CustomerZip column of the CustomerAddress table.

```
CREATE INDEX CustZip
ON CustomerAddress (CustomerZip)
```

A clustered index is created practically the same way as a secondary index, except you designate two or more columns for the index. Let's say that you want to create a clustered index using CustomerLastName and CustomerFirstName from a CustomerContact table. Here's how you write the query:

```
CREATE INDEX CustName
ON custContact (custLastName, custFirstName)
```

Too many indexes can actually slow down the performance of the DBMS, because each index is updated every time a new row is inserted into the table. Therefore, any unnecessary indexes should be dropped.

You drop an index by using the Drop Index statement, as shown here:

```
DROP INDEX CustName ON CustomersContact
```

Inserting a Row

You'll remember from the previous chapter that the Insert Into statement is used to insert a new row into a table. You need to provide the column name and the values that will be inserted into those columns.

Let's say that we want to insert a new row into the CustomerAddress table. Here's how this is done: Notice that we didn't insert a value into the CustomerCtry column, which is the customer country, because previously in this chapter we designed a default value for this column. So if we don't insert a value, the DBMS will automatically insert USA into the CustomerCtry column.

```
INSERT INTO CustomerAddress
(CustomerNumber, CustomerStreet, CustomerCity, Customerstate,
 CustomerZip )
VALUES ('12345','121 West Street','Allendale','NJ','07660')
```

Selecting Data from a Table

We touched upon how to select information from a table in the last chapter. We'll go into more detail in this section and illustrate how to retrieve more complex information. Before beginning, let's expand the CustomerAddress table to include the customer name. The new table should be called Customers, and here are the columns you'll need:

- CustomerNumber CHAR(30) NOT NULL
- CustomerFirstName CHAR(50)
- CustomerLastName CHAR(50)
- CustomerStreet, CHAR(30)
- CustomerCity CHAR(30)
- *CustomerState CHAR(2)
- CustomerZip CHAR(10)
- CustomerCtry CHAR(5) DEFAULT 'USA'

Once you create the table, then insert the following rows into it:

Customer-Number	Customer-FirstName	Customer-LastName	Customer-Street	CustomerCity	Customer-State	CustomerZip	CustomerCtry
12345	Bob	Jones	5 First Street	New York City	NY	07555	USA
67890	Mary	Smith	8 Third Street	Dallas	TX	75553	USA
09876	Sam	Jones	5 First Street	New York City	NY	07555	USA
54321	Mark	Russell	3 Sixth Street	Los Angeles	CA	82272	USA
53465	Susan	Allen	18 Fifth Street	Chicago	IL	45003	USA
87634	Tom	Russell	3 Sixth Street	Los Angeles	CA	82272	USA

You can select all the data contained in the table by using the following query. The asterisk is a wildcard character telling the DBMS to return all the columns. All rows are returned because we didn't include a WHERE clause:

```
SELECT *
FROM Customers
```

Specific columns are selected by using the name of the column in the Select statement. Here's how we retrieve customer names:

```
SELECT CustomerFirstName, CustomerLastName
FROM Customers
```

We can retrieve selected rows by specifying a condition in the WHERE clause of the query. Suppose we want to retrieve all the information about the customer whose last name is Jones. Here's the query we'd need to write:

```
SELECT CustomerNumber, CustomerFirstName, CustomerLastName, CustomerStreet, CustomerCity,
CustomerState, CustomerZip, CustomerCtry
FROM Customers
WHERE CustomerLastName = 'Jones'
```

In the real world, rows are selected according to multiple conditions such as a combination of a customer's first and last names. Multiple conditions are defined in the WHERE clause and are combined by using AND, OR, or NOT.

Let's say that we want to retrieve information about Bob Jones. We'll need two conditions in the WHERE clause. The first specifies the first name, and the next

specifies the last name. These conditions are then joined together using AND to form one compound expression. Both conditions must be true; otherwise, the row isn't returned to your application.

Here's the query:

```
SELECT CustomerNumber, CustomerFirstName, CustomerLastName, CustomerStreet, CustomerCity,
CustomerState, CustomerZip, CustomerCtry
FROM Customers
WHERE CustomerFirstName = 'Bob' AND CustomerLastName = 'Jones'
```

The OR clause is used if we want a row returned if either the first condition is true or the second condition is true. A row isn't returned only if neither condition is true. Let's say that we want information about either Bob or Mary. Here's the query we'd need to write:

```
SELECT CustomerNumber, CustomerFirstName, CustomerLastName, CustomerStreet, CustomerCity,
CustomerState, CustomerZip, CustomerCtry
FROM Customers
WHERE CustomerFirstName = 'Bob' OR CustomerFirstName = 'Mary'
```

We can exclude information by using the NOT clause in the condition. For example, suppose that we want information about all the customers except for Bob Jones. Here's what we need to do. First, we create the compound expression where we specify Bob as the CustomerFirstName and Jones as the CustomerLastName.

Next, we place a NOT in front of the compound expression. The NOT tells the DBMS to reverse the logic of the expression. That is, if the value of the Customer-FirstName column is Bob and the value of the CustomerLastName column is Jones, then don't return the row.

Here's the query:

```
SELECT CustomerNumber, CustomerFirstName, CustomerLastName, CustomerStreet, CustomerCity,
CustomerState, CustomerZip, CustomerCtry
FROM Customers
WHERE NOT (CustomerFirstName = 'Bob' AND CustomerLastName = 'Jones')
```

Relational Operators

Relational operators can be used to create a condition that evaluates a range of values. Relational operators are less than (<), greater than (>), less than or equal to (<=), and greater than or equal to (>=).

Before using these operators, let's revise the Customer table by including a Sales column, which is a NUMERIC data type. Inset the following sales data into the apropriate row of the table. We'll use these values to select rows to return to our application as shown in this table.

Customer-Number	Customer-FirstName	Customer-LastName	Customer-Street	Customer-City	Customer-State	Customer-Zip	Customer-Ctry	Sales
12345	Bob	Jones	5 First Street	New York City	NY	07555	USA	50000
67890	Mary	Smith	8 Third Street	Dallas	TX	75553	USA	20000
09876	Sam	Jones	5 First Street	New York City	NY	07555	USA	50000
54321	Mark	Russell	3 Sixth Street	Los Angeles	CA	82272	USA	30000
53465	Susan	Allen	18 Fifth Street	Chicago	IL	45003	USA	40000
87634	Tom	Russell	3 Sixth Street	Los Angeles	CA	82272	USA	30000

Let's begin by selecting customers who have sales of $50,000. Two customers are returned. These are Bob Jones and Sam Jones, both of whom live at the same address. Other customers are excluded because they don't have sales of $50,000.

```
SELECT CustomerNumber, CustomerFirstName, CustomerLastName, CustomerStreet, CustomerCity,
CustomerState, CustomerZip, CustomerCtry
FROM Customers
WHERE Sales = 50000
```

Now let's take a look at the less-than operator. We'll use it in the next example to retrieve customers whose sales are less than $50,000. Four rows are returned—all but the two Joneses.

```
SELECT CustomerNumber, CustomerFirstName, CustomerLastName, CustomerStreet, CustomerCity,
CustomerState, CustomerZip, CustomerCtry
FROM Customers
WHERE Sales < 50000
```

The greater-than operator is used in a similar way in the next example, except only customers whose sales are greater than $40,000 are returned. If you run this, only the two rows containing the Joneses are returned, because the other customers have sales less than or equal to $40,000.

```
SELECT CustomerNumber, CustomerFirstName, CustomerLastName, CustomerStreet, CustomerCity,
CustomerState, CustomerZip, CustomerCtry
FROM Customers
WHERE Sales > 40000
```

In the previous examples, customers whose sales were greater than $40,000 were excluded. However, you can include those customers by inserting an equal sign. The expression is then less than or equal to or greater than or equal to, as illustrated in the next two examples.

```
SELECT CustomerNumber, CustomerFirstName, CustomerLastName, CustomerStreet, CustomerCity,
CustomerState, CustomerZip, CustomerCtry
```

```
FROM Customers
WHERE Sales <= 50000

SELECT CustomerNumber, CustomerFirstName, CustomerLastName, CustomerStreet, CustomerCity,
CustomerState, CustomerZip, CustomerCtry
FROM Customers
WHERE Sales >= 40000
```

Another way to select rows using a range of values is to use the Between operator. The Between operator requires you to provide a range of values. Rows whose values fall within the range are returned to your application.

The range must be a sequential series of values such as from 100 to 200. All values within the range including the first and last values are considered when the DBMS evaluates the value of a column. That is, a row with the value of 100 or the value of 200 is returned.

Here's how you use the Between operator:

```
SELECT CustomerNumber, CustomerFirstName, CustomerLastName, CustomerStreet, CustomerCity,
CustomerState, CustomerZip, CustomerCtry
FROM Customers
WHERE Sales BETWEEN 20000 AND 39999
```

Sometimes you won't know the exact value stored in a column, but you'll know a portion of the value. For example, you may know that a customer's last name begins with the characters Smi. However, the name could be Smith or Smite. You can have the DBMS search for a partial match and return those customers whose last name is like Smi. You do this by using the Like operator.

The Like operator requires you to use a wildcard character in place of unknown characters. Here are the wildcards that are used with the Like operator:

- **Underscore (_)**   A single-character wildcard. For example, if you are unsure if the customer's last name is Anderson or Andersen, you can use the underscore in place of the character that is in question, such as Anders_n.

- **Percent (%)**   A multicharacter wildcard used to match any number of characters. For example, Smi% is used to match a value of a column where the first three characters are Smi, followed by any other characters.

Here's the query you'd write to find customers whose last name begins with Smi:

```
SELECT CustomerNumber, CustomerFirstName, CustomerLastName, CustomerStreet, CustomerCity,
CustomerState, CustomerZip, CustomerCtry
FROM Customers
WHERE CustomerLastName LIKE 'Smi%'
```

A common real-world problem that you will encounter is to identify rows that are missing data in a column. You can then update the table with the missing data.

For example, which customers don't have a ZIP code on file? A column that doesn't have a value is referred to as NULL. NULL means that the column is devoid of any value. Don't confuse NULL with zero. Zero is a value.

If you want rows returned that have a column whose value is NULL, then you use the IS NULL operator in a query. The next example returns customers whose CustomerZip column is NULL—that is, devoid of any value:

```
SELECT CustomerNumber, CustomerFirstName, CustomerLastName, CustomerStreet, CustomerCity,
CustomerState, CustomerZip, CustomerCtry
FROM Customers
WHERE CustomerZip IS NULL
```

Another real-world problem that you'll encounter is having too many rows returned to your application. Let's say that you want to send a flyer to your customers. The Customers table has names and addresses of all your customers. You could simply retrieve all rows from the table; however, suppose more than one customer lives at the same address. This means that you'll be sending multiple copies of the flyer to the same address.

A better approach is to send one flyer to each distinct address. You can ask the DBMS to filter duplicate addresses by using the Distinct modifier. Here's what you need to write:

```
SELECT DISTINCT CustomerStreet, CustomerCity, CustomerState, CustomerZip, CustomerCtry
FROM Customers
```

Still another common problem occurs when you need to select rows according to a set of values that are not in a sequence. Let's say that a sales representative is going to be on the road and wants to visit customers within specific ZIP codes. The ZIP codes are in no particular order.

The solution is to use the In modifier. The In modifier is used to define a set of values. The set is then compared to the value of a column that you specify in the query. The row is returned if the value is within the set.

Here's this query. If the value of the sales column is $20,000 or $30,000 or $40,000, then the row is returned:

```
SELECT CustomerNumber, CustomerFirstName, CustomerLastName, CustomerStreet, CustomerCity,
CustomerState, CustomerZip, CustomerCtry
FROM Customers
WHERE Sales IN (20000, 30000, 40000)
```

You can also reverse this process by using the Not In modifier. The Not In modifier tells the DBMS to return the row if the value of the column is not one of the values in the set. Here's a rewrite of the previous example. Rows whose sales column isn't $20,000 or $30,000 or $40,000 are returned:

```
SELECT CustomerNumber, CustomerFirstName, CustomerLastName, CustomerStreet, CustomerCity,
CustomerState, CustomerZip, CustomerCtry
FROM Customers
WHERE Sales NOT IN (20000, 30000, 40000)
```

Updating Tables

You can change information already in a table by using the Update statement, which was introduced in the last chapter. Before exploring how to update a table, let's revise the Customers table so that you'll be able to follow along with examples shown within this section. Insert the following data into the table:

- CustomerNumber CHAR(30)
- CustomerFirstName CHAR(30)
- CustomerLastName CHAR(30)
- CustomerStreet CHAR(30)
- CustomerCity CHAR(30)
- CustomerState CHAR(2)
- CustomerZipCode CHAR(10)
- Discount LONG
- Price LONG
- DiscountPrice LONG

Customer-Number	Customer-FirstName	Customer-LastName	Customer-Street	Customer-City	Customer-State	Customer-Zip	Discount	Price	Discount-Price
12345	Bob	Jones	5 First Street	New York City	NY	07555	10	100	
67890	Mary	Smith	8 Third Street	Dallas	TX	75553	20	200	
09876	Sam	Jones	5 First Street	New York City	NY	07555	11	300	
54321	Mark	Russell	23 Eighth Street	Los Angeles	CA	82272	16	400	
53465	Susan	Allen	18 Fifth Street	Chicago	IL	45003	15	500	
87676	Kelly	Russell	32 Fourth Street	Los Angeles	CA	82272	15	600	

As you'll recall from the preceding chapter, the Update statement is used to change values in one or more columns in one or more rows of the table. The Update statement requires that you provide the name of the table and a Set clause that identifies column names and new values that will be placed in the column. The new values overwrite the column's existing values. An Update statement updates all rows unless you include a WHERE clause, which specifies a condition that must exist in a row before the row is updated.

Let's say that you want to change Bob Jones' address to 5 Main Street. Here's what you need to write in the query:

```
UPDATE Customers
SET CustomerStreet = '5 Main Street'
WHERE CustomerFirstName = 'Bob' and CustomerLastName = 'Jones'
```

Only one row is updated by the previous query because only one customer is named Bob Jones. If another customer has the same name, then his street address would also be changed. In the real world, a customer number rather than a customer name is used to identify a customer so that only the proper customer information is updated.

Sometimes, you'll want to update multiple rows by replacing a sales representative with a new one. You could find rows that contain the current sales representative and then replace it with the new sales representative.

There are four common WHERE clause expressions that are used to update multiple rows of a table. These are

- **The IN test**   Updates only if a value matches a value in the IN clause.
- **The IS NULL test**   Rows that don't have a value in the specified column are updated when the IS NULL operator is used in the WHERE clause expression.
- **The comparison test**   You've seen this used in the preceding example.
- **All rows**   A query can direct the DBMS to update the specified column in all rows of a table by excluding the WHERE clause in the query.

Be cautious whenever you execute a query that updates multiple rows, because an error in a query is multiplied by the number of rows in a table.

The IN clause provides two or more values that are compared to the value of the designated column in the IN clause. Rows whose columns contain one of these values are updated by the UPDATE statement. This is shown in the next example, where the value of the Discount column is changed to 25 if the current value of the Discount column is either 12 or 15:

```
UPDATE Customers
SET Discount = 25
WHERE Discount IN (12,15)
```

The IS NULL test determines if the column is NULL, that is, if the column is devoid of any value. If so, then the column is updated. The next example uses the IS NULL test to update the Discount column if there isn't a last name in the CustomerLastName column:

```
UPDATE Customers
SET Discount = 0
WHERE CustomerLastName IS NULL
```

Another common use of the Update statement is to change the value of a column according to a calculation. For example, we can calculate the discounted price of an item by using the value of the Price column and the value of the Discount column. The result of the calculation can then be inserted into the DiscountPrice column.

Here's how this is done:

```
UPDATE Customers
SET DiscountPrice = Price * ((100 - Discount) / 100)
```

Deleting Data from a Table

One or more rows can be removed from a table by using the Delete From statement. Before doing so, however, make sure that the information you are deleting is no longer needed and won't impact other tables in your database (see "Joining Tables").

There are two ways in which to delete rows. First, you can remove all rows of a table by using the Delete From statement without a WHERE clause. The other way is to specify rows you want to delete by using a WHERE clause. This is illustrated in the next example, where we delete the row that contains information about Sam Jones:

```
DELETE FROM Customers
WHERE CustomerLastName = 'Jones' and CustomerFirstName = 'Tom'
```

Joining Tables

As you learned in Chapter 9, rows of two tables can be linked together by joining the tables using a value that is common to each of them. For example, a table containing customer information can be joined to a table that contains customer orders by using a customer number, which appears in a column in both tables.

Tables are joined in a query using a two-step process. First, both tables must be identified in the FROM clause. Next, an expression is created in the WHERE clause that identifies the columns that are used to create the join.

Before learning how this is done, let's create another table called Orders and insert the data shown here:

- OrderNumber Character(30) Primary Key
- ProductNumber Character(30)

- CustomerNumber Character(10)
- Quantity NUMBER
- SubTotal NUMBER

OrderNumber	ProductNumber	CustomerNumber	Quantity	SubTotal
122	5237	87676	1	325
334	3255	54321	1	250
365	3255	54321	4	1000
534	7466	67890	3	1596
587	5237	12345	1	325
717	1052	54321	2	200
874	7466	12345	1	532

Let's retrieve the customer name and the subtotal for all orders. Here's the query that you'll need to write. The Select statement contains the names of the columns that we want the DBMS to return to our application.

The From clause must contain the names of both tables that are being used by the query. Each name is separated from the next by a comma. The WHERE clause is where the join occurs. It is here that you need to specify the column name of each table that is used to join the tables. Both columns must have the same value and the same data type; otherwise, rows won't be joined together.

Whenever the same column name appears in both tables, you'll need to preface the column name with the table name. This is the case with CustomerNumber. Both the Customers table and the Orders table have a column called Customer-Number. Therefore, we need to explicitly identify which column we're referring to. Notice that the table name and the column name are separated by a period.

```
SELECT CustomerFirstName, CustomerLastName, Subtotal
FROM Customers, Orders
WHERE Customers.CustomerNumber = Orders.CustomerNumber
```

The preceding example returned all rows. However, you can specify the rows that you want returned by setting criteria in the WHERE clause. To do this, you create an expression, as you learned earlier in this chapter.

Suppose we want to return only the customer name and subtotal for customer number 87676. Here's what you need to do:

```
SELECT CustomerFirstName, CustomerLastName, Subtotal
FROM Customers, Orders
WHERE Customers.CustomerNumber = Orders.CustomerNumber AND Customers.CustomerNumber =
'87676'
```

A query can become unreadable to you—not to the DBMS—if you need to explicitly use table names to preface column names in the query. The names are simply too long. You can shorten the name of a table just for the query by using a table alias. A table *alias* is an abbreviation that can be used in place of the name of the table in the query.

Here's how this is done: The abbreviation is placed alongside the table name in the From clause. You create your own abbreviation. Where possible, use the first letter of the table. The abbreviation is then used in place of the table name in the query, as shown here:

```
SELECT CustomerFirstName, CustomerLastName, Subtotal
FROM Customers C, Orders O
WHERE C.CustomerNumber = O.CustomerNumber AND C.CustomerNumber = '87676'
```

Calculating Columns

The DBMS can calculate values in a table using one of five built-in calculation functions. You place the name of the column that you want calculated within the parentheses of the calculation function. These are the functions:

- SUM() tallies values in a column that is passed to the built-in function.

  ```
  SELECT SUM(Quantity)
  FROM Orders
  ```

- AVG() averages values in a column that is passed to the built-in function.

  ```
  SELECT AVG(Quantity)
  FROM Orders
  ```

- MIN() determines the minimum value in a column that is passed to the built-in function.

  ```
  SELECT MIN(Quantity)
  FROM Orders
  ```

- MAX() determines the maximum value in a column that is passed to the built-in function.

  ```
  SELECT MAX(Quantity)
  FROM Orders
  ```

- COUNT() determines the number of rows in a column that is passed to the built-in function. Rows without values in the column are excluded from the count.

  ```
  SELECT COUNT(Quantity)
  FROM Orders
  ```

The Count() function is also used to count the number of rows in a table. You do this by using the wildcard character (asterisk) within the parentheses of the function as shown here:

```
SELECT COUNT(*)
FROM Orders
```

You can perform multiple counts by extending the Select statement to reflect each count. For example, here's how we determine the total number of rows in the table and the total value of the Quantity column:

```
SELECT COUNT(*), COUNT(Quantity)
FROM Orders
```

You can restrict the scope of a built-in calculation function by using a WHERE clause expression to specify the criteria for a row to be included in a calculation. Any valid WHERE clause expression can be used to filter rows to be excluded from the calculation.

Let's say that you want to calculate the total number of orders, the average, and the total of the values in the Quantity column. Here's how you do it:

```
SELECT COUNT(OrderNumber), AVG(Quantity),   SUM(Quantity)
FROM Orders o, customers c
WHERE o.CustomerNumber = c.CustNumber
```

There are two common problems that occur when using built-in functions. Some rows won't contain any values, and others will contain duplicate values. Both of these conditions can affect the calculation.

You can solve these problems by using the IS NULL operator and the Distinct modifier in your query. Both of these were explained in detail previously in the chapter.

Grouping and Ordering Data

Rows can be grouped or sorted by using the GROUP BY clause or the ORDER BY clause. Grouping organizes rows according to similar values within the same column. Let's say that you want to see a quantity for each product. The selected columns can be grouped by product number.

Sorting organizes rows in natural order. A DBMS is capable of simple and complex sorting. A simple sort is when the values in a single column are used for the sort. A complex sort is when multiple columns are used for the sort; for instance, rows may be sorted by customer last name and, within customer last name, by customer first name.

Here's how to group rows: The Select statement contains columns that will be returned to your application. The Group By clause groups these by product number. This means that rows that have the same product number appear one underneath the other.

```
SELECT ProductNumber, SUM(Quantity)
FROM Sales
GROUP BY ProductNumber
```

You can also create a subgroup within a group. This is illustrated in the next example, where the product number group is further grouped by customer number. The results are shown in Table 11-1.

```
SELECT ProductNumber, CustomerNumber, SUM(Quantity)
FROM Sales
GROUP BY ProductNumber, CustomerNumber
```

The number of rows that are included in a group can be limited by including a conditional expression in the query. A conditional expression is similar to the WHERE clause expression discussed previously in this chapter, except instead of the WHERE clause a Having clause is used.

In the next example, we use the Having clause to return rows whose Quantity column has a value that is greater than 1. Table 11-2 shows the results.

```
SELECT ProductNumber, CustomerNumber, SUM(Quantity)
FROM Sales
GROUP BY ProductNumber, CustomerNumber
HAVING Quantity > 1
```

ProductNumber	CustomerNumber	Quantity
1052	54321	2
3255	54321	1
3255	54321	4
5237	12345	1
5237	87676	1
7466	12345	1
7466	67890	3

Table 1-1 Rows Are Grouped by ProductNumber and Then by CustomerNumber.

ProductNumber	CustomerNumber	Quantity
1052	54321	2
3255	54321	4
7466	67890	3

Table 1-2   Rows Are Grouped by ProductNumber and Then CustomerNumber if They Have a Quantity Greater than 1.

Columns that are empty can create unexpected results when you execute a query. This is because sometimes the empty column is included or excluded from the operation, depending on the nature of the query.

The DBMS may include or exclude a row in a group, depending on the conditional expression. Here's how this works:

- A row is included in a group if the empty column isn't used to group rows or used in the conditional expression in the HAVING clause.

- A row is included in the group if the empty column is used to group rows. Rows containing the empty column are placed in their own group.

You can sort values returned to your application by using the Order By clause as shown here, where the rows are sorted by ProductNumber:

```
SELECT ProductNumber, CustomerNumber, Quantity
FROM Sales
ORDER BY ProductNumber
```

Rows are sorted in ascending order unless you specify descending order by using the DESC modifier as illustrated here:

```
SELECT ProductNumber, CustomerNumber, Quantity
FROM Sales
ORDER BY BY ProductNumber DESC
```

You can also sort using a second column within the original sort by specifying another column in the Order By clause. Here we're sorting by ProductNumber, and within ProductNumber, we're sorting by CustomerNumber:

```
SELECT ProductNumber, CustomerNumber, Quantity
FROM Sales
ORDER BY ProductNumber, CustomerNumber.
```

Looking Ahead

Queries have the DBMS perform various database tasks, such as creating and deleting a table. When creating a table, you can specify whether a column must have a value and set a default value for a column, which is used if a new row doesn't have a value for the column.

You can increase the efficiency of locating rows by creating an index, which is similar to an index of a book. In addition to primary keys, there are two kinds of indexes: secondary indexes and a clustered indexes. However, having too many indexes might slow inserting and updating rows because each time this happens all the relative indexes must be updated.

There are various ways to write a query to select data from one or multiple tables. You can select all the columns from all the rows or use the WHERE clause to specify criteria for selecting rows. The selection criteria consist of a simple or compound expression that can use relational operators to specify one value or a range of values.

The selection criteria don't have to exactly match values in a column, because you can use the Like modifier combined with wildcard characters to partially match values in a column. This enables you to locate the name Smith if you know only that the name begins with Smi.

Rows of two tables can be linked together by create a join using a column in each table that contains the same value. You join tables by specifying the table names in the From clause and creating an equivalent expression in the WHERE clause. Once tables are joined, you can select any column from those tables.

SQL has built-in functions that are used to perform calculations on columns of a table such as tallying values in a column or simply counting the number of rows in a table. You can fine-tune any calculation by using the WHERE clause to specify the columns that you want included in the calculation.

Information returned by the DBMS can be organized into groups and sorted. Grouping rows is used for aggregations and causes the DBMS to place together all rows that have the same value for a column. Sorting causes the returned rows to be sorted in ascending or descending order, according to the value in the column that you specify in the Sort By clause.

In the next chapter we'll finish our look at how to work with a database by showing how you can bind data to a web control to minimize the code that you'll need to write.

Quiz

1. The selection criteria can be a set of values that are not in any sequence.
   a. True
   b. False

2. What operator would you use to specify a range of values in a WHERE clause?
   a. From To
   b. To From
   c. Between
   d. None of the above

3. SET is used to
   a. Create a table alias.
   b. Specify the column and the value to update within a table.
   c. Specify the value for inserting a new row.
   d. Specify the selection criteria.

4. The underscore
   a. Is a single-character wildcard.
   b. Is a multiple-character wildcard.
   c. Represents any number of tables.
   d. Represents any number of indexes.

5. How would you reverse the logic of an expression in the WHERE clause?
   a. !
   b. ELSE
   c. NOT
   d. None of the above

6. How do you designate a primary key for a table?
   a. The first column is always the primary key.
   b. Use CONSTRAINT *KeyName* PRIMARY KEY (*ColumnName*).
   c. The last column is always the primary key.
   d. Place PRIMARY KEY at the end of the column name.

7. DROP JOIN removes a join.

   a. True

   b. False

8. You cannot set a default value for a column.

   a. True

   b. False

9. A clustered index consists of two or more columns.

   a. True

   b. False

10. Updating a column overwrites the current value in the column.

   a. True

   b. False

Answers

1. a. True

2. c. Between

3. b. Specify the column and the value for updating a table.

4. a. Is a single-character wildcard.

5. c. NOT

6. b. Use CONSTRAINT *KeyName* PRIMARY KEY (*ColumnName*)

7. b. False. There's no need to "remove" a join—you just discard the result set.

8. b. False. You set the default value for a column with the DEFAULT clause.

9. a. True

10. a. True

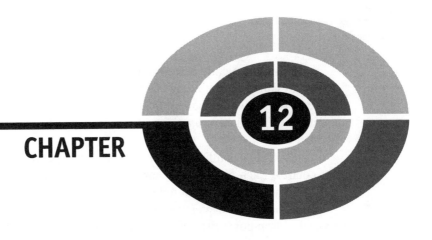

Binding Data to Controls

Developers are always looking for efficient ways to streamline an application and reduce lines of code to write. One of those ways is to link data directly to a web control so that it appears automatically every time the web page is displayed.

Linking data to a web control is called data binding and is the topic of this chapter. Data can come from a variety of sources, but the most common source is from a database. In this chapter, you'll learn how to bind data to a web control and then use that data and web control within your application.

Data Binding Basics

In previous chapters you learned how to retrieve information from a database and display the information on your web page. Many times this information is displayed in a control such as a drop-down list box or a text box on a web form.

You can dynamically assign information from a database to a control by using a process called data binding. *Data binding* links the value property of a control to a data source while your application is running. The data source can be data from a database. The data source can also be an expression, methods, or properties of another control.

Each control has a DataSource property that specifies the source of the data for the control. Each control also has a DataBind() method. You call the DataBind() method whenever you want to bring the data source into the control.

Throughout this chapter we'll show how to bind data from a database to a Repeater control, a drop-down list control, a radio button control, and a list box control.

The Repeater Control

The Repeater control is used to display records from a database and is declared by using the following ASP.NET tags. The <asp:Repeater> tag requires two attributes. These are ID and Runat, both of these you've learned about throughout this book. The ID attribute uniquely identifies the Repeater, and the Runat attribute specifies that this control runs on the server.

Within the Repeater tag is the ItemTemplate. The ItemTemplate specifies what is to be displayed. Here you reference data returned from the database. (You'll see how to retrieve data later in this section.)

The ItemTemplate tag in turn contains a data binding expression, which is used to reference this data. This expression begins with <%# and ends with %>. The expression itself calls the DataItem() method of the Container object and passes it the column name that identifies the column from the bound data source that the control displays. A Container object is an object that contains other objects.

```
<asp:Repeater ID="RepeaterID" Runat="Server">
   <ItemTemplate>
      <%# Container.DataItem("ColumnName") %>
   </ItemTemplate>
</asp:Repeater>
```

Data is retrieved from the database using techniques that you learned in Chapter 10. You'll recall that you need to open a connection to the database and then pass the database management system (DBMS) a query. A reader is then used to access the result returned by the DBMS.

Data that is retrieved from the DBMS must be bound to the Repeater control. This is accomplished by assigning a reference to the reader to the DataSource property of the Repeater control, and then by calling the Repeater control's DataBind()

method. Every control has a DataBind() function that binds (links) the data source to the control. The control then displays the data once the data source is bound to the control.

Connecting to the database, running the query, and binding the control to the data source typically occurs once in your application. It makes sense to do this when the page is loaded. Therefore, place the code that links to the data in the Page_Load subroutine as shown here. This example connects to the Microsoft SQL Server database, but you can connect to another database, as illustrated in Chapter 10.

This example begins by declaring SqlConnection, SqlCommand, and SqlDataReader variables. Next, a connection is opened to the DBMS by creating a SqlConnection object and passing it login information.

An instance of the SqlCommand object is then created, passing it the query that will be sent to the DBMS to retrieve our data. The connection is then opened by calling the Connection object's Open() method, and data is returned to the reader by calling the SqlCommand object's ExecuteReader() method.

A reference to the reader is assigned to the DataSource property of the Repeater control, and then the DataBind() method is called to bind the data to the Repeater control. The reader and the connection are then closed.

```
Sub Page_Load
  Dim conCust As SqlConnection
  Dim cmdSelectRows As SqlCommand
  Dim dtrCust As SqlDataReader
  conCust = New SqlConnection( "Server=server;UID=userID;
          PWD=password;
          Database=database" )
  cmdSelectRows = New SqlCommand( "query", conCust)
  conCust.Open()
  dtrCust = cmdSelectRows.ExecuteReader()
  RepeaterControlID.DataSource = dtrCust
  RepeaterControlID.DataBind()
  dtrCust.Close()
  conCust.Close()
End Sub
```

Let's assemble these pieces and retrieve data from the Customers table that you created in Chapter 11. The following code shows how this is done. We begin by defining the Page_Load subroutine. The database is called CustomerContactData. Replace MyID and MyPassword with your user ID and password. We'll use a very simple query that retrieves all the rows and all the columns from the Customers table.

Next, we create a form on our web page that contains the Repeater control. The Repeater control has a data binding expression that calls the DataItem() of the Container object to access the CustomerLastName column of the data returned to the application by the DBMS in response to our query.

```
<%@ Import Namespace="System.Data.SqlClient" %>
<Script Runat="Server">
Sub Page_Load
  Dim conCust As SqlConnection
  Dim cmdSelectRows As SqlCommand
  Dim dtrCust As SqlDataReader
  conCust = New SqlConnection(
  "Server=localhost; UID=MyID;PWD=MyPassword; Database=CustomerContactData" )
  cmdSelectRows = New SqlCommand( "Select * From custContact", conCust)
  conCust.Open()
  dtrCust = cmdSelectRows.ExecuteReader()
  rptCust.DataSource = dtrCust
  rptCust.DataBind()
  dtrCust.Close()
  conCust.Close()
End Sub
</Script>
<html>
    <head><title>Repeater Control Data Binding</title></head>
    <body>
       <form Runat="Server">
          <asp:Repeater ID="rptCust" Runat="Server">
             <ItemTemplate>
                <%# Container.DataItem("custLastName") %>
             </ItemTemplate>
          </asp:Repeater>
       </form>
    </body>
</html>
```

A Closer Look at Templates

The ItemTemplate for the Repeater control is just one type of template. Templates can contain data retrieved from the DBMS, HTML tags, and inline ASP.NET statements. There are five templates that can be used with the Repeater control:

- **HeaderTemplate**   Used to format the header section of the Repeater control
- **ItemTemplate**   Used to display and format data displayed in the Repeater control

- **AlternatingItemTemplate**   Used to display and format alternate data items
- **SeparatorTemplate**   Used to separate data displayed by the Repeater control
- **FooterTemplate**   Used to format the footer section of the Repeater control

The following example is a modification of our previous example and illustrates how to use these different templates in an application. All rows and columns are retrieved from the Customers table. We'll display the CustomerFirstName and CustomerLastName columns in a table.

The HeaderTemplate is the first template used in this example. The HeaderTemplate contains HTML tags that create a table with two columns: Customer First Name and Customer Last Name.

The ItemTemplate appears next. This is nearly identical to the ItemTemplate in the previous example; however, besides having it access data from the DBMS, we've also included HTML tags that define a row and columns of the table. The data is displayed in a blue font.

The AlternatingItemTemplate defines the format for alternating items that appear in the Repeater control, that is, the second, fourth, and so on items. The format is the same as for the ItemTemplate; however, the data appears in red instead of blue.

The FooterTemplate is the last template in this example and contains the HTML closing tag for the table.

```
<%@ Import Namespace="System.Data.SqlClient" %>
<Script Runat="Server">
Sub Page_Load
  Dim conCust As SqlConnection
  Dim cmdSelectRows As SqlCommand
  Dim dtrCust As SqlDataReader
  conCust = New SqlConnection( "Server=localhost;UID=
MyID;PWD=MyPassword;Database=CustomerContactData")
  cmdSelectRows = New SqlCommand( "Select * From Customers", conCust)
  conCust.Open()
  dtrCust = cmdSelectRows.ExecuteReader()
  rptCust.DataSource = dtrCust
  rptCust.DataBind()
  dtrCust.Close()
  ()
  conCust.Close()
End Sub
</Script>
<html>
<head><title> Repeater Control Data Binding </title></head>
<body>
    <form Runat="Server">
      <asp:Repeater ID="rptCust" Runat="Server">
        <HeaderTemplate>
            <table border=1 cellpadding=5>
```

```
        <tr>
          <th>Customer First Name</th>
          <th>Customer Last Name</th>
        </tr>
      </HeaderTemplate>
      <ItemTemplate>
        <font color="blue">
        <tr>
          <td><%# Container.DataItem("custFirstName") %></td>
          <td><%# Container.DataItem("custLastName") %></td>
        </tr>
      </ItemTemplate>
      <AlternatingItemTemplate>
        <font color="red">
        <tr>
          <td><%# Container.DataItem("CustFirstName") %></td>
          <td><%# Container.DataItem("CustLastName") %></td>
        </tr>
      </AlternatingItemTemplate>
      <FooterTemplate>
          </table>
      </FooterTemplate>
    </asp:Repeater>
  </form>
</body>
</html>
```

Drop-Down List

Data can also be bounded to the DropDownList control by assigning the column name to the DataTextField property of the DropDownList control in the Page_Load method. This is illustrated in the next example, where we load the last name of customers into a drop-down list when the page is loaded.

Notice that we connect to the database and execute the query in the Page_Load subroutine much as we did in the previous example, with one difference. The database connection is made within an If statement that evaluates the status of the IsPostBack property.

A postback occurs when the page calls itself. A visitor loads a page for the first time by entering the page's URL into the browser address box or by clicking a hyperlink contained on a different page. This is not a postback. However, once the page is displayed, the page can request itself. This is a postback.

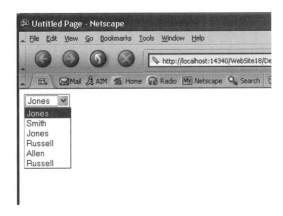

Figure 12-1   The last names shown in the DropDownList control are from the database.

If the page is a postback, then the IsPostBack property is true; otherwise, the IsPostBack property is false. Data connection and data binding occur only when the page isn't a postback. Therefore, we need to test the value of the IsPostBack property before connecting to the DBMS and binding the data. We do this by reversing the logic of the IsPostBack property. That is, if the IsPostBack property is false (the page is loaded the first time), then we make the condition expression true so that statements within the If statement (connect to the DBMS and bind the data) are executed.

The web page itself is different than the previous example because we created a form that contains the DropDownList. The DropDownList control is populated with the last name of customers from the Customers table (Figure 12-1).

There would be other controls in a real-world application such as a button that when selected causes the selected customer last name to be processed (see Chapter 8).

```
<%@ Import Namespace="System.Data.SqlClient" %>
<Script Runat="Server">
Sub Page_Load
  If Not IsPostBack Then
    Dim conCust As SqlConnection
    Dim cmdSelectRows As SqlCommand
    Dim dtrCust As SqlDataReader
    conCust = New SqlConnection( "Server=localhost;UID=
MyID;PWD=MyPassword;Database=CustomerContactData")
    conCust.Open()
    cmdSelectRows = New SqlCommand( "Select cistLastName From
custContact", conCust)
    dtrCust = cmdSelectRows.ExecuteReader()
    deleteCust.DataSource = dtrCust
```

```
         deleteCust.DataTextField = "custLastName"
         deleteCust.DataBind()
         dtrCust.Close()
         conCust.Close()
      End If
   End Sub
   </Script>
   <html>
   <head><title>Drop-Down List Control Data Binding</title></head>
   <body>
      <form Runat="Server">
         <asp:DropDownList ID="deleteCust" Runat="Server" />
      </form>
   </body>
   </html>
```

Radio Button

As you learned in Chapter 8, radio buttons are a convenient way to display a group of options from which the visitor selects only one option within the group.

You can store in a table names of radio buttons that are within the same group. This enables you to dynamically define members of the group according to values in the database. For example, a customer might qualify for a unique set of delivery options, as shown by the customer's profile. The set can be stored in a table.

Data contained in a table is linked to a radio button using the same techniques as are used to link the DropDownList control. For instance, you can assign the column name to the DataTextField property of the radio button control as shown in the next example. For the following example, you'll need to modify the custContact table to include the DeliveryOption column before running this program.

```
<%@ Import Namespace="System.Data.SqlClient" %>
<Script Runat="Server">
Sub Page_Load
   If Not IsPostBack Then
      Dim conCust As SqlConnection
      Dim cmdSelectRows As SqlCommand
      Dim dtrCust As SqlDataReader
      conCust = New SqlConnection( "Server=localhost;UID=
MyID;PWD=MyPassword;Database=CustomerContactData")
      cmdSelectRows = New SqlCommand( "Select DeliveryOption
         From custContact Where Critera='45'", conCust)
      conCust.Open()
      dtrCust = cmdSelectRows.ExecuteReader()
```

```
      radioButtonSelection.DataSource = dtrCust
      radioButtonSelection.DataTextField = "DeliveryOption"
      radioButtonSelection.DataBind()
      dtrCust.Close()
      conCust.Close()
   End If
End Sub
</Script>
<html>
<head><title>Radio Button Control Data Binding </title></head>
<body>
   <form Runat="Server">
      <asp:RadioButtonList ID="radioButtonSelection" Runat="Server" />
      <p>
   </form>
</body>
</html>
```

Check Box

Check box controls are stored and retrieved identically to how radio buttons are stored and retrieved. The only difference is that you are using a check box instead of a radio box. The next example shows how to create a check box that uses the customer's last name as its label. Refer to Chapter 8 for more information about how to incorporate a check box control into your application.

```
<%@ Import Namespace="System.Data.SqlClient" %>
<Script Runat="Server">
Sub Page_Load
   If Not IsPostBack Then
      Dim conCust As SqlConnection
      Dim cmdSelectRows As SqlCommand
      Dim dtrCust As SqlDataReader
      conCust = New SqlConnection( "Server=localhost;UID=
MyID;PWD=MyPassword;Database=CustomerContactData")
      cmdSelectRows = New SqlCommand("Select custLastName From
custContact", conCust)
      conCust.Open()
      dtrCust = cmdSelectRows.ExecuteReader()
      checkBoxSelection.DataSource = dtrCust
      checkBoxSelection.DataTextField = "Customer Last Name"
      checkBoxSelection.DataBind()
```

```
      dtrCust.Close()
      conCust.Close()
   End If
End Sub
</Script>
<html>
<head><title>Check Box Control Data Binding</title></head>
<body>
   <form Runat="Server">
      <asp:CheckBoxList ID="checkBoxSelection" Runat="Server" />
   </form>
</body>
</html>
```

List Box

The List Box control is bound to data much as you bind data to the drop-down list box, which you learned how to do earlier in this chapter. The actions of connecting to the database, sending the query, and binding data occur within the Page_Load subroutine. Statements required to execute these tasks should be enclosed within an If statement that executes if the IsPostBack property is false, which means that the page is being loaded for the first time (see the earlier section "Drop-Down List").

The following example illustrates how to bind data to a list box control. In this example we're populating the list box with the CustomerLastName column from the Customers table. Notice that once again the column name is used in the Page_Load subroutine to bind the custLastName to the DataTextField property of the list box.

The web page consists of a form that contains the list box control. Only the list box control is used in this example (Figure 12-2). You can insert other controls (see Chapter 8) after you are comfortable binding data to the list box.

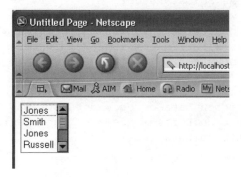

Figure 12-2   The list box contains last names from the database.

```
<%@ Import Namespace="System.Data.SqlClient" %>
<Script Runat="Server">
Sub Page_Load
  If Not IsPostBack Then
    Dim conCust As SqlConnection
    Dim cmdSelectRows As SqlCommand
    Dim dtrCust As SqlDataReader
    conCust = New SqlConnection( "Server=localhost;UID=
MyID;PWD=MyPassword;Database=CustomerContactData")
    conCust.Open()
    cmdSelectRows = New SqlCommand("Select custLastName From
custContact", conCust)
    dtrCust = cmdSelectRows.ExecuteReader()
    lstCustomerLastName.DataSource = dtrCust
    lstCustomerLastName.DataTextField = "custLastName"
    lstCustomerLastName.DataBind()
    dtrCust.Close()
    conCust.Close()
  End If
End Sub
</Script>
<html>
    <head><title>List Box Control Data Binding</title></head>
    <body>
        <form Runat="Server">
            <asp:ListBox ID="lstCustomerLastName" Runat="Server" />
        </form>
    </body>
</html>
```

Hyperlinks

A very common practice is to dynamically create hyperlinks on a web page. As you'll remember from when you learned HTML, a hyperlink consists of at least two attributes. The first is the text or image that appears on the web page, and the second is the URL that is called when the visitor selects the hyperlink.

In the next example, both attributes are stored in a column of a table and are then bound to a Repeater control in the Page_Load subroutine when the web page is loaded.

Let's modify the Customers table (see Chapter 11) by inserting the following two columns so that we can use those columns in the next example:

- CustomerCompany CHAR(30)
- CustomerURL CHAR(30)

Statements in the Page_Load subroutine are nearly the same as those you saw earlier in the case of the Repeater control (see the earlier section "The Repeater Control"), except the query returns the CustomerCompany and the CustomerURL from the Customers table.

Statements in the web page are also similar to statements you saw in the web page of the Repeater control, except for the HyperLink control within the ItemTemplate. We assign column names to the Text attribute and to the NavigateURL attribute.

The CustomerCompany column is assigned to the Text attribute, and the CustomerURL column is assigned to NavigateURL. This is called when the visitor selects the hyperlink.

```
<%@ Import Namespace="System.Data.SqlClient" %>
<Script Runat="Server">
Sub Page_Load
  If Not IsPostBack Then
    Dim conCust As SqlConnection
    Dim cmdSelectRows As SqlCommand
    Dim dtrCust As SqlDataReader
    conCust = New SqlConnection( "Server=localhost;UID=
MyID;PWD=MyPassword;Database=CustomerContactData")
    cmdSelectRows = New SqlCommand(
        "Select CustomerCompany, CustomerURL From Customers",
        conCust)
    conCust.Open()
    dtrCust = cmdSelectRows.ExecuteReader()
    hyperLinks.DataSource = dtrCust
    hyperLinks.DataBind()
    dtrCust.Close()
    conCust.Close()
  End If
End Sub
</Script>
<html>
   <head><title>Hyperlink Data Binding</title></head>
   <body>
   <form Runat="Server">
      <asp:Repeater ID="hyperLinks" Runat="Server">
         <ItemTemplate>
           <ASP:HyperLink Text='<%# Container.DataItem("CustomerCompany") %>'
NavigateURL='<%# Container.DataItem("CustomerURL") %>' Runat="Server" />
         </ItemTemplate>
      </asp:Repeater>
   </form>
   </body>
</html>
```

Quiz

1. The line <td><%# Container.DataItem("CustomerFirstName") %></td> inserts data from the CustomerFirstName column into a column of a table on the web form.

   a. True

   b. False

2. If IsPostBack is true, then

   a. The web page is loaded for the first time.

   b. The web page called itself.

   c. The web page sent data to the database.

   d. None of the above.

3. The AlternatingItemTemplate

   a. Defines the format for all items that appear in the Repeater control.

   b. Defines the format for first item that appears in the Repeater control.

   c. Defines the format for alternating items that appear in the Repeater control.

   d. Defines the format for alternating items that appear in the list box control.

4. DataBind()

   a. Removes a data binding from a control.

   b. Binds data to a DBMS.

   c. Binds data to a database.

   d. Binds data to a control.

5. Data binding most commonly occurs in the

   a. OnClick() method

   b. MouseOver() event

   c. Page_Load event

   d. None of the above

6. Data for data binding can come from

   a. A database

   b. An expression

   c. A property of another control

   d. All of the above

7. Calculated results from a database cannot be bound to a list box control.

   a. True

   b. False

8. The Repeater control is visible on the web page.

   a. True

   b. False

9. Separator-Template: Used to separate data displayed by the Repeater control.

   a. True

   b. False

10. Data binding is restricted to data that the user ID is authorized to retrieve.

   a. True

   b. False

Answers

1. a. True

2. b. The web page called itself.

3. c. Defines the format for alternating items that appear in the Repeater control.

4. d. Binds data to a control.

5. c. Page_Load event

6. d. All of the above

7. b. False

8. b. False. The control itself is not visible. On the other hand, the data output by the control is visible.

9. a. True

10. a. True. The success or failure of any attempt to retrieve data depends on having the necessary permissions.

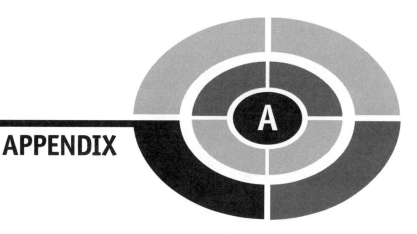

Final Exam

1. An index is used to
   a. Quickly find information in another index.
   b. Quickly find information in a database.
   c. Quickly find information in a table.
   d. Quickly find information in one column.
2. Normalizing a database does not remove most redundant data.
   a. True
   b. False
3. A database management system is subdivided into groups called
   a. Tables
   b. Data
   c. Subdatabases
   d. None of the above

4. Identifying information that you need to store in your database is the first step in designing a database.

 a. True

 b. False

5. Microsoft Access is a database management system.

 a. True

 b. False

6. A clustered index is based on only one column.

 a. True

 b. False

7. A foreign key is a secondary key of a different table.

 a. True

 b. False

8. Another name for joining tables together is

 a. Relating

 b. Merging

 c. Combining

 d. Gluing

9. A primary key uniquely identifies tables of a database.

 a. True

 b. False

10. The database schema is the

 a. Design of data

 b. Design of a table

 c. Design of the database

 d. None of the above

11. What information don't you need when declaring a parameter in a function or subroutine?

 a. The AS keyword

 b. Parameter name

 c. Parameter data type

 d. Parameter size

12. A function cannot be called from an expression.

   a. True

   b. False

13. A subroutine's return value

   a. Is always assigned to a variable.

   b. Is always used in an expression.

   c. May or may not be used in an expression.

   d. A subroutine doesn't return a value.

14. You must declare parameters for all functions.

   a. True

   b. False

15. The data type of the return value doesn't have to be specified when declaring a function that returns a value.

   a. True

   b. False

16. ParamArray is used

   a. To declare an array that is used as a return value of a subroutine

   b. To declare an array that is used as a return value of a function

   c. Because you need a variable number of arguments to pass

   d. To declare an array that is used as a return value of a function that is called from an expression

17. A subroutine is another name for a function.

   a. True

   b. False

18. You return a value from a function by using

   a. Submit

   b. Apply

   c. Ret

   d. None of the above

19. The return value from a subroutine must be used in an expression.

   a. True

   b. False

20. A subroutine is usually defined in the

    a. Page_Login event

    b. Code section of an application

    c. Page_Upload event

    d. Page_Download event

21. Page_Load

    a. Is the way a client requests a page from the web server.

    b. Starts the web server.

    c. Starts the ASP.NET engine.

    d. Is the name of the event handler for the Page_Load event.

22. The expression runat="server" means

    a. Start the web server.

    b. Start the ASP.NET engine.

    c. Execute the code on the client side.

    d. None of the above.

23. An ASP.NET web page is divided into an HTML portion and a source code portion.

    a. True

    b. False

24. The tag <%@ Page Language="VB" %> is a directive.

    a. True

    b. False

25. What controls the ASP.NET instructions that use an HTML class in .NET Framework?

    a. HTML markup code

    b. An HTML server control

    c. A web control class

    d. A web browser

26. Event handlers must be defined within the web page.

    a. True

    b. False

27. An object is an instance of a class.

    a. True

    b. False

28. A property of a class is

    a. An action associated with a class

    b. Data associated with a class

    c. An instance of a class

    d. None of the above

29. What executes in reaction to a specified event?

    a. Reaction method

    b. Event handler

    c. Response handler

    d. Reaction handler

30. What method sends characters to the client?

    a. The Response.Send() method

    b. The Response.Read() method

    c. The Response.Write() method

    d. None of the above

31. Literal values must be enclosed within quotations.

    a. True

    b. False

32. You must convert from one data type to another using casting.

    a. True

    b. False

33. A property is

    a. A temporary storage place in memory

    b. A value associated with a control

    c. A value that can be changed

    d. All of the above

34. A customer name is a(n)

    a. Integer

    b. Short

    c. Long

    d. None of the above

35. The AndAlso logical operator tells the ASP.NET engine

    a. Not to evaluate the second logical expression if the first logical expression is true

    b. To evaluate the second logical expression if the first logical expression is true

    c. Not to evaluate the second logical expression if the first logical expression is false

    d. None of the above

36. An arithmetic operator is used to define the condition for ASP.NET to make a decision.

    a. True

    b. False

37. The Jump operator tells the ASP.NET to

    a. Skip evaluating the expression.

    b. Skip evaluating the expression only if the expression is false.

    c. Reverse the logic of the expression after evaluating the expression.

    d. None of the above.

38. The < operator is used to determine if the value on the left side of the operator is

    a. Equal to the value on the right side of the operator.

    b. Not equal to the value on the right side of the operator.

    c. Less than the value on the right side of the operator.

    d. Greater than the value on the right side of the operator.

39. An expression using the Or operator is true if both the logical expressions joined together by the Or operator are true.

    a. True

    b. False

40. Initialization means assigning

    a. The first value to a variable

    b. A value to a variable

    c. A string to a variable

    d. An integer to a variable

41. The best place to open a connection to a database is

    a. The On_Click event handler

    b. The Page_Load subroutine

    c. In the SQL query

    d. In the query

42. Which SQL clause or statement defines the subset of rows that contain information that you want to return to your application?

    a. Return

    b. Where

    c. From

    d. Select

43. A query parameter can be assigned values the visitors enter into a form on your web site.

    a. True

    b. False

44. A namespace defines objects.

    a. True

    b. False

45. A stored procedure is not sent from your web page to the DBMS each time you execute a query.

    a. True

    b. False

46. Your application can determine the number of rows that were returned by the DBMS.

    a. True

    b. False

47. What clause or statement identifies the table that contains information you want returned to your application?

    a. Where

    b. From

    c. Select

    d. None of the above

48. You open a connection a database by using

    a. ConnectDB

    b. DBConnection

    c. SQL Server for SqlConnect or OleDbConect for Access

    d. None of the above

49. Which SQL clause or statement specifies the columns you want returned to your application?

    a. Return

    b. Where

    c. From

    d. None of the above

50. You can pass information to a stored procedure.

    a. True

    b. False

51. What would you use if you want a block of statements to be executed only if a condition isn't true?

    a. If...Then

    b. If...Then...Else

    c. A For loop

    d. A For in loop

52. Statements within a For loop cannot reference the For loop variable.

    a. True

    b. False

53. What loop executes statements if a condition is partially true?

    a. A Do While loop

    b. A Do Until loop

    c. An Until loop

    d. None of the above

54. A Case statement must have a default Case.

    a. True

    b. False

55. The DEFAULT clause is used in a While loop to set default values.

    a. True

    b. False

56. What loop executes statements if a condition is false?

    a. A Do While loop

    b. A Do Until loop

    c. An Until loop

    d. None of the above

57. A Case statement isn't ideal to use to evaluate an option from a large menu selected by a visitor to your web site.

    a. True

    b. False

58. A For loop cannot skip values in the counter range.

    a. True

    b. False

59. What is the purpose of If in an If...Then...Else statement?

    a. It contains statements that are executed only if the conditional expression is true.

    b. It defines another conditional expression the ASP.NET engine evaluates if the first conditional expression is false.

    c. It contains statements that are executed only if the conditional expression is false.

    d. It is used to nest an If statement.

60. The initializer in the For loop is used to

    a. Increase the expression by 1.

    b. Determine the range of values used to control the iterations of the loop by the ASP.NET engine.

   c. Limit the number of statements that can be contained in the code block.

   d. None of the above.

61. ASP.NET can be used to create

   a. E-commerce web sites

   b. Intranet web sites

   c. Corporate web sites

   d. All of the above

62. Classes are contained in

   a. The customer database

   b. The .NET Framework

   c. The Account database

   d. All of the above

63. ASP.NET cannot generate web pages that contain images or audio.

   a. True

   b. False

64. You can use a word processor to write an ASP.NET web page.

   a. True

   b. False

65. The .NET Framework is required for the

   a. .NET OS

   b. ASP.NET engine

   c. .NET source code

   d. None of the above

66. ASP.NET web pages are static web pages.

   a. True

   b. False

67. The ASP.NET engine runs

   a. On the router

   b. Client-side

   c. Both server-side and client-side

   d. None of the above

68. ASP.NET cannot generate HTML markup code.

    a. True

    b. False

69. ASP.NET Web Pages are not written using

    a. VB.NET

    b. C#

    c. VBScript

    d. None of the above

70. The server side runs

    a. ASP.NET web pages

    b. The web browser

    c. Both the web browser and ASP.NET web pages

    d. None of the above

71. What is assigned to the Value property of an item in a DropDownList Box if you don't assign anything to the Value property?

    a. Nothing is assigned to the Value property.

    b. The value of the ID property.

    c. The value of the Text property.

    d. You must assign a value to the Value property.

72. The selection of a check box does not affect the status of other check boxes.

    a. True

    b. False

73. The ID property of a check box is used to identify the check box within your code.

    a. True

    b. False

74. What happens when the Boolean value of an item is set to true in a drop-down list box?

    a. The item appears as the selected item when the box is first displayed.

    b. The item isn't displayed.

    c. The name of the item is set to true.

    d. The name of the item is set to false.

75. Unless you use the UP ARROW and DOWN ARROW keys to change the order, in what order do items appear in the DropDownList Box?

   a. The order in which they are entered

   b. Alphabetical order

   c. Numerical order

   d. Random order

76. The best control to use when there is one of a small set of mutually exclusive options from which to select is a

   a. DropDownList Box

   b. Radio Button

   c. Check box

   d. None of the above

77. The selection of a radio button affects the selection of every radio button within its group.

   a. True

   b. False

78. You cannot set a default selection for a drop-down list box.

   a. True

   b. False

79. You don't have to set the Value property of an item on the drop-down list box.

   a. True

   b. False

80. An ElseIf statement might be used to evaluate a check button because

   a. You must evaluate all check boxes that appear within the same group.

   b. You must evaluate all check boxes including those that appear outside the group.

   c. If one check box is true, you need to examine other radio buttons outside the group.

   d. None of the above

81. The testing phase is where you write code for your application.

   a. True

   b. False

82. What operator is used to combine values?

    a. The equal sign

    b. The assignment operator

    c. The equivalence operator

    d. The plus sign

83. CreateAccount.Visible = True means

    a. Making an element visible

    b. Making an element invisible

    c. Making an element accessible

    d. None of the above

84. You create an event handler for a button control by single-clicking a button on the Design tab.

    a. True

    b. False

85. You store information into a text box from within your code by using

    a. The equal sign

    b. The copy property

    c. The equivalent operator

    d. The plus sign

86. What property is used to uniquely identify an element?

    a. The Text property

    b. The Value property

    c. The ID property

    d. None of the above

87. The planning phase is where bugs are discovered and fixed.

    a. True

    b. False

88. Variable values must be enclosed with quotations in your code.

    a. True

    b. False

89. The best way to prevent a visitor from changing the value of a text box element is by

    a. Setting the Visible property

    b. Setting the Invisible property

    c. Setting the ReadOnly property

    d. None of the above

90. You can change the value of an element by

    a. Using the Check pane

    b. Using the Visible property of the element

    c. Using the ReadOnly property of the element

    d. None of the above

91. What method would you use to reset values of an array?

    a. Reset()

    b. Copy()

    c. Clear()

    d. Reboot()

92. An array can have elements of different data types.

    a. True

    b. False

93. The length of an array is equal to the index of the last element of the array.

    a. True

    b. False

94. What method is used to copy a segment of an array to another array?

    a. Cpy()

    b. SigCopy()

    c. PartCopy()

    d. None of the above

95. How many elements are there in this array?

    Dim productsA() AS String = {" ", "Water", "Pizza",}

    a. 2

    b. 3

c. 4

d. None

96. The Sort() method only sorts numbers in numerical order.

   a. True

   b. False

97. An array element cannot be used the same way a variable is used.

   a. True

   b. False

98. This is the first element of the products array: products(0).

   a. True

   b. False

99. What method is used to search for a value in an array?

   a. Index()

   b. LastIndex()

   c. Search()

   d. None of the above

100. What method is used to compare two arrays?

   a. Comp()

   b. CompareArray()

   c. Compare()

   d. None of the above

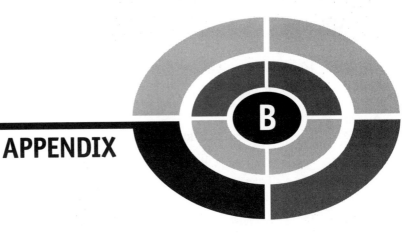

Answers to Final Exam

1. c. Quickly find information in a table.

2. b. False

3. d. None of the above. The database management system is the software that manages the data, not the data itself.

4. a. True

5. a. True

6. b. False

7. b. False. A foreign key is a primary key of a different table.

8. a. Relating

9. b. False. A primary key uniquely identifies rows of a particular table. Tables are uniquely identified by their table names.

10. c. Design of the database

11. d. Parameter size

12. b. False

13. d. A subroutine doesn't return a value.

14. b. False. Not all functions have parameters.

15. a. True. However, as a matter of sound programming style, the return value types of functions should always be declared.

16. c. Because you need a variable number of arguments to pass

17. b. False

18. d. None of the above. You return a value from a function by using the Return statement, or by assigning the return value to a variable whose name is the same as the function itself.

19. b. False. There is no return value from a subroutine.

20. b. Code section of an application

21. d. Is the name of the event handler for the Page_Load event.

22. d. None of the above. It means to execute the code on the server.

23. a. True

24. a. True

25. b. An HTML server control

26. b. False. The definition of event handlers is optional.

27. a. True

28. b. Data associated with a class

29. b. Event handler

30. c. Response.Write() sends characters to the client.

31. a. True

32. b. False

33. d. All of the above

34. d. None of the above. It is a String.

35. c. Not to evaluate the second logical expression if the first logical expression is false.

36. b. False. The If statement is used to define a condition for branching.

37. d. None of the above. There is no Jump operator.

38. c. Less than the value on the right side of the operator.

39. b. False.

40. a. The first value to a variable

41. b. The Page_Load subroutine

42. b. Where

43. a. True

44. b. False. A namespace provides a way of organizing objects hierarchically to prevent naming collisions.

45. a. True. A stored procedure resides in the database itself (that's why it's stored).

46. a. True

47. b. From

48. c. SQL Server for SqlConnect or OleDbConect for Access

49. d. None of the above

50. a. True

51. b. If...Then...Else. The Else block is executed if the condition specified by If is not true.

52. b. False. In fact, one of the most common uses of a For loop is to iterate an array, which requires that the loop counter be used.

53. d. None of the above

54. b. False. Although it can have a default case (and it's often a good idea to provide one), it is by no means required.

55. b. False. While does not have a default clause.

56. b. A Do Until loop

57. b. False

58. b. False. The Step clause allows the For loop to skip values in the counter range.

59. a. It contains statements that are executed only if the conditional expression is true.

60. d. None of the above. It's used to set the starting value of the loop counter.

61. d. All of the above

62. b. .NET Framework

63. b. False

64. a. True

65. b. ASP.NET engine

66. b. False

67. d. None of the above. It runs on the server.

68. b. False

69. c. VBScript

70. a. ASP.NET web pages

71. c. The value of the Text property

72. a. True

73. a. True

74. a. The item appears as the selected item when the list box is first displayed.

75. a. The order in which they are entered

76. b. Radio Button

77. a. True

78. b. False

79. a. True

80. d. None of the above

81. b. False

82. d. The plus sign

83. a. Making an element visible

84. b. False. One of the ways you can create an event handler is by double-clicking a button on the Design tab.

85. a. The equal sign

86. c. The ID property

87. b. False

88. b. False. Only the literal values of String variables must be enclosed in quotation marks.

89. c. Setting the ReadOnly property to True

90. d. None of the above

91. c. Clear()

92. a. True

93. b. False. The length of an array is usually one greater than the index of its last element.

94. d. None of the above. You use the array's Copy method to copy an array.

95. b. 3

96. b. False. The Sort method is also capable of sorting strings.

97. b. False

98. a. True

99. d. None of the above. The methods used to search an array are IndexOf, LastIndexOf, and BinarySearch.

100. d. None of the above

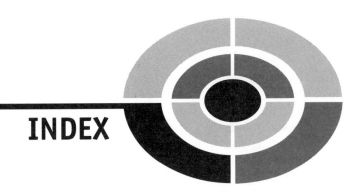

INDEX

References to figures are in italics.

The fast and easy way to understanding computing fundamentals

- *No formal training needed*
- *Self-paced, easy-to-follow, and user-friendly*
- *Amazing low price*

0-07-225454-8

0-07-225363-0

0-07-225514-5

0-07-225359-2

0-07-225370-3

0-07-225364-9

0-07-225878-0

0-07-226134-X

0-07-226171-4

0-07-226170-6

0-07-226141-2

0-07-226182-X

0-07-226224-9

0-07-226210-9

For more information on these and other McGraw-Hill/Osborne titles, visit www.osborne.com.